94A6325

Coming of Age in the Era of Mass Incarceration

DR. KIRK "JAE" JAMES

Published by
Daraja Press in conjunction with **Maat Media**
https://darajapress.com
Wakefield, Quebec, Canada
2026

ISBN: 978-1-997742-33-3 (soft cover)
ISBN: 978-1-997742-34-0 (ePub)

Library and Archives Canada Cataloguing in Publication

Title: 94A6325: coming of age in the era of mass incarceration / Dr. Kirk "Jae" James.
Other titles: Coming of age in the era of mass incarceration
Names: James, Kirk (Kirk Jae), author.
Description: Includes bibliographical references.
Identifiers: Canadiana (print) 20260157473 | Canadiana (ebook) 20260159212 | ISBN 9781997742333 (softcover) | ISBN 9781997742340 (PDF)
Subjects: LCSH: James, Kirk (Kirk Jae)—Imprisonment. | LCSH: Prisoners—United States—Biography. | LCSH: Ex-convicts—United States—Biography. | LCSH: Discrimination in criminal justice administration—United States. | LCSH: Jamaican Americans—Biography. | LCSH: College teachers—United States—Biography. | LCGFT: Autobiographies.
Classification: LCC HV9468.J36 A3 2026 | DDC 365/.6092—dc23

Table of Contents

Prologue vii
Introduction xv
Dedication xxi
Polo Dedication xxiii

1994 1

Verse 1: Genesis 2
Verse 2: Sankofa 12
Exhibit A: Charges 35
Verse 3: Rikers Island 42
Verse 4: Legal System 48
Verse 5: Faith, Hope & Allah 52
Verse 6: Keiana James 54
Verse 7: Hurt People Hurt People 57
Verse 8: Plea For Mercy 60
Exhibit B: Sentence 65
Verse 9: Going Upstate 66
Verse 10: The Cat 70
Verse 11: Moya 76

1995 81

Verse 1: Survival 82
Verse 2: Power 2 The People Then And Now! 86
Verse 3: Mess Hall Crew 90
Photos: Coxsackie CF, 1994 to 1995 94
Verse 4: Greene 95
Verse 5: M-2 Dorm 97
Verse 6: OJ 101

1996 103

Verse 1: Who am I? 104
Verse 2: Y.A.P. 107
Verse 3: Killing Me Softly 111
Verse 4: 1996 Immigration Laws 113
Exhibit C: Immigration Warrant 116

1997 123

Verse 1: Deportee 124
Exhibit D: Deportation Order 131
Verse 2: Parole Board #1 132
Exhibit E: Parole denial + Transcript 141
Verse 3: Jailhouse Lawyer 152

1998 155
Verse 1: El Hefe 156
Verse 2: The Dentist 159
Verse 3: Exodus 161
Photos: Greene CF, 1995-98 165
Verse 4: Auburn 167
1999 171
Verse 1: Attica 172
Verse 2: Wyoming 174
Verse 3: Bliss & Kye 176
Verse 4: The Mountains 179
Verse 5: The Consortium 183
Verse 6: Parole Board #2 184
Exhibit F: Parole denial 188
Verse 7: The Box 189
2000 193
Verse 1: Phoenix 194
Verse 2: Human Relations Therapeutic Program 197
Verse 3: Jedi School 199
Verse 4: Family 202
Verse 5: Pre-Honor Dorm 204
2001 207
Verse 1: Parole Board #3 208
Exhibit G: Parole denial 209
Verse 2: Honor Dorm Crew 210
Verse 3: INS v. St. Cyr 212
Verse 4: 9-11-01 214
Verse 5: 212c 216
2002 217
Verse 1: A Change is Gonna Come 218
Exhibit H: 212c document 224
Verse 2: Victory?! 225
Verse 3: The Graduate 227
Verse 4: Evolve 229
Verse 5: Christmas Gift 232
Photos: Wyoming CF, 1999-2002 234
2003 237
Verse 1: Arthur Kill 238
Verse 2: Parole Board #4 241
Verse 3: The Dragon 243
Exhibit I: Release document 245
Epilogue 246
About the Author 249

If we—and now I mean the relatively conscious whites
and the relatively conscious blacks, who must, like lovers,
insist on, or create, the consciousness of the others—
do not falter in our duty now, we may be able,
handful that we are, to end the racial nightmare,
and achieve our country, and change the history of the world.

— James Baldwin

Prologue

Today in the United States—the self-proclaimed paragon of democracy—fascist tools are no longer hiding in the shadows. Fear, division, propaganda, surveillance, hate speech from political leaders, and an insatiable capitalist greed that threatens humanity and the planet stand boldly at podiums, write policy, and broadcast in high definition.

Distrust in media; ICE; book bans; anti-immigrant legislation; police-, state- and federal-sanctioned violence coupled with attacks on higher education, reproductive freedom, LGBTQ+ rights; imperialism; mass surveillance; and the rewriting of history feel less like democracy and more like George Orwell's *1984*.

What we are witnessing *now* is not a democracy in crisis—it is an *old world order*, committed to maintaining the status quo, reasserting itself. Resistance, and a *new world order* cannot occur with surface-level analysis. Our elder sister and comrade, Angela Davis, teaches us that to dismantle oppressive structures and bring about the change we desire, we must go to the root.

The root of what we call "America" lies in manifest destiny, White supremacy, settler colonialism, Indigenous genocide, Chinese labor exploitation, and the enslavement and extraction of over 10 million Africans from their home, among countless other atrocities.

The United States Constitution—often held up as a sacred social contract—was written by and for White land-owning men. The social contract was never designed to include non-White people or even White women. Ironically, Thomas Jefferson, a slave owner and architect of the document, warned in a letter to James Madison on September 6, 1789, that "no society can make a perpetual constitution, or even a perpetual law. The earth belongs always to the living generation…"

Jefferson understood that a constitution that failed to evolve would incarcerate future generations in outdated beliefs. Jefferson's prophecy is alive in today's backlash against "Critical Race Theory" (CRT), Diversity,

Equity and Inclusion (DEI), immigration, and "wokeness"—a term born in Black communities to signal a consciousness of the "isms" we exist within. A term indicative of a willingness to think critically has been twisted into a slur—and weaponized by a nation that prefers its citizens deaf, dumb, and blind to history.

Fyodor Dostoevsky, the famous Russian writer, was arrested in 1849 and sentenced to death in a society much like today for daring to imagine freedom from oppression. His sentence was ultimately commuted to life in a Siberian prison camp, where he experienced and witnessed immense human suffering.

An oppressive government, a death sentence, years of inhumane imprisonment, and exile profoundly shaped Dostoevsky as a writer—and as the author of classic works such as *Crime and Punishment, The Idiot*, and *The Brothers Karamazov*. From this lived experience emerged one of his most enduring observations: "The degree of civilization in a society can be judged by entering its prisons." By Dostoevsky's measure, the United States is profoundly uncivilized. With less than five per cent of the world's population, it cages nearly 25 per cent of the world's incarcerated people in conditions not fit for animals.

For decades, prior to the mass wave of immigration detention and deportations perpetuated through the gross gestapo-like aggressions of ICE—the United States held the dubious distinction of incarcerating more people than any country in the world.

More than two million human beings—with mothers, fathers, brothers, sisters, children, and friends—are locked away; millions more are surveilled through parole, probation, and immigration detention. Black people are imprisoned at five times the rate of Whites. Women are the fastest-growing incarcerated population. And we cage more children than any other nation.

This wave of racialized hyperincarceration is not a broken system—it is the continued exploitation of Black and Brown labor, land, and resources which feed the machinery of White supremacy—whose ideological roots stretch back to the 15th-century Doctrine of Discovery—formalized, through a series of papal bulls (official decrees) granting and incentivizing European nations the *divine* right to conquer, colonize, commit genocide, and enslave non-White non-Christian peoples.

The Doctrine of Discovery birthed imperialism, colonialism, and chattel slavery. It also produced the myth of race—a fictional idea, but deadly practice which sustains a global caste system with whiteness at the top and everyone else scrambling for proximity. These beliefs—justified through religious doctrine—became law, policy, and culture.

In the landmark US Supreme Court case *Johnson v. M'Intosh* (1823), the court ruled that "Discovery is the foundation of title, in European nations, and this overlooks all proprietary rights in the natives…."

Utilizing the "Discovery Doctrine," the Supreme Court effectively codified into law the idea that Indigenous people did not "own" their land in a way the US government was bound to respect.

The legacy of the Doctrine of Discovery is evident within the Thirteenth Amendment of the United States Constitution. Though widely celebrated for abolishing slavery, the Amendment contains a striking exception which reads:

"Neither slavery nor involuntary servitude, *except as a punishment for crime whereof the party shall have been duly convicted,* shall exist within the United States, or any place subject to their jurisdiction."

The loophole in the 13th Amendment allowed slavery to be legalized and rebranded through Black Codes and later Jim Crow laws. Every day, Black life, inclusive of walking on the same sides of the street as Whites, not having a job, working for yourself, not being able to care for your children, or even looking them in the eye, was criminalized.

White men—historically positioned by colonialism, imperialism, capitalism and a distortion of religious texts as the arbiters of a fixed morality perpetually bent in their favor—created racialized ideas, practices, institutions, and laws forcing theoretically freed Black people back onto plantations as "convicts," "inmates," "prisoners," "bad people," cheaper to exploit, and thus more disposable than slaves.

The "docile slave" became the "dangerous criminal." Plantations became prisons; slave owners became wardens; branding became prison numbers; chains became handcuffs; slave catchers became police. The uncivilized continent became a highly criminalized project, favela, slum, or any other name given to places where historically marginalized people are forced to dwell. What was once slavery became the modern carceral state—an intentional racialized tool of social control and labor exploitation rooted in anti-Blackness—emblematic of White supremacy.

How do we reform a system operating exactly as it was designed?

The United States does not need reform. It needs reckoning. What we are witnessing is not democracy under attack—it is White supremacy fighting for its life. And to resist it, we must dare to imagine something beyond nationalistic, imperialistic, and exploitative governments stuck in perpetual states of war and ideological psychosis.

Love and imagination—often incarcerated within systems of oppression, are a few of the tools necessary in moving us beyond war and the scarcity of the world we exist within.

We must imagine new versions of ourselves, communities, and a global order rooted in abundance, justice, and love for all people!

As a young child visiting the Statue of Liberty in 1983, I was awestruck by her size and the promise she held for humanity. I learned she was a beacon of hope for immigrants—a safe place for all people—especially those most vulnerable.

The trip to the Statue of Liberty in 1983 is a day I will never forget. Living in Jamaica was pretty diverse. But New York City was another dimension—so many new smells, sounds, buildings, cars, languages, faces, foods, clothes, and cultures.

Coming of age in Queens, New York, with friends whose families—like mine—had come from all over the world, we crowded into living rooms after school and on weekends to watch wrestling. Immigrants and first-generation kids, intoxicated by monkey flips and power slams, arguing passionately over whose favorite wrestler was the best. In those moments, America truly felt like the promised land. And even now, decades later, I can admit without shame—I still get a little teary-eyed when I hear Hulk Hogan's theme song, and the words: "*I am a real American… fight for the rights of every man.*" Back then, I believed it. I believed America meant belonging, dignity, and protection—for all human beings.

A belief shattered and stomped out by my lived experience as a Black man *coming of age* in the era of mass incarceration.

Years later, in my search for truth, my research into human rights led me back to the Statue of Liberty—only to discover that her creators were

French abolitionists who imagined her not only as a beacon of hope for immigrants, but as a symbol of Black liberation, holding broken chains at her feet.

Those chains are still there, partially hidden beneath her robes—like so much of American history, visible yet unseen.

Change can occur only when we face the truth hidden in the darkness. However, Audre Lorde reminds us that there are no single-issue struggles. The darkness within "mass incarceration," and the oppression in Gaza, Haiti, across Africa, South America, and the Caribbean are not separate crises—they are *intersectional* expressions of the same machinery of White supremacy, racialized violence, and imperial rule.

Frantz Fanon warned that every oppressive system requires a "dangerous other." For Israel—and for the global silence that accompanies genocide—Palestinians must be rendered existential threats to justify siege and annihilation. For the US, Black people, colored people, trans people, Muslims, immigrants, and other marginalized minorities must be cast as inherently criminal to justify policing, prisons, surveillance, and deportations.

The same global order that bombs hospitals in Gaza funds militarized policing in American cities. The same legislators who minimize and seek to suppress the Epstein Files, defend imperial violence by Israel and the United States—while passing anti-protest laws, mandatory minimums, and policies that further police historically marginalized communities of color.

I believe we must stand in love with all people on this planet! Condemning state violence—from Gaza to Rikers—is not anti-anyone! The calls for Palestinian liberation and Jewish safety are not oppositional—they are interdependent. No community's freedom can rest on the subjugation of another.

Safety built on domination is an illusion. Collective liberation requires dismantling and abolishing every idea, system, and practice rooted in dehumanization, militarism, and racial hierarchy—including the global carceral order itself.

James Baldwin wrote that he criticizes America *because he loves her* and refuses to accept the betrayal of her own ideals. Dr. King warned that "a time comes when silence is betrayal." Critique of oppressive systems and practices is not disloyalty—it is love refusing to surrender to hate—It is accountability to *E pluribus unum.*

And so, as we-the-people arrive at this transformational moment within the United States—a moment when public education, social institutions, and hard-won rights are being dismantled with alarming speed—we must recognize that this moment is also an invitation. A call to question ideas, systems, and practices—including police, jails, and prisons—that have governed our lives without empirical evidence that they deserve our trust.

I believe in abolition—a historical human rights movement, championed by conscious Black and White freedom fighters committed to dismantling cages (both material and ideological), while co-creating new ways of being that truly allow for safety and collective evolution.

No matter your identity, if you believe in love, justice, and the liberation of all people, you must actively resist the onslaught of White supremacy, global insecurity, war, imperialism, and genocide—within and outside of ourselves.

We must commit to building and imagining new ways of being outside what we have been programmed to be. Decolonizing our minds and actions towards liberation will require the co-creation of social contracts, new forms of governance, somatic and trauma-informed practices, education, and relationships—rooted in love, collective care, dignity, and the boundless potential of human life.

The world feels dark, but history, our own lives, and *the hero's journey*—evident across all cultures—are the reminders that the light arises from the darkest hour. We are who we have been waiting for. We are the architects. And in your hand, in my hand, is the power to co-create what comes next!

I'm for truth, no matter who tells it.
I'm for justice, no matter who it is for or against.
I'm a human being, first and foremost, and as such
I'm for whoever and whatever benefits humanity as a whole.

— Malcolm X

Introduction

Peace!

Music carries the history and memory of each generation. My coming of age soundtrack gave testimony to the afterlife of slavery—Black Codes, convict leasing, Jim Crow, redlining, and the continued assault of Black and Brown communities through a carceral genocide known as "mass incarceration."

The music of my generation held our pain, our analysis, and our contradictions. Our music spoke vulnerably about prisons, poverty, capitalism, violence, numbness, and survival.

In the era of the "Central Park Five," The "1994 Crime Bill," the "1996 Immigration Laws," and Black men being labeled "Super Predators," our music did more than describe the *Amerikkkan nightmare.* Our music was revolutionary. It was resistance, imagination, ancestry, joy, and love within a system designed to destroy us.

I am many things—but most of them, I am not.

For the sake of brevity, I am Dr. Kirk "Jae" James—a Black Jamaican immigrant—whose African ancestry was destroyed by slavery.

I am a father of three, a scholar, and an activist committed to human rights for all people. I am a graduate of Hunter College in New York City and the University of Pennsylvania's School of Social Policy and Practice. I currently serve as a Clinical Associate Professor at the New York University Silver School of Social Work, where I direct the Clinical Doctoral Program and the Evolving Justice initiative.

I believe no human being is their worst action. I believe people closest to the problem are closest to the solutions—and that they have a right to tell their own stories. Not to have their pain theorized, extracted, or commodified by imperial scholarship detached from lived experience.

I believe, as James Baldwin did, in the *possibility of America*, while also recognizing that we are standing at a historical crossroads. If this nation is ever to become what it claims to be, we must confront the truths it has long refused to face.

My work interrogates and resists the systems that normalize domination—particularly White supremacy and the carceral logics that sustain it. These systems have long relied on the erasure, exploitation, and disappearance of Black and Indigenous peoples through violence, incarceration, and ideological conditioning. My work seeks to cultivate root knowledge—that awakens consciousness, restores humanity, and compels action toward collective liberation in praxis (theory-reflection and action).

94A6325 is a coming-of-age story in the era of "mass incarceration"—a euphemistic term utilized to describe a complex legal system that has allowed the United States to incarcerate more people, specifically poor, Black, Latinx, women, and children, than any nation in recorded history. The story highlights the experience of people impacted by New York City's and New York State's carceral apparatuses (aka police, jails, prisons, and immigration) in an *era* where one in three Black men were confined—so many that *The New Jim Crow* proclaimed that there were more Black men incarcerated during the 1990s than their enslaved counterparts of 1850.

94A6325 is the historical impact of the 13th amendment of the United States; it's a story of contemporary Black codes in the form of "tough on crime," the "war on drugs," "the 1994 crime bill" and "the 1996 immigration laws"—racialized policies and practices which allowed the police and the "alphabet boys" (aka the FEDS, DEA, ATF, INS, etc.) to be the slave catchers of my generation. Stealing millions of Black and Brown men, women, and children from their communities and transporting them to jails akin to the "door of no return." Where they remained trapped for months and sometimes years before being convicted, sold, and shipped out like animals to barren diasporic lands—where they toiled for months, years, decades, and often life under the brutality of plantations renamed "correctional facilities."

94A6325 is a story emblematic of 1990s hip-hop classics like "You're All I Need" by Method Man and Mary J Blige; Wu-Tang's "C.R.E.A.M"; Nas's "One Love";" Capone-N-Noreaga's "Live on Live Long"; and of course, Tupac's soul-bearing "Dear Mama"—revolutionary music that illuminated the plight of *unfortunates* trapped in the bowels of jails and prisons across the United States. Music and lyrics struggled to capture the historical violence, racism, trauma, poverty, and systemic oppression of a generation. 1990s hip-hop was a cry for help, yet no one was *really* listening!

94A6325 implores the reader to consider how historical racism along with antiquated concepts like "good and bad" are often weaponized through "tough on crime" jargon like "convict" and "super predator" to feed and stoke public fears—which are then utilized to drive criminalization—and how we engage, or not, in a critical dialogue that explores the root issues and intersectionality of what we call "crime," and who we label as "criminals."

94A6325 is a New York State prison number—a branding similar to slavery that dehumanizes and commodifies people as property. It is a book title that many people who have not experienced mass incarceration are baffled by, struggle to remember, and have suggested I change—however, that *discomfort* is precisely my aim. Invisibility, as Ralph Ellison teaches us, is produced. Labels and numbers make it easier to skim, dismiss, and forget that we are speaking about *people*. This logic extends beyond prisons—to immigration systems, policing, welfare offices, hospitals, and borders—where people are often reduced to files and numbers. And for the millions of people incarcerated, or trapped in various oppressive systems, remembering their *number* is the only way to maintain family relations, visit, communicate, or advocate for their humanity and freedom.

94A6325 is my story! It officially commenced on April 13, 1994, when I was arrested and charged under the Rockefeller drug laws, which mandated a sentence of 25 years to life for the possession or sale of as little as four ounces of cocaine. So, despite being only 18 years old, a semester removed from college with no prior criminal history—I was denied bail and sent to Rikers Island—and just six months after my arrival, I was sentenced to life in New York State prison—where I remained caged in various plantations for 3,268 days.

94A6325 comprises ten chapters, each divided into subsections called "verses," which chronicle my arrest on April 13, 1994, to my release on March 25, 2003—a period spanning almost a decade—a period in which every day was my *worst* day. The subsections of this book are titled *verses* because this is more than a narrative—it is a song, a prayer, a witness. Like music, verses carry an energy that cannot always be spoken; like scripture, they hold prophecy, memory, and hope. Shaped by ancestral knowledge, these verses recognize that liberation is often sung before it is seen. Each verse carries immense pain, but also joy—and a spirit compelled to be FREE.

94A6325 is a narrative-driven recollection grounded in my current research and scholarship—often through footnotes. Much of the story derives from my journal notes, memory, and conversations post-release. However, at key moments in the narrative, I include legal documents presented as "Exhibits." I also include "Pics," which are images that capture different eras of my incarceration with family, friends, and my daughter, who was born just months after I was imprisoned. These materials are not included to sensationalize the experience, but to offer transparency and evidence within a system that often relies on lies.

94A6325 utilizes the Ghanaian principle of *Sankofa*—symbolized by a bird looking back over its shoulder—implying that you need to know and reexamine the past to understand the present and future. *Sankofa* differs from Western thought in that it employs a holistic, intersectional approach to understanding people and the societies in which they exist. However, my story and the stories of the millions of people impacted by the carceral apparatus acting in concert with immigration systems are never pretty—a realization made more daunting by the inability of the English language to capture, synthesize, and relay the perpetuity of suffering inflicted *daily* by systems of oppression.

94A6325 is a plea for humanity to examine our carceral system and see for themselves critically—through empirical, longitudinal, and historical data that the mass incarceration of Black and Brown mothers, fathers, and children in the United States is rooted in the same ethos as slavery—and just like the "Slave Narratives" of Fredrick Douglass, Sojourner Truth, and others gave a first-person account that challenged a white-washed revisionist history—it's equally important that the stories of people impacted by "mass incarceration" be centered, and told by them, in their words, voice, and truth!

94A6325 is a call to embrace abolition—a historical theory of change and intersectional movement made up of Blacks and Whites older than the formation of the United States—that called for not only the eradication of slavery, police, jails, and prisons but also demand a profound reevaluation of our societal ideas, norms, and structures that perpetuate scarcity, inequality and racialized oppression.

Abolition teaches us that no one is their worst action. No one is a name, a charge, a file, or a number. From the beginning of time, human beings have carried within us the capacity for both tenderness and terror, creation and destruction, love and harm, joy and pain…

Human beings exist along a spectrum shaped by what we are fed, what we are starved of, and what we are taught to believe about ourselves and one another. The darkness we rush to exile in others—the parts we want to label, cage, or call inhuman—also lives within us. It is only when we dare to look at this without flinching, when we sit with the tension instead of fleeing it, that we can begin to evolve.

Change is rarely easy. But when we commit to both personal and systemic transformation, new worlds emerge: systems rooted not in disappearance, but in presence; not in punishment, but in restoration; not in despair, but in the radical belief that all people—like gardens—will grow roses—even from concrete, when fed by the light of the sun.

Thank you for choosing this book—I humbly request that you utilize an embodied reading approach in which you move beyond the intellect and imagine yourself as a teenager navigating the carceral system.

Decolonizing our minds from the program of White supremacy will require collective labor! Please *labor* with me and think more critically about the *system*, people, and experiences I encounter on my almost decade-long journey through jails, prisons, emotions, and experiences that words fail to honor.

Please research words and terms that may be unfamiliar. If you are new to these issues, please form discussion groups and read alongside books such as Michelle Alexander's *The New Jim Crow* or Ava DuVernay's documentary *13th*. Meet and speak with impacted, incarcerated, and formerly incarcerated people. And finally, please utilize a trauma-informed approach—something as simple as a "conscious breath" as you read this book.

Thank you for honoring *my* story! And thank you for your labor on this journey toward our collective liberation.

Till all are one.

Forward ever!

- Jae

Dedication

This book is dedicated first to my mother—and to all mothers who have endured the heartbreak of loving a child behind bars. It is also dedicated to the many people whose care, sacrifice, resistance, and love made this work possible, including countless others whose names may not appear here but whose presence is no less felt and honored.

To Miss Tiny (R.I.P.), Aunt Karen, Grandma Yvonne, John (R.I.P.), Andre, Kareem, Aaron, Alicia, and the Alexis family.
To Oronde and the Nelson family.
To Heather and the Goodman family.
To Nathalee and family.
To Will (R.I.P.), Taren (R.I.P.), and my forever brother, Bliss (R.I.P.).

To 90s hip-hop—and every artist whose words became the soundtrack of my bid.
To Eric, Gav, Rodney, Ed, Moya, and my Brooklyn and Queens family.
To Zero (R.I.P.) and my Ground Zero family.
To Nicole and the Dominguez family.
To Aunt Audre (R.I.P.), Keith, and Uncle Morrow.
To Aunt Yola (R.I.P.) and my MoBay family.

To X, Kingston, and my Lion Vanguard family.
To Five, Pia, TC, Alex, Abe, Baz, Marlon, Malik, and my BTA family.
To my NYC, NYU Silver, NYU, SP2, Penn, GRI, Rutgers, and Philly family.
To Kathy (R.I.P.), Cheryl, Cam, and my Columbia family.
To Manny, Kevin, IDP, and Families For Freedom.
To Daryl, Terry, Jerry, Phyllis, Lorri, and my Chicago family.

To Amanda Applegate, Tamara Nopper, Bonnie Coker, Charlotte, Chrissy, Kajal, and to everyone who read, edited, held, and carried this story toward completion.

To my children—Keiana, Keiam, and Brooklyn—and to all children who have endured the pain of parental incarceration.

This book is for "Pops," and for all my brothers and sisters caged across the globe. For the ancestors, abolitionists, and freedom fighters who have resisted—and continue to resist—every form of bondage.

With deep gratitude to Firoze, Ayo, Russell, and Daraja Press for believing in and supporting this work.

Finally, *94A6325* is dedicated to George Jackson, "The Dragon," and to the men of Attica who, in September 1971, rose up and gave their lives to be treated as human, declaring:

> *We are men. We are not beasts, and we do not intend to be beaten or driven as such. The entire prison populace has set forth to change forever the ruthless brutalization and disregard for the lives of the prisoners here and throughout the United States.*

Polo Dedication

I could never have imagined the trouble, the rupture, and the reverberations my actions would send through our lives—and through history itself. For that, I am deeply sorry.

I am also forever grateful—for your love, your strength, and your unwavering friendship as we battled the beast, together!

May you rest in power!

1994

VERSE

01

Genesis

Do *you* ever wonder how life began?

Who created the creator?

Or when the world you know will end?

I'm not trying to be deep!

But when you've survived the things I have, *life* changes you on a molecular level.

You start thinking around corners… Reflecting on space, time, and matter—in ways most people take for granted.

I have many questions—that may not be answered—in this lifetime. But to commence with the story, I invite—no, I *implore*:

The conscious,

The seekers of truth,

The believers in democracy, human rights, and a world for, and by the people, to breathe, pause, and consider:

What is FREEDOM?

As far back as I can remember, there was "Miss Tiny."

My great-grandmother.

A believer in the oneness of God and all beings.

She warned me never to take life for granted!

"God-willing," she'd say—before any dream, any plan, or promise that involved a future date or time.

Miss Tiny—born in 1910 on the British colonial island of Jamaica—epitomized ancestral wisdom. She lived a century, shining love and light into the lives of all who encountered her. I was sad when she transitioned in 2010. However, somewhere deep down, I knew her wisdom—would live with me forever!

But in complete transparency, it took years—and a life-altering event on *April 13, 1994*—to truly overstand and put into practice the gifts my great-grandmother bestowed on me.

And *now*, the truth of my words will appear somewhat oxymoronic, but believe me, *I will never forget the moments after death!*

April 1994

It was the morning of April 14, 1994!

I remember the first rays of sunshine, the chirping birds, lively conversations, and booming sound systems.

I remember the impatient drivers blowing horns in synchronized chaos as commuters made their way along Queens Boulevard.

I remember the winter chill slowly giving way to the warmth of spring—there was an energy to the morning that often led to a dope New York City day—but today wasn't good, and would begin an onslaught of bad days lasting almost a decade.

I was wide awake in a nightmare—a bizarro world where nothing made sense, and no matter how hard I tried—I couldn't escape. But I wasn't the only one *entrapped.*[1]

Polo interrupted the attorney and demanded to know:

"How much time are we facing?"

The attorney, as if anticipating the question, responded immediately: "*Probably* 25 years to life, or less if you plead guilty."

I looked for some hint of a joke, but the young, White, court-appointed attorney was devoid of emotion as he read the slew of charges from the free side of the human cage—buried deep within the bowels of the Queens Boulevard courthouse.

I quickly turned towards Polo—who looked similarly confused. I pivoted back, faced the attorney, gripped the steel bars tightly, and proclaimed:

"We didn't kill anyone! Are you sure you're looking at the right case?!"

The attorney appeared annoyed by our inability to accept the validity of anti-Black laws made up by White men. Signaling to the guards that

1 Understanding this term, and how the financial insecurities of marginalized people are exploited by law enforcement to artificially produce "crime" is essential to understanding my story. See *Mathews v. United States*—where the Supreme Court ruled that a "valid entrapment defense has two related elements: government inducement of the crime, and a lack of predisposition on the part of the defendant to engage in the criminal conduct." Two other stories that highlight the utilization of entrapment by law enforcement are the John Delorean (1982) and Elaine Bartlett (1983) cases.

our meeting was over, he returned the legal documents to his briefcase. But he left us this warning:

"You're both being charged with multiple A-1 felonies under the Rockefeller drug laws[2]—which is the equivalent to mass murder—and means the judge will most likely deny bail!"

As the words fell from his lips, the nonstop noise gave way to an eerie silence. This *process* played out countless times throughout the night—it was an automated system—court-appointed attorneys meeting *unfortunates*[3] trapped in cages. First came a hushed reading of the charges, then a discussion of bail; however, *plea bargaining*—for less time—became the only way out once the reality became apparent.

I glanced at my Tag Heuer as the hour hand approached 11 am and quickly did the math. Polo and I were trapped in Queens Central Booking for nearly half a day—by now, we knew the drill—it was where they took you to get "processed" into the system—and where you officially became a number.

Yet, I still believed everything would make sense when we saw the judge. But unbeknownst to us, Polo and I were already *invisible men*[4]—our charges had trumped the depths of our humanity. We were typecast and forced to play roles devoid of range.

Handcuffed, the armed court officer forced us up from the pews and onto our feet. Then, a booming voice, perched high above the mountaintop, called out "Kirk James" and "Duane Adams" before commanding us to swear allegiance and truth to his god. Once affirmed, the judge took a few minutes to review a legal folder, which I assumed contained our charges.

I took advantage of the break and quickly scanned the courtroom—where a sea of Black and Brown people nervously awaited the fate of

2 Enacted in 1973, and to this day is considered one of the most draconian policies ever as it mandated a minimum sentence of 15 years to life, and a maximum of 25 years to life for possessing as little as two ounces of cocaine.

3 This term is an ode to Raekwon's 1995 song "Rainy Dayz" from *Only Built 4 Cuban Linx…*, where he raps *"the unfortunates layin' in mountains, countin'…"* I use *"unfortunates"* deliberately throughout this book to provoke critical reflection on how people come to be captured by carceral systems—not to negate individual accountability, but to disrupt the moral binaries of "good" and "bad" that obscure systemic and historical causes. Genuine accountability and lasting change, I argue, require going to the root of what we call "crime," whom we label "criminal," and the conditions that make cages an inevitable outcome for poor, non-White people.

4 Ralph Ellison's *Invisible Man* names a structural condition—the experience of being unseen while fully present—that Black men routinely navigate in the world of White supremacy. After emancipation, this invisibility was codified through Black Codes and convict leasing; today, it persists through mass incarceration, where names become numbers and people are rendered socially absent while physically confined. The carceral system is thus a preeminent tool of invisibility: it institutionalizes erasure, making human suffering easier to ignore and humanity easier to disappear.

their beloved. I turned to my right and saw them towards the back of the court—Mom, Grandma, and Moya all forced smiles as we made eye contact. But our exchange was short-lived as the judge impatiently demanded:

"How do they plead?!"

I wanted to scream my objection to this primitive sacrificial ritual designed for the colored interloper. But I was learning fast and understood the question was not ours to answer. Instead, Polo and I were inactive participants—or rather bad objects devoid of inquiry or the illusion of justice.

I watched anxiously and perplexed as the White judge conversed with the White attorney and prosecutor in hushed tones. After what felt like a million lifetimes, the court-appointed attorney returned and addressed the court:

"They plead 'not guilty',' your honor."

However, the prosecutor, who cared little for the presumption of innocence and even less for our humanity, angrily retorted:

"We have a lot of evidence against the defendants…"

I glanced at the attorney for his response, but there would be no more conversation. I was shocked as the judge slammed the gavel to signal an adjournment—and even though the farce was over, the drama was just beginning.

With no bail, an armed court officer escorted Polo and me out of the Queens Boulevard Courtroom and back to the holding cells buried deep in the dark sub-basement of the enormous building—which was a hideous place, reminiscent of slave dungeons, filled to the brim with countless Black and Brown bodies awaiting a terrifying uncertainty.

Once secured in the human cages, Polo, who was a few years older and familiar with the system, began preparing me for the journey ahead. He said they would probably send me to "C-74"—which was the infamous adolescent housing unit at Rikers—Biggie Smalls, Nas, Wu-Tang Clan, Tupac, Mobb Deep, Capone-N-Noreaga, and pretty much most of New York City hip-hop[5] rapped about it.

5 Hip-hop emerged in the 1970s Bronx from communities shaped by redlining, deindustrialization, and state abandonment. Early mainstream visibility—most notably the Sugarhill Gang's "Rapper's Delight" (1979)—spoke to social issues including mental health, poverty, racism, and police violence. By the 1990s, amid the War on Drugs and the rapid expansion of prisons, hip-hop became an archive of mass incarceration, chronicling how poverty, policing, and punishment colluded to render criminalization routine long before policymakers and academics coined the term "mass incarceration."

I was terrified! I didn't know what was fact or fiction. But with my head up, I looked Polo in the eye while secretly processing the implications of his words, which proved prophetic as a short time later, the CO called my name for the bus to Rikers.

As the door of no return opened, Polo hugged me and whispered:

"Stay strong; they will test you."

Polo's warning held a truth necessary for me to survive—so I held tight to his words and armored up as I was shackled, led from the cell, and escorted through a series of maze-like tunnels out of Central Booking to an awaiting "jail bus."

As we prepared to leave through retracting barbed wire fences, my palms were sweating, and my heart rate steadily increased. Yet everything around me slowed down—except for the bus, which sped quickly along the Grand Central Parkway towards the Triborough Bridge. It was all strangely familiar—from Forest Hills High School and Flushing Meadow Park to Shea Stadium—they were all staples of the Queens neighborhoods I grew up in after migrating from Jamaica in 1986 with Mom.

However, the sights of so many of my childhood memories were short-lived as a large sign announced our arrival to hell—which had one way in and one way out.

My body tensed as the bus sped up. Anticipation rose as we climbed towards the arch of the drawbridge. Through meshwire-reinforced windows, I watched the receding sunlight give way to darkness. I stared at the illuminated silhouette of Manhattan and its Twin Towers. And as the bus reached the bridge's apex, I glanced down at LaGuardia Airport below to the far right.

The sight of the airport triggered memories of past trips back home to Jamaica and the excitement I felt when the plane landed in "Mobay." And for a minute, everything was back to normal. But the darkness ahead began to take shape and stole my attention.

The bus was eerily silent as we descended onto the Island—framed by multiple project-like buildings with layered fences—first chain-link, then razor wire, then walls topped with more blades. Even the grass and trees appeared hostile. There were also towers with guns and cameras, capturing every movement.

Eighteen years in an anti-Black world conditioned me to dissociate[6] and normalize the perpetual violence of White supremacy. But this now was different!

Words won't ever do this experience justice!

Please, take a moment and labor with me:

Imagine yourself facing life in prison at eighteen.

No bail!

Trapped on a bus to Rikers Island—an overcrowded jail designed for the confinement and torture of people—with forty other young men?

Ponder *that,* and add that you're confined by forward-facing handcuffs, with a small black box attached in the middle—which then connects to a 5-pound chain-waist belt. And as the chain tightens, both hands get pulled towards the stomach, as if in an act of reverence.

Finally, each *unfortunate* is chained together via the ankles to seal the deal!

It's an understatement to say "I was terrified" as the bus finally arrived at C-74. But I remembered Polo's words, took a deep breath, and prepared myself for the infamous adolescent building. However, my grand entrance to C-74 was delayed.

My partner and I struggled to exit the bus via the stairs—a task requiring a bit of coordination that neither of us could execute in our current mental and physical state. As a result, each misstep drove the cold circular steel cuff deeper into my shin and extracted blood.

I was hurting in more ways than one. However, fear and adrenaline muted the physical pain as they marched us further into the building towards the "why-me?" cells—a name given by *unfortunates* to commemorate the moment you arrive at C-74 and learn the illusion of liberty is no more—and that you, your family, or loved ones have no power to save you. So, you curse your oppressor and beg of your creator: "*Why me?*"

For Black men, surviving Rikers Island, jails, prisons, and ghettos throughout the US was a lot like "Mandingo fighting"—a period that

6 James Baldwin's assertion that to be Black and conscious in America is to live in a constant state of rage identifies a rational psychological response to systems that deny Black humanity while demanding compliance. For the oppressed, dissonance functions as a rage mitigator—an adaptive survival mechanism involving internal splitting that enables functioning amid persistent contradiction—paralleling W.E.B. Du Bois's concept of double consciousness and Frantz Fanon's analysis of colonial psychology. For the oppressor, dissonance manifests differently: as moral disengagement, denial, and rationalization that permit participation in domination while preserving a self-image of innocence or benevolence. In both cases, dissonance is not incidental but structural—produced by systems that require psychological distortion to sustain racial hierarchy and normalized violence.

forced enslaved Black men to fight each other for their survival and the profit and entertainment of White men. An internalized conditioning that still results in Black men seeing each other as the enemy. So, the "why me?" cells are also where recently captured "detainees" first get to size each other up to determine who would feast and who would famine. But I was mostly spared the scrutiny as a few teenagers accused of raping a woman in Coney Island arrived just as I did.

The "Coney Island" case was all over the news, increasing the detained teenagers' risk of harm. As a result, they were being processed and sent to the protective custody (PC) unit of the jail—a "safe" place in theory from the scrutiny and likely assaults from guards and other captives who viewed people accused of rape as subhuman.[7]

I quietly watched the drama unfold until a CO came and got me from the cell to commence the intake process—which was just a few feet away behind a row of curtain partitions—where another CO stood eagerly awaiting.

With my back against the wall, the new CO menacingly towered over me and commanded me to undress. His words land, and I hear him, but it's hard to compute. Eventually, I dissociate and retreat into my safe space, as autopilot takes the wheel and slowly removes my clothes.

Fully naked, I faced the White CO, rooted my feet, and stood defiantly proud as he inspected my Black body.

With hate in his eyes and contempt in his words, the CO spat orders at me in rapid fire:

"Raise your hands above your head!"

"Palms out!"

"Wiggle your fingers!"

"Bring your hands up to your mouth!"

"Use your middle fingers to open your mouth wide!"

"Lift your tongue!"

"Move it side to side!"

"Lift your dick!"

"Lift your balls!"

7 Carceral logic depends on a moral hierarchy of crime. People accused of sexual violence—particularly rape—are often rendered permanently subhuman and beyond context or transformation, while some perpetrators of extreme violence, such as Charles Manson, are culturally mythologized. We must refuse the premise that any person can be reduced to their worst act. Genuine safety and accountability, emerge not from disposability and cages, but from conditions that allow for truth-telling, responsibility, repair, and transformation.

"Turn around and hold up the wall!"

"Lift your right foot and wiggle your toes!"

"Lift your left foot and wiggle your toes!"

"Bend over, spread your ass, and cough!"

"Get dressed!"

I felt violated after the *process*, but knew deep down—like a survival program in my DNA—that this wasn't a time for feelings! So I kept my armor up as the CO escorted us further into the building, where the hallways were dark and gray and gave the illusion of never-ending intestinal tubes. The only distinguishing features were metal detectors and doorways leading to what I assume are housing units.

A strong smell of cleaning solution laced with bleach permeated the air. It was a little after midnight, but no one was sleeping when the lights went on in Mod 5—where the COs were primarily Black and Brown overseers—many, from the same neighborhoods, the same communities, and the same traumas. But similarly to chattel slavery and the legacy of *overseers,* they have been poisoned by greed and blinded by the illusion that control over their people affords them superiority—and has somehow saved them from a system(s) designed to negate our collective humanity.

I felt fear, anger, and shame as the two Black COs lined us up against the wall and cheerfully handed our folders to two Black housing unit COs, who gave us the law of the land before assigning our beds. But just as we began to leave, one of the COs ordered us to stop, looked us over one last time, laughed, and said, "You better hurry before the lights go out!"

His comment was intensified by the stares we received as we moved deeper into the housing unit. And even though I was afraid, I held firm to Polo's warning and intentionally made eye contact with everyone in my path as I navigated towards my assigned bed—which I found just as the lights went out. I sat with my back against the wall until my eyes acclimated to the dark. I then scanned the dorm discreetly as no one appeared to be sleeping or going to bed anytime soon.

After a few minutes of observation, I focused on a group of about five to seven people in what appeared to be a tactical formation. My adrenaline spiked in anticipation of combat. Finally, I sat up straight, feet on the floor, and positioned my body towards the action. Initially, I couldn't tell what was happening until I saw a young cat who had come to Mod-5 with me heading towards the bathroom. I want to tell him not to go—assess the situation first! But sadly, for my self-preservation, I remained silent.

I watched with knots in my stomach as members of the greeting crew methodically followed the young cat into the bathroom—while others took up posts at the entrance to serve as lookouts. Within a few moments, the scuffling of sneakers and muted murmurs became more distinct.

I looked at the CO station—but no one was in sight. I looked at the other *unfortunates*, who appeared unbothered. And taking my cue, I feigned a similar air of indifference. And after what seemed like an eternity, the tactical team emerged from the bathroom with the swagger of a successful operation. Some moments later, my fellow "new-jack" stumbled out, head down, defeated, and back to his assigned bed.

I sat with dread and tension for hours before the sunlight permeated the rectangular housing unit. I'd fought to stay awake all night, but I was exhausted. I was nearly asleep when I noticed someone moving toward me.

I was foggy, but jumped up immediately to defend myself. Yet, sensing my trepidation, the man paused and slowed his approach. Once he got within arm's reach, he extended a fist pound to show respect and introduced himself. He was a slim cat, slightly older, maybe in his late twenties, and about 6 feet tall. Earlier, I'd observed him moving about the dorm in ways others couldn't.

He introduced himself as "Born" and said he was the "night porter"—and his job was to prevent suicides. I wanted to ask questions, but refrained. Born looked me over casually and said, "I can help with phone calls, cigarettes, or anything else you need?"

I nodded to convey understanding but told Born I was good in the most assertive tone I could muster. Maybe I was a little paranoid, but I knew what happened in Mod-5—the stories were legendary.

Living in highly criminalized communities, there is always a chance encounter at the bodega, on the block, or in the parks in the warmer months with someone you hadn't seen in a minute who had survived Rikers—now mostly muscle-bound looking like the incredible hulk doing push-ups and pull-ups by the hundreds—while weaving intricate tales of cats getting robbed for their jewelry, sneakers or jackets. Stories, probably exaggerated and self-aggrandizing, but true enough that I knew my Timberlands, leather jacket, gold chain, and watch made me a target. So, as Born continued to make small talk, I nonchalantly kept an eye out for an ambush.

Born finally wrapped up our chat and reiterated his willingness to help me before departing with another fist bump. Yet I cautiously watched him as he slowly made his way towards the young man assaulted in the bathroom. And with what appeared to be concern, he *probably* offered him immunity from further assaults for a small fee.

Born finished up with the new jack and moved on towards the assault team. Whose beds were clustered at a 90-degree angle along two adjacent walls—which was not accidental, but a product of many of them being survivors of violent systems, neighborhoods, and youth jails like Spofford—experiences which made them skilled veterans in the art of war: from the psychological to the physical; and masters of creating weapons from just about *anything*. So, as Born neared the assault team, I wasn't sure what to expect. But I was caught off guard as he greeted them with a gang signal and huddled them together as if calling out a play.

I was desperate to escape Rikers Island as I watched Born interact with his crew. Yet I knew something wasn't adding up. And despite the terror of the moment, I kept trying to connect the dots—especially my last encounter with "Eddie" on the night I got arrested. Yet the understanding I sought of my present predicament required an examination of my past, beginning with a conversation I had with "Judas" in 1993.

VERSE

02

Sankofa

March 1993

To provide critical context for my current predicament in 1994, please journey back with me to 1993 as I share a few pivotal stories and conversations that led to my arrest. Let us begin with Judas, who was old enough to be my father—tall, slim, and with mannerisms straight out of the "blaxploitation" era.

Judas was friends with John, my stepdad. They'd met while working at a nursing home in Queens—John's first job after migrating from Trinidad. And as fate would have it, John met Mom at this same nursing home after we migrated from Jamaica in '86.

Judas had a history—he'd done time in Sing Sing and Attica. I was probably twelve or thirteen when we met. My fascination with his stories grew into a weird admiration for him. We were among the best men when Mom and John married in the fall of '91. He was family, or so I thought. However, one day in March of 1993, Judas stopped by our house in Rosedale, Queens. I hadn't seen him in a while, but didn't give it much thought when he asked:

"Do you want to make some easy money?"

Judas didn't wait for an answer before continuing: "I have some good friends looking to buy drugs and guns. They just need a hookup and will pay good money." The conversation with Judas was riddled with lies—on both ends. But let's start with the truth: first, I never sold drugs, guns, or anything before my conversation with Judas. Second, I was only 17 years old, and we had never engaged in such a manner—but my teenage bravado usually spiked when Judas was around. I was always looking to impress him—like when I showed him a 22-caliber handgun with a pearl handle. But it was all a facade—A LIE; I was fronting!

The 22-caliber handgun was readily available[1] and easily purchased in any hood for less than a pair of Jordans; it also didn't work as the firing pin was broken. Yet we passed it around the crew, which was more *A Tribe Called Quest* than *Onyx*, to keep predators away.

Playing with guns—that worked or not—was admittedly a dangerous game. But so were inner-city violence, police brutality, and our survival odds as young men of color growing up in New York City during the carceral genocide of the 1990s. Anyway, my false bravado with Judas made an impression, and he tried to recruit me as the "hookup" for his friends, promising a substantial commission for my help.

I was at a crossroads in my relationship with Judas. But instead of telling the devil "no!" and risk losing "street cred," I lied and naively said, "Let me think about it"—five words that people use every day to avoid a direct answer, and five words that would haunt me for decades to come.

By 1993, I rarely attended school, and my relationship with the New York City Department of Education was broken. I was ultimately "pushed out"[2] of Forest Hills High School, which was shocking to Mom, as she knew I loved to learn and would fight to go to school even while sick when we lived in Jamaica. But she didn't realize how disconnected I felt from the US educational system, which only sought to foster memorization and regurgitation[3] of revisionist White supremacist history.

Also, around spring '93, after leaving Forest Hills High School and speaking with Judas, I took the General Equivalency Diploma (GED) exam and passed it with little preparation. Subsequently, I enrolled at Nassau Community College for the 1993 fall semester with hopes of becoming an attorney—a dormant dream from my childhood in Jamaica, revitalized by my summer youth internship at the New York City Law Department in 1991.

1 The US Department of Justice estimated that as many as 2 million illegal guns were in NYC in 1993.

2 Unlike "dropout," which places the onus on the student, "pushout" emphasizes how systemic factors like racism, zero-tolerance policies and lack of connection with material and educators actively push students out of school. See "school to prison pipeline."

3 See Paulo Freire, *Pedagogy of the Oppressed.* And bell hooks, *Teaching to transgress: Education as the practice of freedom.*

May 1993

By May '93, after a few bumps, my life was coming into focus. Mom rewarded me with a trip to Jamaica for my 18th birthday, where I spent a little time with my dad in Lindsted, where he lived and worked as an environmental scientist for a bauxite company with his wife and kids. After leaving dad, I stayed with my Great Uncle "Zero" in Bogue Heights, Montego Bay (or Mobay).

Zero had a stunning view of the Bay, hotels, and various cruise ships from all over the world. It was always a happy place, but things felt a little different as my Great Aunt, Yola—the family matriarch, who lived about a quarter mile away—had died recently after a battle with leukemia. Like all the women in my family, Aunt Yola was a warrior queen in the mold of "Nanny"—the famous Maroon leader who refused to let the British enslave her people. Her house was where we convened as a community, ate, debated, got wisdom, and loved each other through life's journey. Her transition to the essence not only created grief, but it also destabilized our family core.

Centuries of colonial conditioning and brutality have normalized violence and suppressed vulnerability among Caribbean men. So during much of my time with Zero—who, in many ways, was a paternal figure—his grief over the loss of his older sister made it difficult for him to be fully present—so I spent a lot of time by myself discovering cannabis while hanging at Doctor's Cave Beach, staring at the clouds, and reading *Rasta and Resistance,* which he gave me for my birthday. The book, written by Horace Campbell—one of his best friends—spoke of the evolution of the Rastafarian movement in response to the oppression of White supremacy.

Maybe it was the cannabis, but I was different after celebrating my 18th birthday and leaving Jamaica at the end of May 1993. I was giddy and excited to get back home to New York City. I even clapped with the other Caribbean travelers when the plane landed, and I wasn't even mad standing outside the terminal for almost an hour waiting for John, who was always notoriously late to pick me up. But what threw me for a loop was the surprise he brought when he finally arrived.

She came up from behind me and covered my eyes with her hands.

But I could smell and feel that it was Moya—who I turned and embraced like a long-lost lover. She was Peruvian, tall, talkative, gum-chewing with dark hair and eyes originating from her Inca roots—which, along with her skin, got dark olive in the summer.

Moya was my first love. We met during our first year of junior high school at Halsey. I was excited to see her, but we had a complex history and had dated on and off since 1988. However, that night in May at the airport, and maybe two other times in June, would be the last time I saw her until a tragic night in December, which is for a later story. At that moment, I was just happy to be back in New York City to commence the summer of '93.

July 1993

As the days turned into weeks, I forgot about my conversation with Judas and slowly moved forward after another gut-wrenching breakup with Moya. It helped that I was working at the Mid-Manhattan Library as a clerk, a position Grandma Yvonne secured for me through a friend. I didn't get paid much, but I met many dope people, read cool books, and found joy roaming the city after work, catching free concerts, or hanging out in the West Village, playing handball at the cage for hours.

Exhausted and hungry after handball, we often got pizza and a "quarter water" before heading to Washington Square Park—where we watched the bikers, skaters, girls, hustlers, and occasional hip-hop cyphers.[4]

The Mid-Manhattan Library was also where I met Heather, who was from Brooklyn. Light-skinned with freckles, she rocked bamboo earrings, and embodied the quintessential '90s "b-girl." We clicked immediately and spent many nights hanging together at the boardwalk in Coney Island, playing video games, driving go-carts, and nurturing our inner Darryl Strawberry at the batting cages.

Summer '93 was epic! I even saw the Wu-Tang Clan perform for the first time at the annual Jones Beach Greek Festival. In hindsight, 1993 was *probably* the last time I was truly free—not just from

4 Washington Square Park has always been a hub for social justice movements, musicians, artists, academics and varied activists--which was significantly impacted by then-Mayor Rudy Giuliani's policies, and policing in the form of "Broken Windows" during the 1990s.

incarceration, but from the varied insecurities and prisons that life as an *adult* often triggers. My family also moved from Lefrak City to Hook Creek Boulevard in Rosedale, Queens, which, in theory, was a step up in neighborhoods. However, it was located on the Queens-Long Island border and considered a "2-fare zone," meaning my commute and the cost of traveling to Manhattan doubled.

I usually got home from work around 8 pm when the MTA was reliable. One such day, I arrived home to find Mom seated at the kitchen table. I greeted her and asked if I had any messages—I was looking for jobs closer to home and hoping that one of the many stores I had applied to at Green Acres Mall would call. But Mom's response threw me for a loop. Translated from her thick Jamaican patois, she said:

"Yes, Eddie keeps calling! You should tell him to stop leaving messages, as I'm not your answering machine!"

1993 was the pre-cell phone era, and everyone called your house phone unless you had a pager. So, I was somewhat perplexed, as the only person I knew named "Eddie" went by "Tony" and hated being called otherwise. Yet I didn't give it much thought, so I thanked Mom and went to my room. But over the next few months, I kept getting more messages from this mysterious "Eddie." I even began to think it was a prank until he finally got me on the phone.

"Judas says you can get drugs and guns" was how "Eddie" introduced himself. I should have hung up the phone, but my bravado kicked in again, and the call ended with me giving a vague assurance that I would follow up in a few. And even though we hung up with promises to be in touch, I knew I wouldn't entertain "Eddie's" offer. But as Miss Tiny always said, "You get burned when you play with fire."

September 1993

I excitedly entered Nassau Community College in the fall of '93 and, ironically, majored in criminal justice. I was proud of myself, especially when so many Black men of my generation were doing "bids." However, I had a brutal four-hour commute each day, which I hoped to avoid after getting my first car—a 1983 orange Chevy Chevette acquired from a family friend for a hundred dollars. But one day, toward the end of the summer, while rushing to work at the library, I misread the parking signs.

I left my orange Chevy Chevette by the F train on Main Street and Queens Boulevard in a no-parking zone—and it was towed. This was before computers, so when I called the police, there was no record of the car being taken. For a moment, I thought it had been stolen. When I finally learned it had been towed, the cost to retrieve it was more than I could afford. I was left sad and stranded, stuck in a two-fare zone with a brutal commute, once again at the mercy of the MTA.

The season changed from summer to fall, and Eddie kept calling, promising, and demanding. He was my one constant. My default response was, "I'm still looking," which was far from the truth, but it gave him the green light to keep calling and entice me with *more* money. Which was tempting, but I didn't take it seriously.

I grew up in New York City in the midst of the drug war and knew the perceived reward wasn't worth the risk. I witnessed the destruction of the crack epidemic in the mid-80s. From the pushers to the users, it was a misdirected, genocidal attempt to escape the perpetual insecurities of White supremacy, racialized capitalism, and an unquantifiable level of trauma at the hands of the "isms."

I remember living in Lefrak City—waking up on hot, humid summer mornings with no central air, wondering which of the hustlers on 57th Ave or 98th Street would get shot, or arrested by the *alphabet boys.*[5]I remember weekends with Aunt Audre in downtown Brooklyn on Bergen Street and seeing the sidewalks littered with crack vials and bullet shells—looking almost organic, as if they had rained down from the sky! I knew plenty of people who had dropped out of school to hustle. And I'd had plenty of offers to join them in their enterprises, but it never appealed to me.

November 1993

Being a *dreamer,* I never got too high or too low. But life began to demand more of me—which coincidentally also started with an unexpected phone call. It was Thanksgiving night, 1993. I was with my boy Gav, who was home on break from Maryland Eastern Shore—at his dad's house in

5 The "alphabet boys" were the Feds—the ATF, SWAT, TNT, and a maze of other government agencies unleashed during the "War on Drugs," transforming our neighborhoods into militarized zones of surveillance, raids, and entrapment, where enforcement replaced investment and police power eclipsed care.

Brooklyn, watching the Dallas Cowboys' "snow bowl" when Heather beeped me "911." I knew it was serious as she never used that code.

Gav passed me the cordless telephone, and I called immediately, but it rang forever before she answered. I could hear faint sobs as Heather picked up. I was now officially nervous and asked if she was OK. But no words came, only louder sobbing. I remained silent, not knowing what to say or what was happening. But after what seemed like an eternity, Heather caught her breath and said, "I'm pregnant!"

I was in shock as Gav drove me to meet Heather in Coney Island on 28th Street between Surf and Mermaid Avenues. It was dark by the time we arrived. I stood outside the car, cold and disheveled, waiting for her to come downstairs to meet me in front of the project building. But seeing Heather, who was always *good*, crying and shivering as we stood face-to-face in the parking lot, forced me to get it together.

I embraced Heather, and we stood there, quiet, for a while before she began to cry again. She told me about her dad, who sought relief from his trauma through violence, alcohol, and drugs—before ultimately losing control of his life and abandoning his family. She told me how scared she was to be pregnant, to be a mother, and to raise a child.

While my story wasn't the same as Heather's, I understood—I, too, was the product of an unplanned teenage pregnancy. My mom was a brilliant high school student expected to be a doctor who got pregnant at sixteen years old and had to hide for weeks in shame and fear from her classmates and family. So, as Heather spoke about being afraid and repeating a karmic cycle, I overstood! But I had no words. I just kept listening and let the implications sink in. And when it seemed that Heather didn't have anything more to say, I took a breath, composed myself, and assured her that our story would be different.

From somewhere other than my brain, I declared, "Let's have our baby."

December 1993

Two weeks after Thanksgiving and learning Heather was pregnant, I went out with three of my best friends—Gav, Eric, and Moya. Eric and Gav were my *boyz* from elementary school, Caribbean, from Lefrak

City, and my brothers from another mother. As for Moya, I already told you it was complicated! We hadn't seen each other in months. However, she had reached out a few days prior, and we all agreed to hang out on a blustery, cold Friday night at a local pool hall on Queens Boulevard—where we spent a ton of money and had a lot of fun trying to convince ourselves and each other that we didn't suck at pool.

Gav stayed behind to settle the tab while we made our way back to his car—a burgundy 1990 Hyundai Excel hatchback. Perched on the dashboard was Mr. Potato Head, a faded Happy Meal toy from the day Gav got his driver's license. He'd been there ever since—our lucky charm, our silent guardian, watching over every ride we made in and around the city's war zones.

Moya had her arm around me as we navigated towards the car. We were all buzzed and laughed when Eric fell off the curb and almost landed face down before regaining his balance and launching into a Scarface impersonation. But he barely finished "Say goodnight to the bad guy" before tripping again and falling angrily onto the hood of a parked car.

We stopped laughing long enough to see Eric slowly stand up and playfully brush off his clothes. We marched on behind Eric, zig-zagging towards the car when, out of nowhere, a man jumped like a tiger onto his back, collapsing his tall but skinny frame on contact. Maybe it was the shock of the moment or the alcohol, but my response was delayed.

I slowly took off my new leather jacket and handed it to Moya. But by then, the guy was straddling Eric and throwing punches to his head and face. I grabbed the guy's shoulders to pull him off, but he quickly got to his feet and swung at me, but missed.

The guy cocked his right arm back to swing again, and I saw the knife—but it was too late. I instinctively raised my hands to protect my face, but the blade found its mark in my left arm and burned as it entered right above the elbow. It was like a sudden jolt of electricity, which compelled me to jerk my hand back as the blade made contact with the bone.

"Stop! Stop! Stop!" Moya screamed, and everything froze, leaving me locked in a staredown with the attacker and his butcher's knife. I wanted to ask him why—none of the violence made sense—but adrenaline and anger blocked the words.

Sensing the opportunity, Moya bravely ran between the man with the knife and me and attended to Eric. Our eyes followed her to his limp body on the sidewalk, as his hands grasped at his head and face as if trying to find and clog the leak—but blood was everywhere, and half his Afro was crimson red and slicked down against his head.

The attacker assessed the situation and took off running. Instinctively, I began to chase him, but Moya screamed at me and broke the spell of vengeance, allowing me to see Eric lying on the concrete, muttering incoherently and squinting his eyes to keep the blood out. Moya held his head in her lap and tried to slow the bleeding, to little avail.

"Yo! What the fuck is going on?" I looked up and saw Gav running towards us, but could only stare blankly—unable to translate raw emotion into words. I turned to Moya, who was screaming for help, but no one was coming. I looked at Eric, now slipping in and out of consciousness and muttering repeatedly: "Don't let me die!" and decided we had to act.

Gav and I lifted Eric off the bloody concrete and towards the car, which felt miles away under the weight of his limp body. We were all covered with Eric's blood when we slid him into the back seat next to Moya, who was crying uncontrollably as she held his head in her lap.

I rode shotgun with Gav, urging him to run the red lights on Queens Blvd as we sped towards St. John's hospital, where we simultaneously lifted and dragged his semi-unconscious body up the ramp towards the hospital entrance.

We screamed for help as the sliding door opened, allowing us to enter the emergency room. However, the seated attendant only looked up from the desk to ask us to fill out forms.

The chart colliding against the glass window reverberated like a gunshot. And for good measure, I screamed, "We need help!" I shoved everything off the desk while threatening further damage if Eric didn't get medical attention immediately—which he did, along with hospital security to make sure nothing else got damaged.

Confrontation, rage, even violence—none of it came naturally to me. But at that moment, I knew it was the only way to save Eric's life. And I would have done anything to make sure he didn't die.

Once they rushed him into surgery, Gav and I made what was a tough and emotional call to Eric's mother. After 200 stitches and a few weeks in the hospital, Eric made it home. But something changed that night, shattering our illusion of invincibility forever. And in hindsight, it was a precursor of the violence to come.

I got seven stitches and only missed a few days of class after the attack, but the missed days cost me my job at Gap-Kids in Roosevelt Field Mall. I did, however, finish my first college semester strong and passed all my classes—with grades ranging from an "A" in Debate to a "D" in Juvenile Delinquency (JD).

The "A" in Debate surprised no one. Miss Tiny always said I was born to argue and often *too smart for my own good*. But my grade in JD was disappointing, as surely my shenanigans over the past few months should have factored into the equation!? However, it became clear that the distance between my life and the juvenile justice case studies we read in class was shrinking.

I was excited for my second semester of college despite lingering financial hurdles. Mom had to pay for my first semester out of pocket, as the powers that be deemed our family income too high for any aid. However, the calculations didn't account for the fact that immigrant families were not "traditional" and often supported numerous family members and close friends at home and abroad.

Shortly after the semester concluded, Mom sat me down and explained that she and John could no longer afford to pay for college out of pocket. I was disappointed, but I understood. We were always family first—and I knew how hard they worked to create opportunities for our growing family. But the prospect of ushering in 1994 with a child on the way, no job, and no college didn't feel right. Yet I had no idea just how *wrong* it would be.

January 1994

"Idle time is the devil's playground" was another one of Miss Tiny's idioms that I didn't get, but it was real. Especially after I began taking "Eddie's" calls more seriously. I soon transitioned from working, attending college, and preparing to be a father to becoming the "hook-up."

A coming-of-age story in New York City—albeit with a splash of Ray and Nephew overproof rum—was now Scarface in high definition.

But at the moment, I was more Manolo than Scarface and badly in need of a leading man.

It was one of those frigid, clear-sky days indicative of January in Gotham when I made the call that changed my life and impacted countless others. Yet, even today, I can't tell you what made me do it. What I can tell you is that Eddie's wish list continued to grow and ranged from semi-automatic guns to cocaine—*always* emphasizing that more was better. But since I had no prior experience selling drugs or guns, I reached out to one of my boys from The Flip Side (aka "TFS")—a neighborhood crew of older guys who drove fly cars, dated all the hot girls, and were legends in the schools we attended.

After a few calls, I got the number for a guy I knew in passing. "Polo" was tall, slim, and a pretty boy with Trinidadian heritage—although many people thought he was Hispanic. He was a hustler and had the "hook up" on cell phones in the early '90s before they were even a thing. I sat on his number for a few days before eventually paging him, and it took another few days for us to meet up—but when we did, the first question he asked after I told him about "Eddie" was: "How do you know him?"

My bravado didn't allow for the truth, and I told Polo, "he worked with one of my boys, and we did business occasionally." Sadly, for both of us, the lie worked. Satisfied, he promised to check with some people and get back to me. True to his word, a week later, he called me on the cell phone I'd bought from him and said, "The connect" could get a Smith & Wesson handgun for $500.

Selling guns was new territory for me, but coming of age in a White man's world taught me numerous survival skills—and one of them was to *hustle*. So I excitedly called Eddie and told him I could get a handgun for $1000." Eddie quickly agreed, and we decided to meet in Forest Hills, Queens, not far from Polo's house off 108th Street, once the merchandise was received.

I hung up the phone, not knowing what Eddie looked like. Or any other logistical details. I only knew that he "was a cool dude from Staten Island trying to make money on the side," according to Judas—who I began to wonder if I could trust.

I had many questions and jitters over the next few days. But backing out didn't feel like an option. So when Polo called to confirm everything was ready, I reluctantly called Eddie to set a day and time to meet.

I often remember small details of life from childhood. But I remember very little about the day my life changed forever, except that the vibes didn't feel right when Eddie pulled up in his red Jeep Cherokee with his White, *cop-looking* friend riding shotgun.

Every pore in my body screamed *police*. But I muted my intuitive wisdom and got in the back seat of the Jeep, where we introduced ourselves and exchanged pleasantries.

After a few minutes of nervous chatter, Polo, sitting behind the driver, casually handed the gun to Eddie in the passenger seat. Eddie took a few minutes to inspect it before handing Polo an envelope containing crisp $100 bills. It was, by all appearances, a casual business transaction. We exited the car once everyone was satisfied, but not before promising future deals to make us all *rich*.

My boy Tito and a few friends were parked blocks away in a red 1988 Mustang t-top convertible for safety purposes when the deal went down. After Eddie drove off and Polo and I wrapped up, I made my way over to the car, where they all expressed some valid concerns. But I couldn't hear them.

Making more money in ten minutes than I ever earned from a paycheck instigated a euphoria that negated reason. Eddie also knew *money* would assuage our fears as he led us to Hell. And thanks to "Reaganomics," our hoods were flooded with drugs and guns. So, Eddie paying us above street value made doing business with him a no-brainer. In my mind, it was an opportunity to stack some dough before going back into the real world.

Pretty soon, we had a streamlined operation: Eddie placed an order with me, and I relayed it to Polo, who coordinated with the *connect*. Once the item (or a suitable alternative) was in hand, a delivery day and time were confirmed with Eddie. Usually, on the day of delivery, I met Polo at his building, where he lived with his mother in a two-bedroom apartment. Nothing fancy for Forest Hills. But as an 18-year-old hip-hop-head and child of the '90s, I was enamored with Polo's room.

Polo had a giant TV with a Sega Genesis, Super Nintendo, and game systems that weren't even available for sale in the United States. He was also a "Lo-lifer" with a plethora of Ralph Lauren gear and sneakers in a huge walk-in closet.

Polo's mom was usually at work when I visited. She probably knew he had side hustles but was clueless that her house was now a transit stop for our newly minted drug and gun enterprise—which, after a while, truly began to feel like a *legitimate* business. Yet even with the dissonance, there were times I wondered *who was buying the drugs and guns we sold to Eddie?*

March 1994

It was business as usual one day in March, except that Eddie and Polo were both running late. So, I went to the Forest Hills Community Center directly behind Polo's building. It was always a safe space for people from different neighborhoods, and I always knew someone there. But as I turned the corner onto 62nd Drive, I noticed a large contingent of police cars at the far end of the block.

The tension in the air was palpable, but the cops were lounging around various vehicles as if awaiting instructions. I was on edge and kept moving. But I was naive and told myself that the army of police behind Polo's house—around the same time I was to meet Eddie—was just a coincidence. But in hindsight, I missed another red light and disregarded the stop sign altogether. The allure of fast money drove me blindly towards the intersection—and my day of reckoning.

April 1994

The morning of April 13, 1994, was dark, rainy, and cold—a good day to call in sick and stay in bed. I hadn't slept much, having spent the night watching a documentary and arguing with Moya, who was now *unofficially* living with me as she was feuding with her mom, who hated me because I was Black and presumably a bad influence.

With Heather due in July, Moya and I were at war as she felt I betrayed our relationship—which couldn't be further from the truth, as she dumped me when I got back from Jamaica under really shady circumstances. For weeks, I didn't hear anything from her. I was so worried that I showed up at her mother's house on Woodhaven Blvd unannounced to make sure she was ok. However, my unexpected visit to Moya's mother's house didn't go well and emphatically ended all communication from June until we reconnected in early December of '93.

So we weren't in the best frame of mind when Moya asked, "What happens if you get arrested?" A prophetic question, which at the moment felt like a blow—even though it shouldn't have, since we had *just* watched a documentary on the Attica prison riots. But I was disconnected from the reality that my actions over the last four months constituted a crime, and responded defiantly to Moya, "Only *bad* people go to prison!"

Polo and I planned to meet Eddie at 5 pm—he told us he had a huge deal in the works and wanted to re-up. The sale included cocaine, a bulletproof vest, and a few guns. Eddie was usually a cool customer, but was anxious when we last spoke. He suggested we meet closer to Staten Island, as he didn't want to drive to Queens. I spoke with Polo, and we agreed to meet Eddie in Brooklyn, off the Belt Parkway at Exit 13.

Polo was supposed to pick me up by 4 pm, but the rain and traffic stretched it closer to 5. Once he arrived, I rushed for the door with a heavy purple JanSport backpack on my shoulders—filled with cash, a cell phone, a Glock 9, and a bulletproof vest. I was halfway gone when I ran into Mom.

I froze. Mom was the last face I wanted to see. For months, I had been pulling away while living a lie. But inches from her, with one foot out the door, I felt guilt, and probably, intuitively, sensed the gravity of what loomed.

Mom and I quickly exchanged pleasantries, and I was almost out the door when she asked if I would be home for dinner. I paused, said "no," and shared that I was meeting Moya later for dinner and a movie and wouldn't be home until late. I stepped outside the house and slowly closed the door, with no idea it would be my last interaction with my mother outside of a prison or jail for the next decade.

Polo was parked, anxiously waiting, a block away at Brookville Park. Walking around the passenger side, I noticed someone else in the car, a guy who ran with TFS. Polo introduced us as his passenger stepped out of the two-door sports car to let me in. We bumped fists as I squeezed into the rear of the vehicle. I sat between the two front seats to get a clear view ahead and ease the claustrophobia I often felt in the back seat of small coupes.

I was barely seated when the tires peeled out, and we were on our way. Polo was worried about being late and spoke casually around his boy—which made me a little uncomfortable as we intentionally did not involve other people in our business. Yet I was optimistic we would make up time as the car sped along the South Conduit toward the Belt Parkway. But once we got close to JFK Airport, we were greeted by a steady stream of rain and brake lights.

I paged and called Eddie on his cell, but his line went unanswered. We crawled anxiously in traffic until Polo threw a Ron-G mixtape in the tape deck—and chants of "M-e-t-h-o-d Man" broke the silence. But the tension remained as we crawled in bumper-to-bumper traffic towards Pennsylvania Ave—one exit from where we were to meet with Eddie.

Once we got close to our destination, I asked Polo to turn down the music so I could repeat Eddie's directions: *get off at exit 13, then make a right onto Rockaway Blvd. Drive three blocks, then look for a Pizza Hut on the left in a small shopping plaza across from the projects.*

Shortly after exiting, we saw Pizza Hut in a horseshoe-shaped plaza anchored by a supermarket and the ubiquitous liquor store. Polo navigated around the horseshoe but didn't park. He positioned the car to face the entrance/exit.

I kept calling Eddie, getting no answer, and arguing with Polo that traffic must be heavy coming from the Verrazano Bridge—assuming he was coming from Staten Island. But there was no assuaging our collective anxiety—even Polo was nervous and fidgety as we were all outside our comfort zones.

In a society predicated on *knowing,* we often ridicule people who speak of realities beyond the mind's subjective understanding. But I believe there are senses we have yet to name or discover—like the one deep down in your gut that tells you something is *off,* danger is imminent, and shit is about to hit the fan. *Do you know that one?* If so, then you will overstand when I tell you that my "spider sense" was screaming when a fast-moving vehicle entered the plaza and screeched to a halt between us and the exit.

Everything started to unravel in a surreal, almost slow-motion way. We even had a synchronized "Oh shit…" moment.

We were experiencing the climax of a story we didn't want to be in. But this wasn't a movie—this was real—and it got extremely deadly when the front doors of the car blocking our exit flew open, and two burly White men jumped out.

I watched in slow motion as the man on the passenger side stumbled out of the car, nearly face-planting in his rush toward us—which looked clumsy and made me almost want to laugh. But the gun in his hand and the cold, violent clarity in his eyes erased any illusion of comedy.

The two White men screamed repeatedly for us to "get the fuck out of the car" as they took tactical positions around us. I examined the face of the guy closest to me—he was animated and moving his mouth, but I could no longer hear his words. I could only stare at the gun, less than a foot away—pivoting back and forth between my face and Polo's boy in the front seat.

For a few moments, it was as if time stopped; then the bubble burst, and there were White men everywhere with more guns—dragging Polo and his boy out of the car first. Then, a large hand grabbed me like a hook and ripped me straight out of the rear of the car, up in the air, and face down onto the wet concrete.

I was disoriented but more concerned about my Timbs, leather jacket, and cream-colored jeans getting dirty, so I raised my body off the floor to protest, but was met with a knee to my back, which knocked the air from my lungs and thrust me back down to the wet concrete.

My face was bruised, and I passed out momentarily. When I regained consciousness, my limbs were restrained while someone's hands searched my pockets. Dazed, I turned my head right and saw an army of what looked to be cops around Polo, who was also on the ground a few feet away. He sent a cryptic message as we made eye contact. But it wasn't necessary. We never discussed contingency plans, yet I knew the *code*.

Once we were all restrained and searched, the men stepped away to huddle and discuss strategy. After a few tense moments, they dragged us off the ground and into separate unmarked cars. They attempted to cover my face and head with some type of hood. I verbally protested but was told to "shut the fuck up."

I took my cue and remained silent, nervously. Aside from movies, I had no reference point for my current predicament. Thankfully, the material on my head was breathable and semi-transparent at just the right angle, and I could see that we were heading toward the Belt Parkway. I began to consider the possibility that these guys weren't cops.

No one read me "Miranda Rights." There was only silence in the car as we sped along the parkway. And for a moment, I considered the possibility of a mob hit. Did I piss someone off? *Did someone snitch on me?* But as I began preparing for my imminent demise, one of the men asked, "Do you know Eddie?"

I was startled by the question, which felt weighty, as the guy in the passenger seat turned and stared at me, as if demanding a response. I nodded my head from side to side to signify *no*, I don't know Eddie.

Did Eddie get locked up? Did he snitch on us? I was scared to ask these questions aloud; instead, I listened and nodded with each inquiry. Whatever they asked, my response would be the same: "No."

When the questions finally subsided, I took a chance and asked, "Where are we going?" I was genuinely confused and scared by our route from the Belt Parkway to the Van Wyck Expressway into Queens—as my one semester in college had taught me a *little* about prosecutorial jurisdiction.

Assuming my escorts were cops, I knew they couldn't just take me from Brooklyn to Queens. But they didn't answer my question; instead, they glanced at each other as people do when they share a secret. A few miles of silence ensued before the driver, who hadn't yet spoken, said: "You will see!"

We continued in silence, exiting the highway at Union Turnpike in Kew Gardens, Queens. We proceeded North along Queens Blvd before stopping at the traffic light by Midway Movie Theater and 108th Street—an area I went to school, knew well, and ironically where I had planned to meet Moya later that night.

We proceeded past Yellowstone Boulevard for a quarter mile before slowing and entering a building toward a dark underground garage. The darkness plus the hood made it impossible to see and exacerbated my anxiety. My heart rate increased as the car stopped and the engine went silent. The guy on the passenger side got out and opened my door before palming my head like a basketball and pulling me out of the car. He then looked down at me and asked: "Do you still want to know where you are?" I remained silent, but he responded villainously, almost to himself: "You will soon find out!"

With the hood on my head and no vision, we navigated towards the unknown. We paused and awaited what I presumed was an elevator—which was confirmed by a chime and the opening of doors moments later. We got on and began our ascent. Just as we were about to get off, someone shouted for us to "Stop!"

Frozen by the command, we stood silent outside the elevator, at which point the hood was removed from my head. As my eyes adjusted, I saw what appeared to be a government building with official-looking seals and emblems on the walls. They cleared us to continue after about 15 minutes by the elevator shaft. A big Black guy greeted us halfway down the long corridor, and for the first time, I exhaled—not because he was Black, but because I immediately knew he was a cop, probably a former Marine.

He looked down curiously at me and asked: "What are you doing here? There was even a hint of concern in his voice. And it felt like a very relevant question considering the moment. Yet it caught me off guard, and I had to think about it for a minute before telling him, "I don't know," which elicited laughter from my escorts and prompted them to give me the first clue of what was happening.

The "ATF doesn't just go after anybody." *ATF?* The acronym made no sense. I had vague recollections of the term from the 1993 Waco, Texas standoff with David Koresh. But couldn't understand what they wanted with me.

I got a sad look from the Marine as he walked away, and we got the green light to proceed. We continued down a long hallway, past offices and meeting spaces, before coming up on a crude row of human-sized bird cages—with *people* inside. I couldn't believe my eyes, but as we got closer, I recognized Polo as one of the captives.

I stopped momentarily, and Polo and I stared blankly at each other before my escort nudged me toward another cage. Once securely inside, with nothing but a small bench, my handcuffs were removed, and I was instructed not to talk with the "other prisoners"—it was rule number one… Yet the onset of claustrophobia didn't allow me to hear my captor's orders.

The walls were shrinking, and despair threatened my little resolve as I stood in the cage. I was scared. I tried to pray, but didn't know where to start.

I was raised in the Baptist church, but I struggled to believe in a White male God—with an affinity for *chosen* people.

I sat down to slow my mind and heart rate, but it didn't work. I felt like I was falling into the abyss.

I took a deep breath and slowly stood from the small bench. I glanced down the long hallway towards Polo. After affirming that there were no guards, we communicated through facial expressions and hand gestures. Polo told me about his interrogation and pointed out the office where it took place.

Maybe our captors were secretly watching and listening—as moments later, the interrogation room office door flew open, and a tall White man emerged and came towards me. He unlocked my cage and instructed me to face the wall with my hands behind my head so he could handcuff me. I was then led to a small room and ordered to strip down to my boxers.

The agent attempted to make small talk and asked, "How did you get into this mess?" Like the Marine from earlier, his tone was caring and caught me off guard. Yet I still didn't know what to say and kept hoping I was in the midst of a bad dream—which I got often, *usually,* face-to-face with my imminent demise, maybe falling off a building, or from some high place.

The dreams always felt very real—I knew deep inside that they represented a crossroads—whether physical or spiritual. It was never an easy fight, but I ultimately conjured the will to wake up right before the climactic scene. However, I felt powerless, in a *nightmare* determined to invalidate my humanity.

To dissociate in hopes of normalcy, I told the agent about my college experience and my dream of becoming an attorney. The tall White man's face looked perplexed as he bluntly interrupted, saying, "You can't be a lawyer with a criminal conviction."

The agent's words lingered as a foul odor in the air. We finished in silence before he escorted me to the interrogation office Polo had pointed out earlier. Once inside, two older White men greeted me from the other side of a large desk.

My escort hovered in the background and out of sight as the interrogation team took over and sat me down. For the first time since the parking lot in Brooklyn, my captors identified themselves as agents from a joint Federal and State Task Force. They then asked, again, if I knew why I was there.

I looked at them, staring at me from across the table, and shook my head *no*. They looked at each other before the agent to my right extended a large envelope across the desk, but didn't hand it to me. Instead, he asked me to "pick it up and look inside." I opened the metal clasp with trembling hands, half expecting something to jump out and bite me. But what came next was worse than a bite and highly venomous.

I shuffled through the photographs of various sizes, from different places and times. Some were months old, others from earlier that week. Pictures of Polo, me, friends, family, and people coming in and out of my house in Rosedale. Stunned, I looked up to find the two White men staring at me with big grins, proud of their work.

The agents let the first envelope marinate for a few more minutes before placing a second envelope on the table in front of me. I did not attempt to open it, so one of the agents emptied its contents onto the table for me to view. At this point, I shouldn't have been surprised, but that's precisely how I felt, looking at surveillance photos of the red Jeep Cherokee and all the deals Polo and I had made with Eddie.

The cards were on the table—they had spades—we both knew it. They let it marinate some more before demanding:

"Do you want to cooperate?"

I shook my head and said, "No."

Sensing my vulnerability, they went in for the kill:

"How do you know Polo?"

"How do you know Eddie?"

"Where did you get the guns and drugs?"

"Do you know how much time you're going to get in prison?"

I was overwhelmed by the questions—which came in rapid succession.

I knew they were trying to scare me, and it was working. One of them threw out "45 years to life" as a possible sentence—which sounded crazy to me—but next thing you know, I was running the numbers in my head.

My math, usually good, was slow under pressure, but if the prison numbers the agent threw out were correct, I would be eligible for parole around my 63rd birthday.

I turned away from the agents and looked out the large window onto Queens Blvd. It was overcast and raining, and cars, with windshield wipers moving back and forth in a rhythmic dance, were held captive by red lights.

I scanned the queue of people under umbrellas and wondered if they truly valued their lives and knew how quickly things could change?

I was falling down the rabbit hole of *what if* when the agent said:

"Save yourself!"

"Polo is cooperating!"

I remained silent, letting the tension build as I contemplated jumping out the window. But my fear of heights and falling squashed the thought.

I took a deep breath and broke the stalemate by asking my captors for a call. The agents looked at each other before sliding me a piece of paper. I instinctively gave them Cleve's name and number. He and I grew up off Washington Boulevard in Kingston, Jamaica—and migrated to the United States within a few years of each other. He was like a big brother who always had my back. But today, his phone rang and went unanswered.

Cleve would be the first of many friends I would never see or speak to again after my arrest. The agents let me make two more calls, and I reluctantly gave them my house number, but no one answered. My third and final choice, which probably should have been first, was Will.

Will was my ace and someone I considered a brother. He was a light-skinned, pretty boy with wavy hair and a slick mouth who was always getting into fights for stealing other dudes' girls. I remembered the one time he went too far and messed with our boy Rico's girlfriend. But Rico wasn't having it and got his crew, Baby Face Killers (aka BFK), together and rolled on Will to beat his ass. Luckily for Will, I was nearby and talked Rico into putting away the knives and guns and giving Will a one-on-one.

Will and I met in '86, when he lived with his mom a floor above my Grandma in Park City Estates, a middle-class housing complex in Queens with a sprinkling of colored folks we considered family—people like J-Boogie, Yosan, Carlos, Rodney, Chris Augusto, and Topaz.

I was losing hope when Will finally answered the phone after what felt like a million rings. The ATF agents announced themselves, told Will I was arrested, and that the call was recorded—at which point I expected him to hang up. But he stayed on as they slid the phone receiver across the desk.

My voice trembled as I said little but made my position clear before asking him to call Moya—who I knew would be good at organizing my friends and family for support and bail money.

After the call, there were no more questions. The tall agent returned to escort me back to the holding cell—where I could feel Polo's eyes probing me for signs of treachery. But there was no time to debrief as the agent immediately turned to Polo after securing me in the cell. It was a hush-hush conversation, but I heard the ATF agent ask him if he had "any drugs or guns in the house?"

If Polo didn't cooperate, the agent threatened to execute a search warrant and tear the house apart. They knew Polo lived with his mother and used that as leverage to get information from him—they even promised only to search where he sent them. The conversation took on a more hushed tone, and a short time later, the agent walked away looking satisfied—but Polo looked pissed!

I didn't have any words for Polo, so I looked away. For the first time, I saw his boy, who was with us earlier in the car, a few cells down from me. He was big—over six feet tall—and looked ginormous in the tiny cell. He was too far away to communicate, but I figured they would eventually let him go.

I lay down on the bench and closed my eyes, hoping, once again, to *miraculously* wake up. But thirty minutes later, the tall agent appeared in front of my cell and said I was being transferred to Central Booking as they turned the case over to the State. I didn't understand the legal jargon, but I assumed I was one step closer to seeing a judge and getting bail.

It was after 10 pm on April 13, 1994, when two new agents came to get me from the cage. Handcuffed, they led me back down the long hallway toward the elevator, where we waited in silence. But there was a lot of noise behind an adjacent wall with a closed door.

I listened closely to what sounded like a celebration and had a sick feeling that I knew one of the voices. A chime signaled the elevator's arrival just as the office door opened. But before stepping on the elevator, I quickly glanced at the open door.

I saw his face, and my body went numb. My mind, once again, struggled to compute. We just stared at each other. But he had no handcuffs, no agents escorting him, and his face was defiant.

I slowly expanded my focus beyond his eyes and noticed the metallic badge around his neck. We held eye contact as he stepped back into the room and slowly closed the door. But I couldn't stop staring—even after "Eddie" was no longer visible.

Exhibit A: Charges

SUPREME COURT OF THE STATE OF NEW YORK

COUNTY OF QUEENS

MAY 25 1994

THE PEOPLE OF THE STATE OF NEW YORK

AGAINST

FILED:
INDICTMENT NO. 1946/94

XJ. KIRK JAMES - AFO,VFO
AKA JD KURT
DEFENDANT
94Q012385
94Q012387
94Q012389
94Q012391
94Q012393
94Q012395
NYSID# 7648252P

XJ. DUANE ADAMS - AFO,VFO
AKA JD GOLD AKA: POLO
DEFENDANT
94Q012386
94Q012388
94Q012390
94Q012392
94Q012394
94Q012396
94Q012397
NYSID# 7648253N

265.11-2	CRIMINAL SALE OF A FIREARM IN THE THIRD DEGREE (1)	(JAMES,KIRK) (ADAMS,DUANE)
265.02-4	CRIMINAL POSSESSION OF A WEAPON IN THE THIRD DEGREE (2)	(JAMES,KIRK) (ADAMS,DUANE)
265.11-2	CRIMINAL SALE OF A FIREARM IN THE THIRD DEGREE (3)	(JAMES,KIRK) (ADAMS,DUANE)
265.01-1	CRIMINAL POSSESSION OF A WEAPON IN THE FOURTH DEGREE (4)	(JAMES,KIRK) (ADAMS,DUANE)
220.41-1	CRIMINAL SALE OF A CONTROLLED SUBSTANCE IN THE SECOND DEGREE, (5)	(JAMES,KIRK) (ADAMS,DUANE) A II
220.16-4	CRIMINAL POSSESSION OF A CONTROLLED SUBSTANCE IN THE THIRD DEGREE (6)	(JAMES,KIRK) (ADAMS,DUANE)
265.11-2	CRIMINAL SALE OF A FIREARM IN THE THIRD DEGREE (7,9)	(JAMES,KIRK) (ADAMS,DUANE)
265.02-4	CRIMINAL POSSESSION OF A WEAPON IN THE THIRD DEGREE (8,10)	(JAMES,KIRK) (ADAMS,DUANE)
265.02-3	CRIMINAL POSSESSION OF A WEAPON IN THE THIRD DEGREE (11)	(JAMES,KIRK) (ADAMS,DUANE)
220.43-1	CRIMINAL SALE OF A CONTROLLED SUBSTANCE IN THE FIRST DEGREE, (12)	(JAMES,KIRK) (ADAMS,DUANE) AI
220.21-1	CRIMINAL POSSESSION OF A CONTROLLED SUBSTANCE IN THE FIRST DEGREE (13)	(JAMES,KIRK) (ADAMS,DUANE) A
265.11-2	CRIMINAL SALE OF A FIREARM IN THE THIRD DEGREE (14,16)	(JAMES,KIRK) (ADAMS,DUANE
265.02-4	CRIMINAL POSSESSION OF A WEAPON IN THE [illegible] DEGREE, (18)	(JAMES,KIRK) (ADAMS,DUANE)
220.18-1	CRIMINAL POSSESSION OF A CONTROLLED SUBSTANCE IN THE SECOND DEGREE (19)	(JAMES,KIRK) (ADAMS,DUANE)
265.11-2	CRIMINAL SALB OF A FIREARM IN THE THIRD DEGREE (20)	(JAMES,KIRK) (ADAMS,DUANE)
265.02-4	CRIMINAL POSSESSION OF A WEAPON IN THE THIRD DEGREE (21)	(JAMES,KIRK) (ADAMS,DUANE)
220.16-4	CRIMINAL POSSESSION OF A CONTROLLED SUBSTANCE IN THE THIRD DEGREE (22)	(ADAMS,DUANE)
265.02-2	CRIMINAL POSSESSION OF A WEAPON IN THE THIRD DEGREE (23)	(ADAMS,DUANE)
265.02-3	CRIMINAL POSSESSION OF A WEAPON IN THE THIRD DEGREE (24)	(ADAMS,DUANE)
265.01-1	CRIMINAL POSSESSION OF A WEAPON IN THE FOURTH DEGREE (25)	(ADAMS,DUANE)
221.10-2	CRIMINAL POSSESSION OF MARIHUANA IN THE FIFTH DEGREE (26)	(ADAMS,DUANE)

A TRUE BILL

FOREMAN

DISTRICT ATTORNEY

FIRST COUNT

THE GRAND JURY OF THE COUNTY OF QUEENS BY THIS INDICTMENT ACCUSE THE DEFENDANTS, DUANE ADAMS, aka "JD GOLD", aka "POLO", AND KIRK JAMES, aka "JD KURT", OF THE CRIME OF CRIMINAL SALE OF A FIREARM IN THE THIRD DEGREE, IN VIOLATION OF PENAL LAW SECTION 265.11(2), COMMITTED AS FOLLOWS:

THE DEFENDANTS, DUANE ADAMS, aka "JD GOLD", aka "POLO", AND KIRK JAMES, aka "JD KURT", ON OR ABOUT JANUARY 24, 1994, IN THE COUNTY OF QUEENS, KNOWINGLY AND UNLAWFULLY POSSESSED A FIREARM, TO WIT: A 9 MM SMITH & WESSON HANDGUN, WITH INTENT TO SELL IT.

SECOND COUNT

THE GRAND JURY OF THE COUNTY OF QUEENS BY THIS INDICTMENT FURTHER ACCUSE THE DEFENDANTS, DUANE ADAMS, aka "JD GOLD", aka "POLO", AND KIRK JAMES, aka "JD KURT", OF THE CRIME OF CRIMINAL POSSESSION OF A WEAPON IN THE THIRD DEGREE, IN VIOLATION OF PENAL LAW SECTION 265.02(4), COMMITTED AS FOLLOWS:

THE DEFENDANTS, DUANE ADAMS, aka "JD GOLD", aka "POLO", AND KIRK JAMES, aka "JD KURT", ON OR ABOUT JANUARY 24, 1994, IN THE COUNTY OF QUEENS, KNOWINGLY AND UNLAWFULLY POSSESSED A LOADED FIREARM, TO WIT: A 9 MM SMITH & WESSON HANDGUN, SUCH POSSESSION NOT BEING IN EITHER DEFENDANT'S HOME OR PLACE OF BUSINESS, THE SUBJECT MATTER OF THIS COUNT BEING AN ARMED VIOLENT FELONY OFFENSE AS DEFINED BY CPL SECTION 1.20.

THIRD COUNT

THE GRAND JURY OF THE COUNTY OF QUEENS BY THIS INDICTMENT FURTHER ACCUSE THE DEFENDANTS, DUANE ADAMS, aka "JD GOLD", aka "POLO", AND KIRK JAMES, aka "JD KURT", OF THE CRIME OF CRIMINAL SALE OF A FIREARM IN THE THIRD DEGREE, IN VIOLATION OF PENAL LAW SECTION 265.11(2), COMMITTED AS FOLLOWS:

THE DEFENDANTS, DUANE ADAMS, aka "JD GOLD", aka "POLO", AND KIRK JAMES, aka "JD KURT", ON OR ABOUT FEBRUARY 14, 1994, IN THE COUNTY OF QUEENS, KNOWINGLY AND UNLAWFULLY POSSESSED A FIREARM, TO WIT: A 9 MM SIG SAUER HANDGUN, WITH INTENT TO SELL IT.

FOURTH COUNT

THE GRAND JURY OF THE COUNTY OF QUEENS BY THIS INDICTMENT FURTHER ACCUSE THE DEFENDANTS, DUANE ADAMS, aka "JD GOLD", aka "POLO", AND KIRK JAMES, aka "JD KURT", OF THE CRIME OF CRIMINAL POSSESSION OF A WEAPON IN THE FOURTH DEGREE, IN VIOLATION OF PENAL LAW SECTION 265.01(1), COMMITTED AS FOLLOWS:

THE DEFENDANTS, DUANE ADAMS, aka "JD GOLD", aka "POLO", AND KIRK JAMES, aka "JD KURT", ON OR ABOUT FEBRUARY 14, 1994, IN THE COUNTY OF QUEENS, KNOWINGLY AND UNLAWFULLY POSSESSED A FIREARM, TO WIT: A 9 MM SIG SAUER HANDGUN.

FIFTH COUNT

THE GRAND JURY OF THE COUNTY OF QUEENS BY THIS INDICTMENT FURTHER ACCUSE THE DEFENDANTS, DUANE ADAMS, aka "JD GOLD", aka "POLO", AND KIRK JAMES, aka "JD KURT", OF THE CRIME OF CRIMINAL SALE OF A CONTROLLED SUBSTANCE IN THE SECOND DEGREE, IN VIOLATION OF PENAL LAW SECTION 220.41(1), COMMITTED AS FOLLOWS:

THE DEFENDANTS, DUANE ADAMS, aka "JD GOLD", aka "POLO", AND KIRK JAMES, aka "JD KURT", ON OR ABOUT MARCH 29, 1994, IN THE COUNTY OF QUEENS, KNOWINGLY AND UNLAWFULLY SOLD TO AN UNDERCOVER DETECTIVE ONE OR MORE PREPARATIONS, COMPOUNDS, MIXTURES OR SUBSTANCES OF AN AGGREGATE WEIGHT OF ONE-HALF OUNCE OR MORE CONTAINING A NARCOTIC DRUG, TO WIT: COCAINE.

SIXTH COUNT

THE GRAND JURY OF THE COUNTY OF QUEENS BY THIS INDICTMENT FURTHER ACCUSE THE DEFENDANTS, DUANE ADAMS, aka "JD GOLD", aka "POLO", AND KIRK JAMES, aka "JD KURT", OF THE CRIME OF CRIMINAL POSSESSION OF A CONTROLLED SUBSTANCE IN THE THIRD DEGREE, IN VIOLATION OF PENAL LAW SECTION 220.16(12), COMMITTED AS FOLLOWS:

THE DEFENDANTS, DUANE ADAMS, aka "JD GOLD", aka "POLO", AND KIRK JAMES, aka "JD KURT", ON OR ABOUT MARCH 29, 1994, IN THE COUNTY OF QUEENS, KNOWINGLY AND UNLAWFULLY POSSESSED ONE OR MORE PREPARATIONS, COMPOUNDS, MIXTURES OR SUBSTANCES OF AN AGGREGATE WEIGHT OF ONE-HALF OUNCE OR MORE CONTAINING A NARCOTIC DRUG, TO WIT: COCAINE.

SEVENTH COUNT

THE GRAND JURY OF THE COUNTY OF QUEENS BY THIS INDICTMENT FURTHER ACCUSE THE DEFENDANTS, DUANE ADAMS, aka "JD GOLD", aka "POLO", AND KIRK JAMES, aka "JD KURT", OF THE CRIME OF CRIMINAL SALE OF A FIREARM IN THE THIRD DEGREE, IN VIOLATION OF PENAL LAW SECTION 265.11(2), COMMITTED AS FOLLOWS:

THE DEFENDANTS, DUANE ADAMS, aka "JD GOLD", aka "POLO", AND KIRK JAMES, aka "JD KURT", ON OR ABOUT MARCH 30, 1994, IN THE COUNTY OF QUEENS, KNOWINGLY AND UNLAWFULLY POSSESSED A FIREARM, TO WIT: A 9 MM TEC HANDGUN, WITH INTENT TO SELL IT.

SEVENTH COUNT

THE GRAND JURY OF THE COUNTY OF QUEENS BY THIS INDICTMENT FURTHER ACCUSE THE DEFENDANTS, DUANE ADAMS, aka "JD GOLD", aka "POLO", AND KIRK JAMES, aka "JD KURT", OF THE CRIME OF CRIMINAL SALE OF A FIREARM IN THE THIRD DEGREE, IN VIOLATION OF PENAL LAW SECTION 265.11(2), COMMITTED AS FOLLOWS:

THE DEFENDANTS, DUANE ADAMS, aka "JD GOLD", aka "POLO", AND KIRK JAMES, aka "JD KURT", ON OR ABOUT MARCH 30, 1994, IN THE COUNTY OF QUEENS, KNOWINGLY AND UNLAWFULLY POSSESSED A FIREARM, TO WIT: A 9 MM TEC HANDGUN, WITH INTENT TO SELL IT.

EIGHTH COUNT

THE GRAND JURY OF THE COUNTY OF QUEENS BY THIS INDICTMENT FURTHER ACCUSE THE DEFENDANTS, DUANE ADAMS, aka "JD GOLD", aka "POLO", AND KIRK JAMES, aka "JD KURT", OF THE CRIME OF CRIMINAL POSSESSION OF A WEAPON IN THE THIRD DEGREE, IN VIOLATION OF PENAL LAW SECTION 265.02(4), COMMITTED AS FOLLOWS:

THE DEFENDANTS, DUANE ADAMS, aka "JD GOLD", aka "POLO", AND KIRK JAMES, aka "JD KURT", ON OR ABOUT MARCH 30, 1994, IN THE COUNTY OF QUEENS, KNOWINGLY AND UNLAWFULLY POSSESSED A LOADED FIREARM, TO WIT: A 9 MM TEC HANDGUN, SUCH POSSESSION NOT BEING IN EITHER DEFENDANT'S HOME OR PLACE OF BUSINESS, THE SUBJECT MATTER OF THIS COUNT BEING AN ARMED VIOLENT FELONY OFFENSE AS DEFINED BY CPL SECTION 1.20.

NINTH COUNT

THE GRAND JURY OF THE COUNTY OF QUEENS BY THIS INDICTMENT FURTHER ACCUSE THE DEFENDANTS, DUANE ADAMS, aka "JD GOLD", aka "POLO", AND KIRK JAMES, aka "JD KURT", OF THE CRIME OF CRIMINAL SALE OF A FIREARM IN THE THIRD DEGREE, IN VIOLATION OF PENAL LAW SECTION 265.11(2), COMMITTED AS FOLLOWS:

THE DEFENDANTS, DUANE ADAMS, aka "JD GOLD", aka "POLO", AND KIRK JAMES, aka "JD KURT", ON OR ABOUT MARCH 30, 1994, IN THE COUNTY OF QUEENS, KNOWINGLY AND UNLAWFULLY POSSESSED A FIREARM, TO WIT: A 9 MM INTERDYNAMIC HANDGUN, WITH INTENT TO SELL IT.

TENTH COUNT

THE GRAND JURY OF THE COUNTY OF QUEENS BY THIS INDICTMENT FURTHER ACCUSE THE DEFENDANTS, DUANE ADAMS, aka "JD GOLD", aka "POLO", AND KIRK JAMES, aka "JD KURT", OF THE CRIME OF CRIMINAL POSSESSION OF A WEAPON IN THE THIRD DEGREE, IN VIOLATION OF PENAL LAW SECTION 265.02(4), COMMITTED AS FOLLOWS:

THE DEFENDANTS, DUANE ADAMS, aka "JD GOLD", aka "POLO", AND KIRK JAMES, aka "JD KURT", ON OR ABOUT MARCH 30, 1994, IN THE COUNTY OF QUEENS, KNOWINGLY AND UNLAWFULLY POSSESSED A LOADED FIREARM, TO WIT: A 9 MM INTERDYNAMIC HANDGUN, SUCH POSSESSION NOT BEING IN EITHER DEFENDANT'S HOME OR PLACE OF BUSINESS, THE SUBJECT MATTER OF THIS COUNT BEING AN ARMED VIOLENT FELONY OFFENSE AS DEFINED BY CPL SECTION 1.20.

ELEVENTH COUNT

THE GRAND JURY OF THE COUNTY OF QUEENS BY THIS INDICTMENT FURTHER ACCUSE THE DEFENDANTS, DUANE ADAMS, aka "JD GOLD", aka "POLO", AND KIRK JAMES, aka "JD KURT", OF THE CRIME OF CRIMINAL POSSESSION OF A WEAPON IN THE THIRD DEGREE, IN VIOLATION OF PENAL LAW SECTION 265.02(3), COMMITTED AS FOLLOWS:

THE DEFENDANTS, DUANE ADAMS, aka "JD GOLD", aka "POLO", AND KIRK JAMES, aka "JD KURT", ON OR ABOUT MARCH 30, 1994, IN THE COUNTY OF QUEENS, KNOWINGLY AND UNLAWFULLY POSSESSED A DEFACED FIREARM, TO WIT: A 9 MM INTERDYNAMIC HANDGUN.

TWELFTH COUNT

THE GRAND JURY OF THE COUNTY OF QUEENS BY THIS INDICTMENT FURTHER ACCUSE THE DEFENDANTS, DUANE ADAMS, aka "JD GOLD", aka "POLO", AND KIRK JAMES, aka "JD KURT", OF THE CRIME OF CRIMINAL SALE OF A CONTROLLED SUBSTANCE IN THE FIRST DEGREE, IN VIOLATION OF PENAL LAW SECTION 220.43(1), COMMITTED AS FOLLOWS:

THE DEFENDANTS, DUANE ADAMS, aka "JD GOLD", aka "POLO", AND KIRK JAMES, aka "JD KURT", ON OR ABOUT APRIL 5, 1994, IN THE COUNTY OF QUEENS, KNOWINGLY AND UNLAWFULLY SOLD TO AN UNDERCOVER DETECTIVE ONE OR MORE PREPARATIONS, COMPOUNDS, MIXTURES OR SUBSTANCES OF AN AGGREGATE WEIGHT OF TWO OUNCES OR MORE CONTAINING A NARCOTIC DRUG, TO WIT: COCAINE.

THIRTEENTH COUNT

THE GRAND JURY OF THE COUNTY OF QUEENS BY THIS INDICTMENT FURTHER ACCUSE THE DEFENDANTS, DUANE ADAMS, aka "JD GOLD", aka "POLO", AND KIRK JAMES, aka "JD KURT", OF THE CRIME OF CRIMINAL POSSESSION OF A CONTROLLED SUBSTANCE IN THE FIRST DEGREE, IN VIOLATION OF PENAL LAW SECTION 220.21(1), COMMITTED AS FOLLOWS:

THE DEFENDANTS, DUANE ADAMS, aka "JD GOLD", aka "POLO", AND KIRK JAMES, aka "JD KURT", ON OR ABOUT APRIL 5, 1994, IN THE COUNTY OF QUEENS, KNOWINGLY AND UNLAWFULLY POSSESSED ONE OR MORE PREPARATIONS, COMPOUNDS, MIXTURES OR SUBSTANCES OF AN AGGREGATE WEIGHT OF FOUR OUNCES OR MORE CONTAINING A NARCOTIC DRUG, TO WIT: COCAINE.

FOURTEENTH COUNT

THE GRAND JURY OF THE COUNTY OF QUEENS BY THIS INDICTMENT FURTHER ACCUSE THE DEFENDANTS, DUANE ADAMS, aka "JD GOLD", aka "POLO", AND KIRK JAMES, aka "JD KURT", OF THE CRIME OF CRIMINAL SALE OF A FIREARM IN THE THIRD DEGREE, IN VIOLATION OF PENAL LAW SECTION 265.11(2), COMMITTED AS FOLLOWS:

THE DEFENDANTS, DUANE ADAMS, aka "JD GOLD", aka "POLO", AND KIRK JAMES, aka "JD KURT", ON OR ABOUT APRIL 5, 1994, IN THE COUNTY OF QUEENS, KNOWINGLY AND UNLAWFULLY POSSESSED A FIREARM, TO WIT: A .25 CALIBER LORCIN HANDGUN, WITH INTENT TO SELL IT.

FIFTEENTH COUNT

THE GRAND JURY OF THE COUNTY OF QUEENS BY THIS INDICTMENT FURTHER ACCUSE THE DEFENDANTS, DUANE ADAMS, aka "JD GOLD", aka "POLO", AND KIRK JAMES, aka "JD KURT", OF THE CRIME OF CRIMINAL POSSESSION OF A WEAPON IN THE THIRD DEGREE, IN VIOLATION OF PENAL LAW SECTION 265.02(4), COMMITTED AS FOLLOWS:

THE DEFENDANTS, DUANE ADAMS, aka "JD GOLD", aka "POLO", AND KIRK JAMES, aka "JD KURT", ON OR ABOUT APRIL 5, 1994, IN THE COUNTY OF QUEENS, KNOWINGLY AND UNLAWFULLY POSSESSED A LOADED FIREARM, TO WIT: A .25 CALIBER LORCIN HANDGUN, SUCH POSSESSION NOT BEING IN EITHER DEFENDANT'S HOME OR PLACE OF BUSINESS, THE SUBJECT MATTER OF THIS COUNT BEING AN ARMED VIOLENT FELONY OFFENSE AS DEFINED BY CPL SECTION 1.20.

SIXTEENTH COUNT

THE GRAND JURY OF THE COUNTY OF QUEENS BY THIS INDICTMENT FURTHER ACCUSE THE DEFENDANTS, DUANE ADAMS, aka "JD GOLD", aka "POLO", AND KIRK JAMES, aka "JD KURT", OF THE CRIME OF CRIMINAL SALE OF A FIREARM IN THE THIRD DEGREE, IN VIOLATION OF PENAL LAW SECTION 265.11(2), COMMITTED AS FOLLOWS:

THE DEFENDANTS, DUANE ADAMS, aka "JD GOLD", aka "POLO", AND KIRK JAMES, aka "JD KURT", ON OR ABOUT APRIL 5, 1994, IN THE COUNTY OF QUEENS, KNOWINGLY AND UNLAWFULLY POSSESSED A FIREARM, TO WIT: A .25 CALIBER JENNINGS HANDGUN, WITH INTENT TO SELL IT.

SEVENTEENTH COUNT

THE GRAND JURY OF THE COUNTY OF QUEENS BY THIS INDICTMENT FURTHER ACCUSE THE DEFENDANTS, DUANE ADAMS, aka "JD GOLD", aka "POLO", AND KIRK JAMES, aka "JD KURT", OF THE CRIME OF CRIMINAL POSSESSION OF A WEAPON IN THE THIRD DEGREE, IN VIOLATION OF PENAL LAW SECTION 265.02(4), COMMITTED AS FOLLOWS:

THE DEFENDANTS, DUANE ADAMS, aka "JD GOLD", aka "POLO", AND KIRK JAMES, aka "JD KURT", ON OR ABOUT APRIL 5, 1994, IN THE COUNTY OF QUEENS, KNOWINGLY AND UNLAWFULLY POSSESSED A LOADED FIREARM, TO WIT: A .25 CALIBER JENNINGS HANDGUN, SUCH POSSESSION NOT BEING IN EITHER DEFENDANT'S HOME OR PLACE OF BUSINESS, THE SUBJECT MATTER OF THIS COUNT BEING AN ARMED VIOLENT FELONY OFFENSE AS DEFINED BY CPL SECTION 1.20.

EIGHTEENTH COUNT

THE GRAND JURY OF THE COUNTY OF QUEENS BY THIS INDICTMENT FURTHER ACCUSE THE DEFENDANTS, DUANE ADAMS, aka "JD GOLD", aka "POLO", AND KIRK JAMES, aka "JD KURT", OF THE CRIME OF CRIMINAL SALE OF A CONTROLLED SUBSTANCE IN THE FIRST DEGREE, IN VIOLATION OF PENAL LAW SECTION 220.43(1), COMMITTED AS FOLLOWS:

THE DEFENDANTS, DUANE ADAMS, aka "JD GOLD", aka "POLO", AND KIRK JAMES, aka "JD KURT", ON OR ABOUT APRIL 13, 1994, IN THE COUNTY OF QUEENS AND ELSEWHERE IN THE STATE OF NEW YORK, KNOWINGLY AND UNLAWFULLY SOLD TO AN UNDERCOVER DETECTIVE ONE OR MORE PREPARATIONS, COMPOUNDS, MIXTURES OR SUBSTANCES OF AN AGGREGATE WEIGHT OF TWO OUNCES OR MORE CONTAINING A NARCOTIC DRUG, TO WIT: COCAINE.

NINETEENTH COUNT

THE GRAND JURY OF THE COUNTY OF QUEENS BY THIS INDICTMENT FURTHER ACCUSE THE DEFENDANTS, DUANE ADAMS, aka "JD GOLD", aka "POLO", AND KIRK JAMES, aka "JD KURT", OF THE CRIME OF CRIMINAL POSSESSION OF A CONTROLLED SUBSTANCE IN THE SECOND DEGREE, IN VIOLATION OF PENAL LAW SECTION 220.18(1), COMMITTED AS FOLLOWS:

THE DEFENDANTS, DUANE ADAMS, aka "JD GOLD", aka "POLO", AND KIRK JAMES, aka "JD KURT", ON OR ABOUT APRIL 13, 1994, IN THE COUNTY OF QUEENS AND ELSEWHERE IN THE STATE OF NEW YORK, KNOWINGLY AND UNLAWFULLY POSSESSED ONE OR MORE PREPARATIONS, COMPOUNDS, MIXTURES OR SUBSTANCES OF AN AGGREGATE WEIGHT OF TWO OUNCES OR MORE CONTAINING A NARCOTIC DRUG, TO WIT: COCAINE.

TWENTIETH COUNT

THE GRAND JURY OF THE COUNTY OF QUEENS BY THIS INDICTMENT FURTHER ACCUSE THE DEFENDANTS, DUANE ADAMS, aka "JD GOLD", aka "POLO", AND KIRK JAMES, aka "JD KURT", OF THE CRIME OF CRIMINAL SALE OF A FIREARM IN THE THIRD DEGREE, IN VIOLATION OF PENAL LAW SECTION 265.11(2), COMMITTED AS FOLLOWS:

THE DEFENDANTS, DUANE ADAMS, aka "JD GOLD", aka "POLO", AND KIRK JAMES, aka "JD KURT", ON OR ABOUT APRIL 13, 1994, IN THE COUNTY OF QUEENS AND ELSEWHERE IN THE STATE OF NEW YORK, KNOWINGLY AND UNLAWFULLY POSSESSED A FIREARM, TO WIT: A 9 MM GLOCK HANDGUN, WITH INTENT TO SELL IT.

TWENTY-FIRST COUNT

THE GRAND JURY OF THE COUNTY OF QUEENS BY THIS INDICTMENT FURTHER ACCUSE THE DEFENDANTS, DUANE ADAMS, aka "JD GOLD", aka "POLO", AND KIRK JAMES, aka "JD KURT", OF THE CRIME OF CRIMINAL POSSESSION OF A WEAPON IN THE THIRD DEGREE, IN VIOLATION OF PENAL LAW SECTION 265.02(4), COMMITTED AS FOLLOWS:

THE DEFENDANTS, DUANE ADAMS, aka "JD GOLD", aka "POLO", AND KIRK JAMES, aka "JD KURT", ON OR ABOUT APRIL 13, 1994, IN THE COUNTY OF QUEENS AND ELSEWHERE IN THE STATE OF NEW YORK, KNOWINGLY AND UNLAWFULLY POSSESSED A LOADED FIREARM, TO WIT: A 9 MM GLOCK HANDGUN, SUCH POSSESSION NOT BEING IN EITHER DEFENDANT'S HOME OR PLACE OF BUSINESS, THE SUBJECT MATTER OF THIS COUNT BEING AN ARMED VIOLENT FELONY OFFENSE AS DEFINED BY CPL SECTION 1.20.

TWENTY-SECOND COUNT

THE GRAND JURY OF THE COUNTY OF QUEENS BY THIS INDICTMENT FURTHER ACCUSE THE DEFENDANT, DUANE ADAMS, aka "JD GOLD", aka "POLO", OF THE CRIME OF CRIMINAL POSSESSION OF A CONTROLLED SUBSTANCE IN THE THIRD DEGREE, IN VIOLATION OF PENAL LAW SECTION 220.16(12), COMMITTED AS FOLLOWS:

THE DEFENDANT, DUANE ADAMS, aka "JD GOLD", aka "POLO", ON OR ABOUT APRIL 13, 1994, IN THE COUNTY OF QUEENS, KNOWINGLY AND UNLAWFULLY POSSESSED ONE OR MORE PREPARATIONS, COMPOUNDS, MIXTURES OR SUBSTANCES OF AN AGGREGATE WEIGHT OF ONE-HALF OUNCE OR MORE CONTAINING A NARCOTIC DRUG, TO WIT: COCAINE.

TWENTY-THIRD COUNT

THE GRAND JURY OF THE COUNTY OF QUEENS BY THIS INDICTMENT FURTHER ACCUSE THE DEFENDANT, DUANE ADAMS, aka "JD GOLD", aka "POLO", OF THE CRIME OF CRIMINAL POSSESSION OF A WEAPON IN THE THIRD DEGREE, IN VIOLATION OF PENAL LAW SECTION 265.02(2), COMMITTED AS FOLLOWS:

THE DEFENDANT, DUANE ADAMS, aka "JD GOLD", aka "POLO", ON OR ABOUT APRIL 13, 1994, IN THE COUNTY OF QUEENS, KNOWINGLY AND UNLAWFULLY POSSESSED A MACHINE-GUN OR A WEAPON SIMULATING A MACHINE-GUN AND WHICH IS ADAPTABLE FOR SUCH USE, TO WIT: A 9 MM INTRATEC HANDGUN.

TWENTY-FOURTH COUNT

THE GRAND JURY OF THE COUNTY OF QUEENS BY THIS INDICTMENT FURTHER ACCUSE THE DEFENDANT, DUANE ADAMS, aka "JD GOLD", aka "POLO", OF THE CRIME OF CRIMINAL POSSESSION OF A WEAPON IN THE THIRD DEGREE, IN VIOLATION OF PENAL LAW SECTION 265.02(3), COMMITTED AS FOLLOWS:

THE DEFENDANT, DUANE ADAMS, aka "JD GOLD", aka "POLO", ON OR ABOUT APRIL 13, 1994, IN THE COUNTY OF QUEENS, KNOWINGLY AND UNLAWFULLY POSSESSED A DEFACED FIREARM, TO WIT: A 9 MM INTRATEC HANDGUN.

TWENTY-FIFTH COUNT

THE GRAND JURY OF THE COUNTY OF QUEENS BY THIS INDICTMENT FURTHER ACCUSE THE DEFENDANT, DUANE ADAMS, aka "JD GOLD", aka "POLO", OF THE CRIME OF CRIMINAL POSSESSION OF A WEAPON IN THE FOURTH DEGREE, IN VIOLATION OF PENAL LAW SECTION 265.01(1), COMMITTED AS FOLLOWS:

THE DEFENDANT, DUANE ADAMS, aka "JD GOLD", aka "POLO", ON OR ABOUT APRIL 13, 1994, IN THE COUNTY OF QUEENS, KNOWINGLY AND UNLAWFULLY POSSESSED A FIREARM, TO WIT: A .380 AMT HANDGUN.

TWENTY-SIXTH COUNT

THE GRAND JURY OF THE COUNTY OF QUEENS BY THIS INDICTMENT FURTHER ACCUSE THE DEFENDANT, DUANE ADAMS, aka "JD GOLD", aka "POLO", OF THE CRIME OF CRIMINAL POSSESSION OF A MARIHUANA IN THE FIFTH DEGREE, IN VIOLATION OF PENAL LAW SECTION 221.10(2), COMMITTED AS FOLLOWS:

THE DEFENDANT, DUANE ADAMS, aka "JD GOLD", aka "POLO", ON OR ABOUT APRIL 13, 1994, IN THE COUNTY OF QUEENS, KNOWINGLY AND UNLAWFULLY POSSESSED ONE OR MORE PREPARATIONS, COMPOUNDS, MIXTURES OR SUBSTANCES OF AN AGGREGATE WEIGHT OF MORE THAN TWENTY-FIVE GRAMS CONTAINING MARIHUANA.

DISTRICT ATTORNEY

VERSE

03

Rikers Island

May 1994

I spent my first few weeks at Rikers trying to understand why Judas[6] set me up with "Eddie." I was mad at myself for being naive and stupid. I was also, at that point, confused as to why the ATF needed to manufacture crime?! However, time to think was a luxury—much of my days on Rikers, especially as the weather got hot, were focused solely on surviving.

Due to overcrowding,[7] they transferred me outside of the C-74 to huge tents situated between the building and perimeter fence outfitted with beds and bathrooms known as the "Sprungs"—considered *safer* than the general population housing units—where guards masqueraded as gang members, drug dealers, and brutal overlords of their domains.

There were jails within jails, each with nicknames like: "murder Mod-8," "3 main the house of pain," and "4 upper the house of suffer"—all vying for supremacy, locked in perpetual states of warfare.

Shaving razors or rug cutters were called "guns"—and like in the hood, they were ubiquitous and available for a price. *Guns* could also be concealed in the anal and oral cavities, making them the most popular combat weapon. But the "bangers" (long, thin, sharpened steel or fiberglass swords with homemade handles) inflicted the most harm.

In C-74, there were no rules! It was common to see hormonal

6 The use of informants and "snitches," such as William O'Neal—who infiltrated the Black Panther Party under FBI direction as part of COINTELPRO (Counterintelligence Program)—played a central role in destabilizing Black liberation and civil rights movements throughout the 1960s and 1970s. These counterinsurgency tactics were later institutionalized during the war on drugs in the 1980s, where the widespread use of confidential informants became a key mechanism driving surveillance, arrests, and what would later be termed "mass incarceration." A 2021 Forbes investigation reported that US federal agencies, including the FBI, paid informants approximately $548 million over several years, often authorizing them to engage in criminal activity and disbursing substantial payments with limited transparency or oversight. For a dramatized account of O'Neal's role in the assassination of Fred Hampton, see *Judas and the Black Messiah* (2021).

7 In 1994, with racialized policing and practices, Rikers Island faced significant overcrowding—with the population reaching approximately 22,000, nearing its maximum capacity. The documentary "Lock-Up: The Prisoners of Rikers Island," filmed in 1994, provides an in-depth look.

adolescent boys—many of whom had experienced multiple adverse childhood experiences[8] (ACEs)—masturbating to female correction officers in plain sight.

Poverty, histories of violence, internalized racism, carceral brutality, undeveloped brains, historical trauma, and toxic masculinity—combined with *hopelessness* and the strong possibility of serious prison time—factored heavily into the culture of violence.

Navigating C-74 required skill and divine intervention—an example of the latter came when I ran into one of my best friends less than 48 hours after arriving at Rikers.

"Serge" was Peruvian and Colombian, got kicked out of Flushing High School, and transferred to Forest Hills High School around 1991. We ended up in the same homeroom, where we got to know each other. But Serge still hung out with a crew from Flushing that stole cars and sold them to chop shops. There were even a few times Will and I hung out with him in stolen vehicles and did dumb shit like going to Palmetto St in Bushwick—an infamous drug block to buy weed.

Serge got kicked out of Forest Hills (depending on who you ask), and we lost contact; yet months later, my boy Ralphy told me he'd been arrested. His crew was allegedly behind a series of taxi robberies in 1992—there was a lot of press around the case, and he was facing "football numbers." I had forgotten all about it, but here we were in 1994, both trapped in the adolescent building on Rikers Island just staring at each other in disbelief until, from halfway across the waiting room, Serge shouted out my name—as if to affirm that it was indeed me.

Attired in the gray prison jumpsuits—required for visits—I excitedly hugged my lost friend as he cried out: "Damn, bro, they got you too!?"—at which I could only laugh sadly. I wished the circumstances could have been different, but I was happy to see Serge. Yet we didn't have much time, as he was coming off a visit and had to return to his housing unit—so we took turns quickly updating each other.

Serge said his last offer from the court was "15 years to life"—and the circumstances were such that he was seriously considering it. He was only

8 Adverse childhood experiences (ACEs) refer to traumatic events in childhood, such as abuse, neglect, and household dysfunction, which significantly impact long-term health and behavior. Studies show that ACEs disproportionately affect marginalized communities due to systemic racism, poverty, and oppression, exacerbating trauma and limiting access to resources that could mitigate harm. High ACE scores are strongly correlated with increased risk of incarceration. Marginalized communities exposed to perpetual stress and instability are more likely to exhibit criminalized behaviors—thus perpetuating the cycle of systemic oppression.

nineteen, but had been trapped on Rikers for over two years and had lost all faith in the system and the possibility of a fair trial. Serge also had a co-defendant that his lawyer felt might be cooperating with the District Attorney.

I was overwhelmed listening to Serge explain his dilemma when the CO shouted my name to begin my visit—which spared me from finding contrived words to console my friend, but it also triggered a wave of sadness as I realized that I might never see him again.

I fought to hold back the tears as Serge and I embraced—after which he held my shoulders, looked me in the eyes, and imparted *cardinal rules of survival,* which included: "No snitching, no gambling, no gangs, no chumps, and if niggas test you, let them know that only Kings come from Queens!"

I slowly turned from my friend, buried my emotions, and went through the curtain partition towards the rows of chairs, tables, COs, and prisoners. Digging deep, I found a smile as Moya and Mom stood to embrace me—for the first time as *a number*—trapped on Rikers Island without bail.

June 1994

A few weeks into June, shortly after my nineteenth birthday, I got transferred to C-73. My first birthday incarcerated lacked the usual festivities, but ushered in a black cloud in my young life that would occupy space and time for many more trips around the sun. Yet the transfer to C-73—with most men in their mid-twenties and early thirties who didn't "pop off" like those in C-74—felt like a belated birthday gift.

Polo, who was 21 years old, got transferred to C-73 a few weeks before I did—but was housed on the other side of the building to keep us separate. I got assigned to Mod-3 Upper, which had a pretty even ratio of Black and Brown *unfortunates*. There were even two White men in the house—who were now the "minority" and relegated to jobs that no one else wanted, like washing clothes, which earned them the nickname: "Maytag One" and "Maytag Two."

I gravitated to some cats who transferred into the dorm around the same time as me. "Dana" was twenty-three, six feet two, and about two hundred and twenty-five pounds from Brownsville, Brooklyn—a neighborhood infamous for poverty, violence, and incarceration rates—the ingredients that forged young men in the mold of "Iron" Mike Tyson. Dana was a smart dude with a juvenile record facing an armed robbery charge, with the judge currently offering him 5 to 15 years.

"Spider" was 19, had a murder charge, and hailed from East New York, Brooklyn—another highly marginalized and overly criminalized neighborhood.[9] Spider had just returned from his first court hearing when we met. Between puffs of his cigarette[10]—a new habit he picked up in an attempt to ease his anxiety—Spider explained that the DA had offered him 20 to life. But he professed his innocence, and within minutes, I knew his entire life story: beginning when cops picked him up in a laundromat on Pennsylvania Ave—while washing his clothes!

Spider was a tall, light-skinned Black male wearing an army jacket, fitting the appearance of "a suspect." Allegedly, the victim couldn't even identify him in the lineup, but the cops convinced them otherwise.

Spider, Dana, and I were Knicks fans. And despite our current predicament, we were excited that they were playing the Houston Rockets in the NBA championship. However, watching the Knicks lose a title wasn't our bonding moment—instead, it was one of those events that most people who remember 1994 can probably tell you where they were and what they were doing when the news broke.

It was June 17, 1994, and we were in a hot, sardine-packed dayroom on Rikers Island, watching the Knicks play, when NBC abruptly cut off the game to provide live aerial coverage of O.J. Simpson and the infamous white Ford Bronco chase. It felt voyeuristic, but it made for great conversation to pass the time, and, in a cruel sense of irony, it gave all of us—Black men trapped on Rikers—a view of how the carceral system operated more humanely along class lines.

Spider and Dana gave me the rundown of Mod-3 Upper and its main characters—essential knowledge to navigate the space successfully. Jails and prisons within the US are an extreme microcosm of the country and were intentionally divided along racial lines. Such as the "Puerto Rican phone," which Hispanics and a few selected Whites were expected to

9 Eddie Ellis, a formerly incarcerated scholar and activist, played a pivotal role in highlighting the spatial concentration of incarcerated populations. In 1979, while imprisoned, Ellis and his study group conducted the "Seven Neighborhoods Study," revealing that 75% of New York State's prison population originated from just seven New York City neighborhoods. See also the concept of "Million Dollar Blocks."

10 Smoking was allowed inside the dorms, which were poorly ventilated, resulting in a permanent cloud of smoke.

use with permission. Then there was a "Black phone" controlled by a "Supreme Team" cat from Queens, who went by "OG." He was probably approaching 50, but looked like an NFL player and commanded attention when he spoke. He gave me a fist bump and a shallow convo to feel me out. But the only thing we had in common was Queens.

The conversation with OG was coded, but the message was clear: He was ruthless in and out of prison, and now, facing *life*, he assured me and everyone else in earshot that he had nothing to lose. But OG was strategic, knew the art of war, and thus understood it would be better to have young lions on his side—or at least indebted to him.

OG gave Dana, Spider, and me 90 minutes of phone time to divide amongst ourselves during "slot time"—typically from 6 to 11 pm. Slot time was when most detainees could reach their families by phone. Considering most of us on Rikers had no bail or couldn't afford it, slot time was as valuable as gold and often a source of conflict during the '90s, when it was still free to make local calls.

July 1994

I was strategic with my phone usage, but soon after arriving at C-73, I lost my cool. It was July 4, 1994, and a gorgeous day. The window above my dorm bed looked out onto the Hudson River, where boats and jet skis were joyfully traversing the water on a beautiful *Independence* Day. But I wasn't in a sunny mood.

Moya was my lifeline to the outside world—we spoke daily, and she visited at least once a week. We had plans to talk during my slot time, but she wasn't home when I called. I tried other numbers, people I hadn't spoken to in a while, but got no answer.

I knew life didn't stop because I was trapped in a cage. I witnessed *unfortunates* lose it when they couldn't reach loved ones, but I naively believed it wouldn't happen to me. However, three months trapped on Rikers Island with no end in sight made me a little reckless. And pretty soon, a few "fuck-you's" were exchanged, but I refused to get off the phone.

"Divine" was probably in his 40s and was finishing up a parole violation. He was under the impression that I should get off the phone if I couldn't reach anyone, which was rational—but I wasn't! How could I be?

Divine and I also weren't particularly friendly; he was a big cat with a nasty attitude and was openly known as a "booty bandit"—for allegedly forcing sexual acts with prisoners "Upstate." Yet I was triggered and irrational, so when he invited me to the bathroom—which often functioned akin to a gladiator pit—I was more than accommodating. But thankfully, Dana stepped in and squashed the situation.

VERSE

04

Legal System

Much of the anger and violence on Rikers stemmed from our frustration with the "criminal injustice system," which perpetually operated beyond capacity.

Court dates happened maybe once a month for trapped people with poor legal representation. On your court date, the COs wake you at about 4 am. Depending on the CO, you *usually* have about 15 minutes to get ready. Next, they escort you to the mess hall for a sad breakfast of cold cereal, toast, and maybe a decent piece of fruit. Detainees are then strip-searched and separated into cells according to the borough of their court hearing.

This herding of people occurs by 5 am, yet the transport buses don't *usually* arrive before 7 am. The holding cells are small, cramped, and only have one toilet with no cover—and are often filled with piss, shit, toilet paper, and won't flush. Everyone is in a bad mood, and the tensions are at an all-time high, leading to many assaults before you even arrive at court.

With little faith in the system, the bus ride is often the highlight of going to court; it's a rare opportunity to leave the confines of Rikers—which was extra special for me as I loved the smell and feel of summer mornings while driving through the Queens neighborhoods I considered home.

Through the barred windows of the jail bus, I caught fleeting glimpses of cars, people, and parks. I scanned the sidewalks, hoping to spot someone familiar, yet silently wishing the reinforced glass would shield me from being seen.

On the bus ride to court, we often tuned in to Hot 97, where instant classics like Biggie Smalls' "Juicy" and Nas' "The World is Yours" dominated the East Coast airwaves. The music reminded those of us trapped in the system that, despite being misunderstood and marginalized, we should never surrender hope—in a world not rooted in our oppression—that awaited, if only we could persevere through what seemed insurmountable.

I fought with all my strength to remain optimistic. But hopelessness was intense, steroid-raging, and often seized control once we arrived at the *human cells*—buried deep—beneath the courthouse.

For hours, detainees anxiously waited for attorneys to visit and cases to be called—with no food except "cop-out sandwiches," consisting of stale bread, old cheese, and mystery meat.

"Pressure-bust pipes" is a phrase often used in jails and prisons. And when they bust, fights, assaults, and robberies pop off on the bus, in holding cells, and even in the courtrooms. Most fights are by hand, but many are with razors, rugcutters, icepicks, and other weapons wrapped in plastic and electric tape—often smuggled in an orifice through pat downs and metal detectors.

If you make it to the judge unscathed, it's that strange ritual again: the White prosecutor speaks to the White judge, who speaks to the White defense attorney, who then possibly speaks to the Black or Brown defendant—and it's not much of a conversation.

The US judicial system is rigged!

Overcrowding, lengthy pre-trial detention, no bail, and the occasional court case are only to determine an acceptable plea.[11] For example, after your arrest, the court offers you ten years at arraignment—which you naturally decline, as you are innocent, or you know the sentence doesn't fit the crime. But with no bail—or bail you can afford—you sit on Rikers for months or years fighting the case.

Poor, and trapped on Rikers, a public defender[12] is your only ally. However, they also represent a few hundred other "detainees"—each desperate for their attention and the possibility of freedom.

Every engagement with your assigned *defender,* who never comes to Rikers to see you or takes calls, is like a first-time meeting; you tell them your name, and they nod violently as if suddenly recalling your story. So, when the plea gets more reasonable, say two years or even time served, you gladly take it—even if you didn't do it.[13]

---

11 During this period, over 90% of cases were resolved through plea bargains. Prosecutors often used the threat of harsher sentences to pressure defendants with poor legal representation into accepting plea deals—making them the default form of verdict in the carceral system.

12 See "Equal Before the Law? New York Counties Face Push to Upgrade Public Defender System" in *Truthout.* Also, "Over-Reliance on Plea Deals is Damaging the Criminal Legal System" in *The Appeal.*

13 Rest in power to Kalief Browder—who fought the system and won, but never recovered from the trauma of

By early July, Polo and I both had private attorneys. But we still had poor legal representation—they never came to see us at Rikers, were never in their office for calls, and always had the same sob story that they were "working hard" on our case, yet had nothing to show for it. But they always needed more time and a lot more money!

I was pretty sure that the attorneys wanted us to "snitch" on each other and cooperate with the District Attorney—which was confirmed over the summer when a CO summoned me from the dorm for what I was told was a "legal visit." But it turned out to be two detectives waiting to take me to the District Attorney's office.

I was surprised by the trip, and spent the ride to Kew Gardens from Rikers going through various angles in my head. I knew they were going to try and pressure me to cooperate. Sure enough, upon arrival, I was met by a team of aggressive cops and prosecutors seeking information about Polo and our supplier. They offered me a reduced sentence, or even time served—depending on what, and whom they were able to acquire through my cooperation.

I badly wanted to go home, but cooperating wasn't an option. I quickly declined the offer and attempted to pivot the conversation by engaging the prosecutors and cops in a discussion about "Judas" and "Eddie," who I reasoned had entrapped us into the crimes we were now being charged with.

I did my best, with my freedom at stake, to articulate mitigating factors I prayed the system would consider in determining accountability. Yet, I was quickly dismissed and ultimately sent back to Rikers Island to end the stalemate. The following week, they tried the same tactic on Polo, who also refused to cooperate.

So, at this point, it's 1994, mid-July. Polo and I are trapped on Rikers Island for months with no bail, poor legal representation, and the District Attorney pressuring us to cooperate at the height of the largest carceral genocide in the history of the world.

In hindsight, I marvel at how strong Polo and I were in fighting a system programmed, incentivized, and determined to negate our humanity. But the odds were stacked against us as we showed up for our first court hearing in months. Yet somehow, maybe delusional, we

Rikers Island. See "Time: The Kalief Browder Story."

still held on to hope. But what we got is a plea bargain our attorneys described as *only* seven years to life in prison.

"What about the entrapment defense we discussed?"

I knew the plea was substantially less than what they first offered. I knew the decisions Polo and I made were wrong, period! However, I knew without a doubt that we were set up and entangled in a dubious system where cops, with the help of paid informants—in the mold of Judas—used money or reduced prison time to exploit and entrap vulnerable populations trying to survive.

No one was willing to fight for us. Our attorneys cared little for talk of systemic oppression or an entrapment defense and warned that if we blew trial—with over 20 counts in the indictment—we would get a sentence of at least 15 years to life.

VERSE

05

Faith, Hope & Allah

The attorney let his words sit before pressing us to decide on the plea deal. But Polo and I insisted we needed more time to discuss the options with our families. However, with no bail and limited resources to defend ourselves, time, faith, and hope were running out.

I made it back to C-73 at 5 pm after our court hearing and contemplated calling Gav and Eric as I had night visits—but decided to hang out in the dorm, as I wasn't prepared to discuss the plea or deal with the post-visit emotional trauma. We also had a nightly ritual in the dorm of *building* spiritually and listening to Funkmaster Flex on Hot 97 to hear the latest hip-hop while doing push-ups, sit-ups, and free weight squats with Ali—a Muslim brother and self-described "freedom fighter" from Palestine.[14]

Ali transferred to the dorm a few weeks after I got there and became a mentor to Dana, me, and Spider. He was in his mid-thirties, spoke several languages, taught us martial arts, and illuminated the similarities between Black and Palestinian struggles. Ali also took us with him to jummah service on Fridays, where the brotherhood, smell of incense, Muslim oils, and fiery *khutbah* often transported me beyond the confines of Rikers and gave me a different perspective on what was possible with religion.

Ali worked in the CO mess hall called the "KK" with Polo—who often sent me food and messages through him. As a result, Ali probably knew more details of our case than anyone else. So, feeling like I needed to speak to someone, I told Ali about the plea offer of 7 years to life. I vented my frustration with the system and our lawyers for not

14 Scholars and activists such as Michelle Alexander and Angela Davis have drawn striking parallels between the US prison system and the Israeli occupation of Palestine. Both rely on the erasure of history and critical discourse, coupled with dehumanizing ideologies, prolonged detention, restricted movement, and systemic control over marginalized populations. These comparisons reveal how state power enforces racialized and colonial hierarchies—whether through mass incarceration in the United States or military and administrative detention in Palestine. See *Freedom Is a Constant Struggle: Ferguson, Palestine, and the Foundations of a Movement* by Angela Davis.

fighting for us. I was in tears and feeling hopeless when Ali quietly and patiently asked:

"Do you want to pray?"

Ali's question shocked me, and I didn't know how to answer it. But eventually, I found myself nodding *yes* in between sobs. Ali's bed was next to mine along the back row of the dorm, which was mostly empty except for the few people who didn't go to the yard. We sat facing each other between our beds.

Ali unwrapped his Quran from his prayer mat and selected a surah, which he began to read in Arabic—slow and melodic. He recited ayat after ayat before bestowing upon me the name "Rahim,"—an attribute of God that translates as "merciful."

Ali reminded me in one of my darkest moments that there was no power greater than God (Allah). From that day forward, "Rahim," and later "Rah" or "Jae-Rah," would become a part of my identity—one rooted in faith, hope, and the "oneness" of God.

Ali prayed aloud for me in English and told me that God would always protect and have mercy on me as long as I remained steadfast on "aṣ-Ṣirāṭ al-mustaqīm"—the straight path, or the way of God.

VERSE

06

Keiana James

July 1994 was scorching in many ways, but with the housing units overcrowded and few working fans, summer felt like an inferno. The rise of the "Bloods" on Rikers Island—beginning in 1993—made going to the yard to cool off a risky proposition. And even though I was considered "neutral," gang warfare was the norm, and someone (neutral or not) usually got stabbed or cut during recreation.

Aside from the hellish conditions, fighting to survive each day, and worrying about going to prison for life, I anxiously awaited the birth of my first child. Some days, I spent hours joyfully imagining how they would look, crawl, or even cry. But there were also dark days when I was furious at myself and wanted to die for not being home to support Heather—and not knowing when or if I would ever get out of jail.

On most nights, it was impossible to sleep. So, once everyone was in bed, I usually read with poor lighting. Then, once the dorm got quiet, I allowed my mind to wander free and explore old memories, which was usually the highlight of my day and the fuel that fed the hope that things could once again be *normal*.

My morning ritual was to do calisthenics and call Heather to check in as soon as the night COs transitioned to the morning team and the phones came out—usually between 7 and 8 am. But on the morning of July 20, 1994, I called and called, but no one answered, which threw off my routine and raised my anxiety to unprecedented levels.

I was frantic until late afternoon when Mom finally picked up the phone. She answered, bursting with excitement—and in her Jamaican patois, she said, "u baby mama belly bus." I didn't even have a moment to process Mom's words before she added: "You're a daddy now!"

Keiana Aurelia James entered the world on Wednesday, July 20, 1994. She was born in Brooklyn at Brookdale Hospital, where my mom was a nurse in labor and delivery—which brought me some solace, but my immediate excitement was tempered.

Don't get me wrong—I was excited, and it's a day I will never forget! But please, try to imagine the unspeakable pain knowing that as your first child is born, you're stuck on Rikers Island, facing life in prison at only nineteen?

I felt horrible for not being there and kept thinking about Thanksgiving night with Heather in Coney Island—and my promise to be better than her father, better than my father. But I was absent on the day our daughter was born! It was hard to hold the joy and pain of the moment simultaneously. Still, I knew my daughter's arrival into this world was special.

The night of Keiana's birth, Polo sent me fried chicken and fries from the KK with Ali—which we combined with food from the commissary and had a celebration party to honor the arrival of my daughter.

Over the next few days, Heather recovered well, and Keiana had no complications—allowing them both to be discharged a few days post-birth. I was excited to speak with her and hear the cries of our new baby girl. And while we both agreed that we didn't want the first time I saw or held Keiana to be in a Rikers Island visiting room, we weren't getting good news from the lawyers.

After a few weeks and many conversations, Heather and I decided that she would bring Keiana to see me on Rikers Island. With everything happening, my emotions were all over the place leading up to the visit. But when I finally saw Keiana, everything changed.

August 1994

Heather gently handed me our daughter as I sat on the opposite side of the visiting room table. She was wrapped tightly in a purple-and-white blanket. Her perfectly round face, full head of hair, button nose, ten fingers, and ten toes melted my heart instantly.

For the first time in months, I lost myself in the now—I was no longer in a Rikers Island visiting room, I was no longer facing life in prison, I was only a father seeing and holding his daughter for the first time. However, I wouldn't be transparent if I didn't tell you that the *high* fell to a devastating *low* when the CO ended the visit 60 minutes later—and I had to watch Heather and my daughter Keiana leave me behind on Rikers Island.

VERSE

07

Hurt People Hurt People

In the hours, days, and weeks after I first saw Keiana, I found myself drowning in a sea of emotions, consumed by a growing desperation to escape—what felt like an inescapable, ever-growing ocean of despair.

One Saturday morning in late August, I lay in bed, half-asleep, daydreaming about Jamaica—which was always my happy place. But it was becoming harder to lose myself in memories of the "good old days." Instead of the familiar aromas of blue mountain coffee, ackee and saltfish, fried fish, and roast breadfruit, the dorm was filled with the scent of Lever 2000 soap and the pungent stench of violence.

Saturday was a popular day for visits, and many people were doing their best to get ready. But most were just trying to wash away the stink after a brutally early wake-up call, which was partially the result of the ever-present racial tension in the dorm that came to a boil when "Chicago," who slept a few bunks away from me and was a stocky self-professed "pimp" and "hustler" from the midwest got jumped, stabbed and ran out the dorm.

Chicago was hilarious, with war stories for days. He was the first person I saw openly using "dope" and "nodding" on Rikers. Nevertheless, Chicago was beloved by all the Blacks in the dorm, so the "Cold War" went nuclear when the Latin Kings assaulted him for an unpaid dope tab.

Ali and Dana took the bangers out of "the stash" during the midnight shift. We were all angry! And even though drug usage and subsequent drama were rampant as trapped people, with generational histories of oppression and traumatic stressors, sought to self-medicate, many Blacks in Mod-3 Upper (myself included) felt that Chicago was only stabbed because he was Black. And it would only be a matter of time—if we did not respond—before it was one of us.

Latino gangs—of which many were *Black*—dominated Rikers, and in the '80s and '90s, they were known to terrorize non-Spanish-speaking

Blacks and other racial groups. Unity was the secret to their strength. "Dominicans," "Cubans," and "Puerto Ricans," it didn't matter; as long as you spoke Spanish—the language of their colonial oppressor—you were down!

Blacks, historically separated, pitted against each other, and taught to hate themselves, didn't have the same unity. Many formed their own smaller cliques for protection, but the Latino gangs reigned *supreme*—and to make matters worse, at least for Blacks, many Latino COs were also proud "bead-wearing" gang members.

Thankfully, the COs in Mod-3 Upper were mainly neutral, but they had snitches and knew something was brewing. They could also sense the tension in the dorm, as almost everyone had extra layers of clothes and jackets—aka "armored up" and prepared for war!

I was up early the morning after Chicago was stabbed, and not the least surprised when, at dawn, a contingent of COs burst into the dorm. They were a special unit nicknamed the "Turtles" by detainees because of their paramilitary gear, including helmets, riot sticks, and shields. They went after everybody in sight, callously swinging their batons at human beings as if they were playing baseball. It was fucked up, and I felt bad for members of the Latin Kings who were targeted, thrown to the ground, and assailed by batons, punches, and kicks to the body.

It was my first time witnessing the Turtles' brutality up close, but everyone on Rikers knew who they were. Yet you could never look at them directly. Whenever they appeared, it didn't matter where you were; you had to immediately face the wall with your hands extended as if holding it up, or the Turtles would make an example out of you.

After pulverizing a few *unfortunates*, the Turtles made us line up against a wall, take off all our clothes, and stand behind each other. "Dick to ass," they screamed with glee. And if you didn't believe they meant it literally, baton blows with the intensity of steroid-fueled home run swings were utilized as reinforcement.

Fear, brutality, and humiliation were the Turtles' calling card—which they made apparent as they dug through the dorm and our personal property, looking for contraband. They found various weapons caches strategically placed in neutral areas of the dorm—thus abdicating guilt by proximity.

Each weapon they found was prominently displayed, as if it were some great archeological discovery. The whole thing lasted about four hours, and many gang members went to the box—a jail within a jail—others had their pictures and trinkets from home destroyed.

I was learning that there were levels to the violence in a place like Rikers Island—as the Turtles' visit instigated a heightened level of hurt, fear, and vulnerability that lingered for days after they left.

VERSE

08

Plea For Mercy

Even though Polo and I were both in C-73, we only saw each other during court or on the days we shared visits. Ali and our families helped out a lot with communication. But as summer neared its end, my relationship with Polo grew strained, especially as the DA continued to pressure us to cooperate.

Our lawyers, who felt like agents of the state, put even more pressure on us to take the plea of "7 years to life" for "drug possession." And as "non-violent offenders," they promised we would qualify for "early release" in three to four years—which *time* would prove to be all lies to make the poison more tolerable for digestion.

Polo and I were trapped; our families were financially drained and probably felt even more paralyzed than we were. Also, as a father, I constantly worried about Keiana's well-being—and understood, in a very real way, the harm I brought home to my family.

I was especially worried about Mom—a Black woman and mother to four Black boys.[15] So when the plea deal was finally put on the table—one that would lock me away for potentially 7 years with a *life sentence* hanging off the end—it felt like I betrayed my family. I knew accepting the plea meant my mother, my siblings, Keiana, and everyone who loved me would wake up every single day worrying whether I was alive, safe, or simply *surviving.*

Going to trial felt no lighter; it meant risking even more time, even more pain, even more uncertainty. The weight of both options was unbearable. I found what little solace I could in the shower—hot water pounding over my head as I cried silently, praying for guidance.

Answers to my prayers didn't come immediately. However, in the midst of my indecision, news spread through the jail that a young

15 I can say without a trace of doubt that calling Mom from Central Booking with the news of my arrest was one of the hardest things I've ever had to do. I could hear the pain in her voice through the phone. I felt horrible knowing what my incarceration would do to her!

brother, about 20 years old, whom Polo and I both knew had gone to trial, lost, and been sentenced to 45 years to life.

The news quickly spread through C-73 and *shook* us pretty badly. Don't get me wrong, we all saw how the courts handed out prison time with no remorse, but 45 years to life, no matter the charge, for a kid whose brain wasn't developed, was fucking ridiculous!

Polo and I were frustrated, and it felt like there was no way out. Our lawyers, supposedly working in our best interest, *strongly* advised us not to go to trial—and repeatedly told us that an "entrapment defense" was too risky.

If I'm being honest, I don't think our attorneys believed us. They were skeptical and would often ask, "Are you sure?" Every time, Polo and I reiterated that Judas and Eddie had set us up.

I often asked the attorneys to consider *whether the prosecutor had evidence that we sold drugs or guns beyond our current charges? Did they care that "Eddie" repeatedly bombarded me with calls and promises of "easy money" for almost six months while I was only 18 years old? Did they care that we were kids and mere pawns in an intentional racial genocide sold as a "drug war"?*

It felt like no one was listening or willing to see us beyond our attributed "criminal" identity—especially in a racialized system predicated on our destruction. Again, I knew our actions were wrong! But there is no such thing as "good'" or "bad" people! We all have experiences and stories that influence our actions—and in a real, democratic, justice-oriented society, they would matter!

I was mad at the dissonant "accountability" zealots who had little understanding of the history that brought us here. And who, ironically, never demand accountability of themselves for stealing land and killing native populations across the globe to build their *democracy.*

Where is the accountability for slavery? For colonialism? For imperialism? For global poverty and the destruction of our planet for the sake of capitalistic greed? Where is the accountability for the US Government deliberately pushing drugs and guns into Black and Brown communities across the globe? And where is the accountability for the police, who continue to gun down poor, unarmed Black, Brown, and White people in the streets of the United States? Where is the accountability for the judicial system—blindly obedient not to justice but to the maintenance of White supremacy and the enforcement of Black-code-inspired laws designed to maintain the historical subjugation and genocide of non-Whites?

The human disregard and hypocrisy inherent in "the system" were maddening! But with no bail, Polo and I had little opportunity to defend ourselves. While we were creative and successfully sent messages (aka "kites") back and forth to each other multiple times a day, it felt as if we had exhausted our collective resources and were out of options—which was hard to accept, given what awaited.

We postponed making an official decision until we spoke with our families again. But eventually, feeling defeated, Polo and I—along with over 90% of the people trapped in the "criminal injustice system" without bail or resources to defend ourselves—took a guilty plea.

The days after we decided to take the plea were dark! But after sitting with so much fear and anxiety for months on Rikers Island, there was also a strange relief knowing my fate—as fucked up as it was. However, communication between Polo and me stopped. But I ran into him in the visiting room holding area the weekend before our plea hearing.

Polo was pacing back and forth as I approached and didn't appear to see me. But as I got closer, he turned suddenly, and a hard left-hand flush to the temple knocked me to the ground.

I was stunned but jumped up, hands up, ready to fight, except I couldn't. So instead, I stood toe-to-toe with Polo and demanded to know: "What the fuck was that!?" Polo, with anger in his eyes and his hands balled up, just stared at me as a crowd gathered and egged us on to fight.

Then, in a rage, Polo screamed: "Your fucking girlfriend doesn't know how to keep her mouth shut!" He explained that Moya, who often drove to Rikers with his girlfriend to see us, shared stories about "other women" visiting him. And while I understood why he was mad, I told him:

"The next time you do some shit like that, I'm fucking you up!"

My statement was only to save face, as I didn't have it in me to fight Polo. But I wasn't afraid of him; it was more my guilt-ridden conscience—*everything* was my fault. Deep down, I felt like I deserved to be punched in the face. I was the catalyst for this catastrophe. Even though Judas and Eddie laid the bait, I was the one who bit, then lied to Polo to bait him—a truth that I would have to live with for the rest of my life.

A few days after our fight and about five months after our arrest in April, Polo and I walked handcuffed into the Queens Boulevard courtroom to accept the plea bargain. It was the first time since the arraignment that the judge addressed us directly as he asked, "Kirk James, Duane Adams, you are here today to plead guilty to 7 years to life for criminal possession of a controlled substance in the second degree." Then he asked:

"Are you taking the plea on your own accord?"

Please, tell me who, especially at 19 and 21, would willingly take a plea that mandated a minimum sentence of 7 years and a maximum of LIFE in prison?

Polo and I were both fathers, with mothers, grandmothers, grandfathers, aunts, uncles, brothers, sisters, and cousins whose lives our plea would impact. Yet none of that mattered; the questions were more for the record and rhetorical. The judge said a few more things before promising us "significant prison time" if he saw us again.

Yet, as CRAZY as his statement was, I knew the judge was telling the truth. The sentence was, by all accounts, "significant," but I knew this peculiar system had no compassion for its captives.

Arbitrary sentencing guidelines did little to address the social, economic, and racial factors perpetuating this vicious cycle of incarceration. As a result, teenage boys were given what *unfortunates* called "football numbers": 5, 10, 15, 20, 25, 30, or even 45 years to life were common sentences.

I felt defeated taking the plea, but considering the carnage around us, I felt *fortunate* that we had a realistic chance of leaving prison sometime in our twenties. However, Polo was not pleased—and it felt like déjà vu as he went from sad to mad as soon as we were out of the courtroom and back in the holding cells.

As Polo started pacing, I got ready. He got in my face and screamed: "It's all your fault!"—which was true! But I knew this wasn't the time for a conversation.

I remained silent as Polo launched more verbal attacks. Maybe Polo took my silence for weakness or felt empowered from our last encounter? Either way, I was prepared!

Polo and I fought a good five-minute round before the guards unlocked the cell to break us up. Yet once they realized we were co-defendants, they decided not to charge us with fighting. Instead, a Morgan Freeman-looking guard sat us down and spoke about the importance of working together to overcome our predicament. He even told us, “You’re going to need each other to survive this system,” which was utterly bizarre coming from him, but it worked as Polo and I tearfully hugged it out.

Exhibit B: Sentence

SUPRE[illegible] NEW YOR[illegible]

INDICTMENT DISMISSED — SEAL ( ) DO NOT SEAL ( ) WITH LEAVE TO RESUBMIT ( )

JUSTICE: PART: DATE:

COURT REPORTER: ADA:

DECISION ON MOTION: SEE ORDER ( ) B.C. ( ) ROR ( ) COMMITTED ( )

730 PSYCHO EXAM. ORDERED ( ) ADJD: COMMITTED TO C.M.H. ( )

ARRAIGNMENT	PENDING SENTENCE
DATE: MAY 26 1994 PART: AA-1	DATE: 8-24-94 PART 1
JUSTICE: PHILIP J. CHETTA	B.C. ( ) ROR ( ) COMMITTED (✓)
REPORTER: [illegible] ADA: [illegible]	SECURING ORDER ENDORSED (✓)
ATTY: DIDIO PRESENT:	PSYCHO EXAM CPL 390:30 ( ) DRUG EXAM ( )
LAS ( ) PVT ( ) 18B ASSIGNED ( )	PREDICATE FELONY FILED DATE:
PLEA: WRNG ( )	A.A.A.A. ( ) DATE: PART:
BAIL FIXED: No Bail	STANDS MUTE ( ) DENIES ( )
B.C. ( ) ROR ( ) COMMITTED ( )	JUSTICE:
SECURING ORDER ENDORSED ( )	ADA:
ADJOURNED TO: AA 6-21	ATTY:
DEFT. ADVISED TRAFFIC 170:10 CPL ( )	REPORTER:

PLEA	SENTENCE
DATE: AUG 11 1994 PART: AA-1	DATE: AUG 24 1994 PART: A
JUSTICE: PHILIP J. CHETTA	JUSTICE: PHILIP J. CHETTA
ADA: TREGLIA	ADA: ~~DIDIO~~ Benton
ATTY: DIDIO	ATTY: DIDIO
REPORTER: ALBERT MUSA	REPORTER: PATRICIA [illegible]
DEFENDANT WITHDRAWS FORMER PLEA AND PLEADS GUILTY (BEFORE) (DURING) TRIAL TO:	REMARKS:

CT.	CRIME	FELONY CLASS	N.Y.S.D.C. (X) N.Y.C.C.I. ( )
	CPCS 2°	ATT	
			7 – L
			MSW SCUA

REMARKS: APPEAL WAIVED

ADVISED 60.35 P.L. SURCHARGE WAIVED ( ) FROM INMATE FUN[DS]
SURCHARGE OF $ TO BE PAID
CRIME VICTIMS ASSISTANCE FEE $
UNDULY HARSH ( ) MITIGATING CIRCUMSTANCES (✓)
ADVISED AND GIVEN NOTICE TO APPEAL ( ) WAIVED ( )

PEOPLE VS. James Kirk INDICTMENT NO. 1946-94

ON THE MOTION OF ADA INDICTMENT IS AMENDED TO SHOW TRUE NAME OF DEFENDANT AS
SEE SECOND PAGE FOR TRIAL ENDORSEMENT ( )

VERSE

09

Going Upstate

September 1994

It was now September, and the seasons were changing again. The morning air had a chill as the temperature began to drop. I could no longer eat or sleep and had lost about ten pounds.

At 19 years old, I was emotionally tethered to fear and anxiety while awaiting a transfer to state prison.[16] And to make matters worse, I was back in C-74 as my life sentence raised my security classification.

I was locked in a cell block where everyone was sentenced, waiting to go upstate, but didn't know when they would get sent hundreds of miles from home. *That* announcement always came at night during the 11 pm count—where there was usually a hushed silence as the CO ensured we were all accounted for while simultaneously calling out names for the morning prison bus to the mountains.

I had to endure two nerve-racking weeks before the CO finally called my name. But *that* night, my anxiety was astronomically high, and I stayed up manic and pacing through the 4 am wake-up call.

The cell door cracked open at 4:30 am. We were allowed clothes on our backs, a religious book, and a picture, which for me was a Quran that Ali gave me. I also had a baby picture of Keiana.

The mood, as expected, was somber as I slowly made my way down the long tier. Blessings of "stay strong" echoed throughout the cells as I stopped to pay respects.

Five other people from my cell block were also going upstate that

16 At the time there were approximately 70 prisons in New York with Attica and Clinton Correctional Facility more than 200 miles from New York City. After the "economic restructuring" in the 1980s-90s, many upstate New York towns faced economic decline and prisons became a key economic driver in these regions, providing jobs and state funding to sustain local economies. Prisoners were counted as residents of the districts where they were incarcerated—which inflated the political representation of rural, predominantly White districts at the expense of urban areas in NYC where most prisoners were from. As a result, these districts gained disproportionate influence in state politics, reinforcing rural political power and perpetuating inequities in representation. Research: "Gerrymandering." See also "Building a Prison Economy in Rural America" by Tracy Huling.

bleak September morning. At 19, I was probably the group's elder. We waited quietly in the dayroom for about 15 minutes before another CO escorted us to a mess hall with about 200 people about to become New York State *property.*

After eating cold cereal and stale bread, we had our body cavities examined, got shackled, and learned our destination. For me, it was "Downstate Correctional Facility," a reception prison for *unfortunates* demanding the highest level of security—often with minimum sentences exceeding five years.

Once on the Greyhound-type prison bus, the CO gave us the rundown of what it meant to be "NY state inmates." But I barely paid attention as I was pretty much immune to the *threat* of physical violence.

I was trapped in thoughts and stared blankly out the window as the bus slowly made its way on the Grand Central Parkway—over the Triboro Bridge, into the Bronx, and onto the Major Deegan Expressway North towards Yankee Stadium—when it occurred to me that I had never been to a game.

I had never seen Don Mattingly play first base or sit with the "bleacher creatures." I was hyper-aware that these *moments* might be my last in New York City.

From Yankee Stadium, to the sad-looking gray buildings framing its perimeter, to the passing cars with drivers robotically navigating along 87 North, to the overcast skies and the elevated subway train in the distance—I savored it all as we sped towards unimaginable horrors. However, the scenery was short-lived.

The prison bus moved quickly over bridges and out of the city towards the mountains—where I wondered if all prisons looked like Attica. Yet when we got there, Downstate was different. It was a relatively new prison, and if not for the electrified barbed-wire fence, it could easily be mistaken for a hospital.

Once inside the prison, they escorted us to the state version of the "why me cell"—where a new CO instructed us to take off our clothes for the customary cavity search.

Naked, they led us to an open shower room where we were bug-sprayed and hosed down like animals. They then gave us shaving razors to cut off all the hair on our heads and faces. Once unrecognizable, we are individually led to a small room to be fingerprinted.

Tattoos, birthmarks, and dental records are also captured for identification purposes. Finally, stripped of all humanity, came the assignment of a New York state prison number—which, like a "branded slave," would live with us forever.

94A6325 was my assigned New York State prison number.

94 Represents the year 1994

A Signifies that I *legally* became the *property* of New York State at Downstate Maximum-Security Prison

6325 means that I was the 6,325th person processed at Downstate Maximum-Security Prison at the time of my arrival in September of 1994.

94A6325 was how the system identified me and expected everyone else to do the same. So, for example, if someone wanted to visit, send mail, or money, they had to know my New York State prison number—I was then assigned State Green pants, shirts, and a sweater with the numbers visible and printed for all to see.

To compound the inhumanity of being processed into the system—my name got changed to "James Kirk" in the database. The intake CO, probably a "trekkie," assumed it was an alias and thought it was hilarious.

Shouting to no one in particular, the CO blurted out, "We got Captain James T Kirk." I didn't laugh! Downstate was no joke and operated like an inpatient psych unit.

Newly arrived prisoners were held in 24-hour solitary confinement except for meals and varied psychological, medical, and educational assessments. We also had occasional periods of recreation at the whim of the on-duty CO.

I had lots of time for *penitence*—which I used to reflect on the extremes of my 19-year-old life and read the Quran. My interest in Islam peaked after I spent time with Ali and read Malcolm X's autobiography on Rikers.

When I wasn't reading the Quran, I gave my attention to the tiny window in my cell—facing a distant road on the side of a mountain. I stared out the window for hours—imagining who the drivers were—

wondering if they knew or cared about what was happening in the valley beneath them?

When I wasn't making up stories about drivers in the distance, I prayed that *someone* would rescue me. When no one came to save me, I tried, also unsuccessfully, to teleport myself back to New York City and my family.

I wasn't allowed packages or commissary and depended on mess hall food for survival. However, the mess hall served many purposes, and since most cell blocks ate there, it was also the primary communication hub for state prisoners—and thus how I knew my co-defendant was also at Downstate.

It took almost two weeks for Polo and me to cross paths in the mess hall. I hardly recognized him with his bald head and shaved face. Our exchange was brief and orchestrated through hand gestures and head nods, concluding with promises to "stay strong" and keep each other updated.

I was happy to see Polo, and he seemed in good spirits, but I returned to the isolation of my cell and cried for hours. I was riddled with guilt and depression—and the weeks following our sentencing tested my will to survive.

I didn't have a suicide plan. But I didn't want to live in a cage!

Each passing day trapped in the mountains of upstate New York—far away from home, my family, and my baby girl Keiana—only further exacerbated my disdain for life. But I held on as the weeks passed, yet I had no idea what plantation I would be sent to next.

The New York State Department of Correctional Services (NYSDOCS) had a secret policy regarding the movement of "prisoners." So my anxiety was *again* super high when the CO finally instructed me to pack up and bring my stuff to the "Draft Room"—where my possessions were cataloged and bagged, then affixed with my last name, NYS number, and a tag color-coded to represent a specific prison—which we weren't supposed to know. My tag was my favorite color, orange, which confirmed my worst fears.

VERSE

10

The Cat

October 1994

Coxsackie Correctional Facility—aka "The Cat"—was one of the only maximum-security prisons specifically designated for adolescents. Referred to as "Gladiator School," The Cat was one of the most violent maximum-security prisons in the United States and possibly the world. The Notorious B.I.G. even referred to Coxsackie in his song "Realest Niggas" as a place where you had to have "ill" hand skills to survive.

I knew there was a strong possibility I would end up in The Cat due to my age and sentence. But again, I held on to hope even as 40 of us in the back of a bus were shackled and herded further upstate into the mountains—where we stopped at various prisons along the way to drop off and pick up other *unfortunates.*

New York state prisons, strategically placed in the forgotten lands of upstate New York as economic engines—were massive, gothic, fear-inducing, inorganic structures designed to last forever.

Great Meadow Correctional Facility (aka Comstock) was our final stop before The Cat. It was an infamous prison about 200 miles north of New York City, amid perpetual grey skies, an ocean of cornfields, farms, and a small town.

Like most maximum-security prisons, Comstock had a brutal reputation and was known to house numerous high-profile prisoners in its bowels. It was an evil-looking structure, with a retracting steel gate that allowed us entrance into the high concrete perimeter wall. Once inside and the gate closed, two COs boarded the bus and relieved the two COs transporting us of their weapons—which were not allowed inside the prison. A roll call was then conducted, and once we were all accounted for, the second gate opened, allowing us passage into the beast.

We rolled slowly into the prison yard, a sprawling expanse about the size of a few New York City blocks, framed by weights and pull-up bars along the perimeter. It was midday, with the sun hanging high at its zenith, scorching the concrete beneath us. The yard, devoid of shade, seemed like a jungle radiating heat. Hundreds, perhaps thousands, of prisoners filled the space, their movements pausing as the bus crept forward. Faces turned, eyes followed.

Stares were heavy with curiosity, suspicion, or indifference. My heart was pounding with fear, and I was glad to be on the bus. Once we got to the receiving room, we dropped off two new jacks and picked up two men with early ’80s numbers emblazoned on their green state jackets.

I ran various equations in my head to calculate how long the men were imprisoned—and while the math was elementary, my brain, surely influenced by my own predicament, couldn’t fathom how people could survive decades in prison!?

The ride from Comstock to The Cat was relatively short and uneventful until we arrived—and one of the men with an ’80s number, who had gotten on at Comstock, *bluntly* refused to get off the bus.

The prisoner’s voice was calm as he stated:

“I would rather go to the box.”

There was a hushed silence as the COs assessed the situation. After a few moments, they instructed everyone else to get off the bus. I pondered his fate briefly, but the uncertainty of my own fate and the continued onslaught of fear left little room for empathy.

Once off the bus, they escorted us through what appeared to be a large industrial area. Along the long hallway, signs above the doors read “Metal Shop,” “Printing,” and “Laundry.” The escorting CO was about five feet tall and probably had a Napoleon complex as he quickly sized me up, took aim, and proclaimed:

“You’re not going to make it!”

I wasn’t sure if the threat was a scare tactic or an astute observation based on experience?

Could he sense my fear?

Was it my size?

The statement seemed to come out of nowhere, but thankfully, at least for my sanity, he made similar proclamations to two other *unfortunates*.

Then, rather jovially, the CO thanked us for arriving to "pay his bills" and put his "kids through college." He then told us he looked forward to meeting our kids one day.

Joke or not? The CO's words instigated a deep anger within me! People on Rikers had warned me about the blatant racism and disregard for our humanity that occurred upstate. Maybe I was overreacting, but at the moment, I couldn't imagine surviving one week in The Cat, much less seven years!

I was losing hope, and that was before I was really inside the prison—which felt unusually quiet and lifeless as we moved through the long hallways with multiple gates and metal detectors. When we finally reached the reception area, the holding cells were old and cold. The paint was peeling, and even with the light on, the cell was dark and smelled of suffering—as if the pain of past inhabitants was trapped and unable to escape.

As the cell door slammed shut behind me, I stood by the entrance and took it all in. The steel bunk to my right was covered in a dingy white sheet and wrapped in an infectious-looking brown blanket. There was a small, barred window above the bed. To my left, less than a foot from the head of the bed, was a stainless-steel toilet with no cover and a built-in washbowl. There was a tiny steel desk with a wooden stool underneath.

I scanned the cell for a little longer before going to the window, which looked out into a small square yard enclosed on all sides. High above the four walls sat towers—with guns aimed and ready to rain down bullets. I was transfixed when, in divine timing, huge flood lights came to life and illuminated "The Center Yard"—a gladiator pit, where prisoners were dumped numerous times a day for a process called "recreation."

After being filtered through metal detectors and invasive body searches, what appeared to be hundreds of prisoners flowed into the tiny shoebox through two huge doors. Many prisoners were grouped up, but most were just spinning the yard clockwise as if bound by some gravitational pull. I even saw a few people I knew from Rikers, including someone who looked like Serge, who I strongly suspected was also in The Cat.

I was taking it all in when my automated defense system went online, and a primal feeling in my body signaled imminent danger. My vantage point allowed me to see it before most in the yard. It looked like a gang assault—via razor tag.

The guy on the wrong side of the attack was trying to neutralize the razors by using his jacket as a shield. But the attackers strategically came from opposite directions, broke his defense, and carved up his face like a pumpkin.

I observed the attack with dread and morbid fascination before feeling compelled to look up at the gun towers, where the guards were also watching and didn't appear bothered or inclined to intervene.

The assault continued for a few minutes before the doors opened, and a contingency of COs in riot gear rushed out and screamed for everybody to get on the floor. But they were too late; the poor guy struggled just to keep his face together.

That first night in The Cat felt like it would never end. I kept thinking about the guy in the yard and the CO saying I wouldn't survive. The urge to give up grew stronger by the minute.

A part of me wished for the peace that oppressed people are inclined to believe came with death. But when it got dark, I escaped to my safe place—filled with beautiful, timeless, and unshackled memories and dreams of a *future* with my daughter, family, and friends—all sustained by an unrelenting belief that *this* wouldn't be my destiny!

I eventually fell asleep and woke just as sunlight pierced the dark cell. Yet I kept my eyes closed and prayed, asking for the strength to survive *whatever* awaited. I felt better after praying, but the day began with a breakfast of cold, sloppy oatmeal served in the cell, delivered with the news that I would be quarantined for at least five days before eventually moving to the general population.

I was allowed one phone call and a visit after a week—which felt like a lifetime away. However, the isolation was a blessing, as it allowed me to settle my mind, journal, and process everything that had happened over the last few months.

Journaling, in particular, allowed me a deep catharsis and became one of my survival tools, and the basis for this story decades later.

I ultimately made it through the week in reception and got a surprise visit from Mom and John. While I was excited to see my family, I wasn't in a sunny mood. The conversations felt forced, as I was depressed and pretty sure they were, too. Yet we all did the courtesy check-in and pretended that I didn't have a life sentence and we weren't sitting in a maximum-security prison visiting room.

To further disassociate, we ate horrible food and drank sodas from overpriced vending machines while passing the time playing mindless games like Uno, checkers, and Monopoly. And when the silence got too heavy, we mixed in some nostalgic banter to lighten the mood.

I felt both sadness and relief three hours later when the CO announced the end of visits. Visitors were directed to the front, and prisoners were sent to the rear of the visiting room. I tried not to look back as I approached the forming queue. I was hurting and doing my best not to crumble as my family exited the visiting room. At that moment, I hated prison visits—but I was torn, as the little bit of humanity they afforded me with family and friends was one of the primary reasons my heart wasn't cold.

I glanced at the other *unfortunates* and saw beneath the mask that they were also hurting. Thankfully, the line moved quickly, and I prepared mentally for the strip search—and dissociated as the White CO examined my naked Black body for contraband. After the search, I went to the package room, where Mom and John left me some canned food, fresh fruits, a pair of shell-toe Adidas, and an army jacket without the lining.[17] But when I got to the package room, the CO in charge couldn't find it.

I began to worry as the package room was infamous for stealing packages or taking a generous percentage. But it turned out the CO couldn't locate my package because it was placed in a different housing unit—as I had been moved to the general population and assigned to cell block B-3, 25 cell.

I arrived after the count to B-3, which was mostly empty, as many *unfortunates* were out for dinner—which spared me the scrutiny I would have received as a new jack with a package. The cell, while dirty, was comparatively cleaner than the one I left in reception; my few belongings were also packed and transported before my arrival. I was able to procure a brand-new sheet set and some other necessities for a few cigarettes[18]

17 Green army jackets were allowed in NY State Prison, but without the lining, which authorities feared would be used to stash weapons. In his song "It Ain't Hard to Tell" from the album Illmatic, Nas raps about sneaking "a Uzi on the island in my army jacket lining"—which is paying homage to the culture of army jackets in jails and prisons.

18 Even though I did not smoke I usually had cigarettes which functioned as currency.

from a 17-year-old with a serious dope habit back in reception. He was being held until space became available in the box—where he had to serve two years in solitary confinement for allegedly stabbing another prisoner.

I was emotionally exhausted after the visit, so I took out the brand-new maroon sheets and began remaking the space before lying down. I fell asleep momentarily but awoke to the loud sound of opening cell doors, bustling energy, and the release of pent-up communication. I quickly jumped off the bed and moved towards the cell door, where I made eye contact and received a head nod from an "OG" in the cell directly across from me.

I glanced to my right and found a familiar face—a dude from Brooklyn known as "Law." I met him in the Sprungs when I first got to Rikers Island. We weren't exactly cool, as he and his crew had *tried* to extort me for commissary. So somewhat playfully, Law acted overly surprised at seeing me before extending his hand towards the cell door to give me a fist-pound. We kicked it briefly before the loud "pop, pop, pop" of opening cell doors, and a command for everybody to "lock it in" halted all communication.

About two hours post-dinner, the CO allowed "Rochester," the porter,[19] out onto the tier. I stood at the cell door patiently for a few minutes before I got his attention. I had gotten pretty good at quick assessments, and he seemed like a cool dude. We were about the same height, except he was maybe a hundred pounds heavier, all solid muscle. But he carried himself with the humility of someone who didn't need external validation.

Rochester poured hot water into my small bucket while handing me a shaving razor—before giving me the rundown of the cell block. *Saturday night was movie night—from 8 to 10 pm in the dayroom at the end of the tier. You could also make collect calls during that time on one of the four pay phones in the back.* He added my name to the recreation list and mentioned that, if things stayed quiet, the CO would likely start rec around 7:30 pm as a reward. But I guess the CO was feeling extra generous—because the cell doors started popping open at 7 pm.

19 Porters are prisoners whose job is to clean and essentially run the cell block in coordination with the CO.

VERSE 11

Moya

November 1994

I quickly got dressed and stepped onto the tier, where bowls of food, popcorn, and various contraband passed rapidly from hand to hand among the *unfortunates*. A chorus of voices and the metallic clatter of cell doors opening and closing echoed through the space as I walked the length of the long hallway, framed by rows of cells, toward the dayroom.

I was slow and deliberate, pretending not to look at what was happening or into anyone's cell while taking mental notes. When I reached the dayroom, I sat in the back and pressed my body against the wall.

It was necessary, upon arrival in new spaces, to observe the land's order. Space and proximity to the TV were usually allocated according to power. To survive, let alone thrive, it was essential to determine who held the throne and who was vying for it, as missteps were often fatal.

After a few minutes of observation, I recognized more people from Rikers Island. We greeted each other as distant acquaintances do. One of them was a Jamaican brother about my age who came up to Downstate with me. He introduced me to other Caribbean folks, who were skeptical of me as I didn't speak in a heavy Caribbean patois.

I quickly assured the men that I was born in Jamaica but grew up in New York. I was also raised by a family of teachers who, to survive and thrive, were conditioned to believe that the "Queen's English" and not patois[20]—a mash-up of various languages and terms used by slaves to communicate without the oppressor's understanding—was to be the official language of Jamaica.

Once authenticated, they offered me a bowl of what looked like fried rice with octopus and calamari, which I had never eaten before,

20 See: "A Patois Revival: Jamaica Weighs Language Change as Ties to Britain Fray" via *New York Times*.

but thankfully accepted, as I had only consumed mess hall food since arriving upstate.

I quickly demolished the bowl of food and made small talk for a little longer before calling Moya—who I hadn't spoken to since I got transferred to The Cat, as she was working, going to school, and less available.

I dialed a few times and got her answering machine each time. I told Mom I would call, so I was extra sad that she wasn't home. But shit, it was a Saturday night. She had just turned 19, and I knew it was selfish to expect her to be sitting at home, waiting by the phone for a collect call from prison.

I hung up the phone and decided to watch the movie. But my mind was preoccupied. I stared at the TV in a stupor for a few moments before realizing that we were watching *Carlito's Way*—which, ironically, Moya and I loved and had watched often.

We knew the lines of our favorite scenes by heart—Moya would play Gail and I, Carlito. Moya was a Scorpio and at times feisty—and thus fond of the scene where Gail angrily confronts Carlito on why he dumped her before going to prison.

Deep down, Moya was a romantic who didn't think 30 years in prison—which was Carlito's sentence—could come between true love. She thought Carlito was selfish and only protecting himself by dumping Gail rather than letting love decide their fate.

"Nothing can stop true love" was our motto.

Moya and I had been through the fire numerous times and believed our love and friendship were strong enough to overcome any obstacle. But we didn't count on our lives mirroring the fictional narrative of our favorite movie.

After the judge sentenced me to seven years to life in prison, Moya joked that I had gotten off easy, since I had 23 fewer years than Carlito. Her humor had a way of sparking hope and joy within me, deepening my love for her.

Moya was my best friend, so unlike Carlito, I chose to let love lead the way and shape our destiny. And as 1994 drew to a close, after a handful of phone calls and letters, we decided to get married.

December 1994

Over the next few weeks, I completed the necessary paperwork, and Moya bought rings. But we didn't want to make a decision as important as marriage, especially considering the circumstances, without putting all the cards on the table. So we scheduled a visit for early December.

Visitor processing didn't usually begin until 8 am—and it could take hours before we got notified of visits. But by 5 am I was ready and pacing in my small cell, anticipating Moya's visit, which we confirmed via collect call the night before. But 9 am crawled to 11 am, and soon it was 1 pm, then 2 pm; slowly, hope began to recede as fear grew stronger.

When 3 pm arrived—the time visits officially ended—my mind ran rampant to find a plausible explanation for why I didn't get a visit from Moya?

The isolation of prison kept me on the brink of insanity—*Maybe she got into an accident? Maybe they didn't let her in? Maybe she missed the bus…* Fear and anxiety took over the tiny cell and began to suffocate me. To make matters worse, I was trapped and unable to make calls until night recreation at 8 pm.

I was manic when the CO finally cracked my cell—and rushed immediately to the dayroom to call. I was tense but could feel my body begin to relax as Moya's "hello" interrupted the ringing; however, before I could say anything, the automated machine announced:

"You have a collect call from a correctional facility…"

I waited patiently, excited to hear her voice. But something unexpected happened: The call was denied! My hands were trembling as I redialed, but the call was denied—again and again, until I couldn't dial anymore.

I told the CO I wanted to "lock in," left the dayroom, and navigated alone, along the long dark tier back to my cell. As the door slammed behind me, I collapsed onto the steel bed and cried. Fear, anger, anxiety, grief—emotions I didn't yet have language for—rose all at once, and fought viciously for my attention. In a matter of months, my whole world was turned upside down. I was literally trapped inside a small, dark cell, hundreds of miles from home—with a life sentence. I was suffocating when my defense mechanism kicked in, and rage started to grow. I was mad at the blatant racism and inhumanity inherent in police, courts, jails, and prisons. I was mad at God for allowing systems of oppression and what I deemed unnecessary suffering to exist. I was mad at myself for making foolish decisions. And aside from my daughter's birth, I was mad at every day, every hour, and every minute of 1994!

1995

VERSE

01

Survival

January 1995

I couldn't escape The Cat, even in my sleep!

The omnipresence of violence was overwhelming. *Shit* was always going down. Fistfights were archaic—razors, shanks, ice-pics, or bone crushers were the weapons of choice—often sold by COs—who instigated drama, utilizing "COINTELPRO" tactics to infiltrate, divide, and create wars among the various factions from the yard, to the mess hall, housing units, programs, and religious services.

Nowhere was safe!

Violence in The Cat was always percolating. So when I heard the screams, I sat up in bed, focused my attention, and listened for a minute to make sure I wasn't dreaming. But in no time, it became clear that the screams were real.

I moved quickly from the bed towards the cell door and caught a whiff of the cannabis permeating the air. I stared in disbelief at the rolls of toilet paper tossed around the tier like confetti. There was also music as fists crashed against cell doors—metal on bone—turning cages into drums, and beats for the various chants.

The scene was more spiritual than a celebration. It was a conjuring of *faith* and *hope*, which guided and sustained caged human beings each New Year as they remained trapped in the belly of the beast.

I felt joy and even allowed myself a smile as the countdown began. And by the time it got to "3," I was yelling in unison. As 1995 arrived, the cell doors rattled louder and louder, and the counting became liberating chants of "freedom, freedom, freedom…"

Blame it on the second-hand contact or drumming, but I felt better than I had in weeks. I didn't know what to expect in 1995. But I laughed nervously to myself, and imagined it couldn't be worse than 1994—

which finally came to a close when I got transferred out of B-3 cell block a few days before the New Year.

I knew the move was imminent, as I saw the "Program Committee" shortly after arriving in The Cat—and they assigned me to the mess hall—which housed workers in either "A-1" or "B-1" cell blocks.

I was sad to leave B-3. Even though I was technically still in the same jail. Going to a different cell block meant there was a *possibility* I would never see my people from B-3 again—which was just as hard and traumatizing as *suddenly* moving away from your neighborhood, school, family, and friends.

The emotional bonds men build in prison are often some of the deepest and most vulnerable relationships—yet are not openly acknowledged or discussed due to internalized homophobia and negative narratives associated with jails and prisons. But for me, there was a sense of community on B-3 amidst the chaos of The Cat that sowed the seed of survival—and would serve me for years to come.

B-3 was where I learned to cook using "the stinger"—an electric coil taken from the "hot pots" they sold in the commissary and used to heat a bucket of water—which cooked various dishes seasoned and prepared in separate plastic trash bags. While I can't speak to the long-term health impact of cooking in plastic bags, I can tell you that this cooking method wasn't just genius;[1]it produced some of the best meals I had in and out of prison.

When we weren't in the yards or at programs, we made music using books, cups, spoons, cell doors, walls, and the human body as instruments—especially on Friday and Saturday nights, which often began and ended with dudes freestyling reggae and hip-hop tighter than most people you heard on the radio.

There was this one dude called "Critical," whose verses captured the darkness, resilience, and resistance of prison life with unnerving precision. One line in particular—*"You can put me in a box, and another box, and another box..."*—was etched into collective memory, and recited verbatim by nearly everyone in The Cat.

Critical's verse wasn't just about confinement; it captured the layered, metaphysical architecture of incarceration itself—cells within

1 See "Sous Vide" - a famous French cooking style that uses the same slow cook bag in water method.

cells, ideologies within ideologies, systems within systems—stretching far past the prison walls.

Rochester, one of the porters in B-3, devised a way to connect a tape player to "the wall"—which was code for the three audio jacks in all the cells—so that he could DJ, play music, and give shoutouts to everyone listening on tiers throughout The Cat. It was as if we had an underground radio station. Rochester had an eclectic taste in music but loved Tupac—and for about two weeks straight, we woke up every morning to "Dear Mama" or "Str8 Ballin" from the *Thug Life* tape.

The COs on B-3 were also mostly cool—which was a rarity in The Cat. However, one incident, instigated by a CO, quickly reminded me that very few people working in maximum-security prisons were "cool." The CO, who often worked in relief, was known for going out of their way to get prisoners in trouble.

One day, the CO instructed the porters that a young White teenager, who had been recently transferred to the B-3, and was allegedly convicted of a sexual crime involving a minor, *couldn't live on the tier*. The CO made it clear that we would all pay the price if *nothing* happened.

COs often spread lies about people they didn't like to keep us at each other's throats. But accusing someone of a sexual offense involving a minor was akin to a death sentence in many prisons. So, I wasn't surprised when a few days later, we learned that the White kid got "burned out"—meaning his cell was set on fire, thankfully while he was out for programs.

I was assigned to work the breakfast and lunch shifts in the mess hall. We began at 5 am with sarcastic echoes of "time to make the doughnuts." New Year's Day '95 was my first day, and I was physically and emotionally exhausted as we traversed the dark, quiet, haunting, cold prison hallways in our mess-hall whites.

It was my first time outside the cell at such an early hour, and I was loopy from waking up so early—which made the journey ahead feel a little daunting. But I prepared as best as possible and got schooled on the politics of the mess hall: for instance, "New Jacks" got "pots & pans." But if you had time or clout in prison, you often gained access to "cook" or "clerical positions"—which also paid better.

I got assigned a "tabletop" position—which had pros and cons but was much better than being trapped in the back of a hot prison kitchen washing dishes and pots covered in mystery mess hall slop. Also, while everywhere was dangerous, the kitchen naturally had more things that could be used as weapons.

It was my job to wipe down a section of tables in the mess hall after each housing unit finished eating. Once all the housing units were fed, I had to sweep and mop the floors. The task itself wasn't challenging, but it meant interacting with various housing units and prisoners used to being the alphas of their domain—which meant someone was often getting tested.

On my first day, I stood close to the food trays, which I figured would make a good shield if something popped off—and watched as the prisoners entered and made their way around the long perimeter of the mess hall before turning into the main dining hall. I was fascinated by the dress, the walk, and the ubiquitous screwface; all choreographed to tell a story—which always seemed to germinate from the same traumatic misfortunes that lead people *not to give a fuck*—which paradoxically, is the safest and most dangerous survival tool for young Black men coming of age in varied projects, jails, prisons, and *systems* designed for their subjugation.

Thankfully, my first breakfast ended without incident. I cleaned up and headed to the recreational area in the back of the mess hall, where everyone passed the time between meals. Some were doing pull-ups and calisthenics, some were playing cards, while others were watching TV.

After wavering for a while, I decided to give the pull-up bar my attention. I knew a few of the guys were "super setting" pull-ups, dips, free-weight squats, and push-ups, and felt comfortable joining them.

VERSE

02

Power 2 The People Then And Now!

"Pops," who had been down since 1979, jokingly welcomed me to the group by proclaiming: "We got fresh meat." I smiled, thinking I would have little trouble with the routine. However, I was wrong—pull-ups required a muscle group that was foreign to me. I jumped onto the bar easily but struggled to do three pull-ups without my body shaking as if I were having a seizure. Meanwhile, at least twenty years my senior, Pops was wide-gripping fifteen a clip. He raised himself with ease till the bar tapped his lower chest—where he would stay as if magnetically attached, hanging motionless for a five-count before surrendering to gravity. But once his arms were fully extended and his feet mere inches off the ground, he would do it again, and again, and again with perfect form.

A guy I knew from Rikers Island introduced me to Pops in the yard when I first got to The Cat. Pops was a cook in the mess hall, but also worked as a night porter in the Center Yard. Pops was well respected and had his own court, a mini yard within the yard, with weights, dips, and a pull-up bar, where he reigned supreme.

One day in the yard, still new to The Cat, I *apparently* bumped into a gang leader who thought I was being intentionally disrespectful and sent a soldier to stab me. Pops thankfully diverted the hit and arranged a pow-wow with the gang leader to squash the one-sided beef.

I was grateful for my relationship with Pops and considered him a mentor. Our cells were right across from each other on A-1. One morning, he handed me a stack of books on the way to the mess hall. I took the books, stared at his grinning face, and couldn't help but laugh at how much he resembled a Black version of Lee Van Cleef in *The Good, The Bad, And The Ugly.* Yet he was no cowboy.

Pops was a Black revolutionary with a graying afro who often greeted me with a raised fist and the mantra: "Power to the people then and now, comrade!"

Pops introduced me to George Jackson, Assata Shakur, Angela Davis, Frantz Fanon, Karl Marx, Steve Biko, Kwame Nkrumah, Che Guevara, Fred Hampton, and other revolutionaries. He taught me terms like fascism and imperialism while challenging me to think critically about the Black and HUMAN experience in a historical, political, and global context.

In "Redemption Song" by Bob Marley, he sings about the need to emancipate our minds from mental slavery—it was one of my favorite songs, but it wasn't until my time with Pops that I understood what the practice entailed. There was no subject beyond question. I felt my foundation shifting as we discussed and massaged topics like "intersectionality," oppression, democracy, genocide, dissonance, racism, and White supremacy while pondering what it meant to be genuinely FREE???

Pops would often quiz me between sets while working out. At first, I didn't take it seriously—I was trying to play it *cool*, so I got most of the questions wrong. But one day, Pops, feeling insulted, bluntly told me not to waste his time. He pulled me aside from the rest of the crew and shared his story with me over the next few days.

Pops told me about growing up in Harlem in the 1950s and '60s. Stories about the civil rights movement, James Baldwin, and Malcolm X—whose murder led him angrily to the Black Panther Party with dreams of revolution. But the United States wanted no part of a "Black Messiah" and took extreme measures to destroy Black Panther chapters, utilizing fascist propaganda, drugs, informants, and varied forms of state-sanctioned violence.

Pops and two other party members were arrested and charged with robbery and murder in the late '70s. The state had little evidence, but Pops' co-defendants accepted 15-year-to-life pleas rather than go to trial.

Pops, who was only 25 years old, couldn't imagine taking a plea for something he didn't do and decided to go to trial—which he lost and got a sentence of 30 years to life. Both of his co-defendants went home in 1994. But Pops had another 15 years in prison before he would even be eligible for parole. Yet even with the remaining years aside, he wasn't hopeful of getting out.

Pops was considered a "radical" to the powers that be and felt he would die in a maximum-security prison. And in a scene deserving of an Oscar consideration, Pops looked me in the eye and said, "You have a chance to get out, a chance to share our stories, and a chance to tell the truth—which will destroy the system, and I will help to prepare you!"

I laughed nervously at his proclamation and unwarranted belief in me. But he got my attention, and I took my reading and our time together more seriously. Once I got going, I would read as many as three books every week. I journaled extensively, and we discussed my journal entries whenever we could. After a few weeks, I began to see my life, history, and future possibilities through the eyes of my newfound "comrades"—most notably George Jackson—who was, and is, for many prisoners, the penitentiary equivalent of Jesus!

George Jackson, once conscious, gave his life to liberate Black people from the bondage of White supremacy. His books *Blood in My Eye* and *Prison Letters* became my bibles. George was only 18 when he was sentenced to life in prison for allegedly stealing $50 from a gas station. George was fearless and knowledgeable. He was the dragon, and his words conveyed an understanding of the perpetual humiliation that Black men trapped in poverty, projects, jails, and prisons throughout the United States experience. Even in death, his legacy inspired resistance and hope for prisoners throughout the system.

Like Ali on Rikers Island, Pops was instrumental in my spiritual journey. Pops was Muslim and invited me to the Jummah service, where the teachings and brotherhood resonated deeply with me. After a few weeks of preparation, I took my shahada on the eve of Ramadan. Pops even taught me a few Arabic surahs (prayers) to prepare me for the month-long fast, during which we would not eat from sunrise to sunset.

Pops cautioned, "Ramadan is not just abstaining from food. It's going inside yourself to find your connection with God." I didn't quite know what he meant then, but Islam felt different—it allowed me to choose *my* relationship with the creator for the first time. I spent much of Ramadan praying and reading the Quran, which shed light in many dark places.

My family couldn't understand my newfound faith and wrote it off as a "prison thing." However, they were very excited when I told them I could go to college while incarcerated.

Getting access to higher education in prison felt like a blessing. I had only two classes in the '95 spring semester. But they met twice a week and offered me an opportunity to escape mentally from the chaos of The Cat. I also saw my growth as a student and critical thinker from my days at Nassau Community College. For the first time in a long while, I began to see some light in what had been thus far a really dark experience. But the rumor mills were churning, and the word on the street was that my first semester could also be my last.

The 1994 crime bill[2] proclaimed "college was creating smarter criminals," and enacted provisions to eliminate federal college aid for incarcerated people. The college administrators believed that, even without federal aid, they could raise enough money to keep the program going. While we were grateful for their passion and commitment to us, we were less optimistic.

Pops loved that I was attending college, but constantly pushed me to do more. He believed oppressed people had to move beyond a scarcity mindset and seize every opportunity for growth. During Ramadan, while working in the mess hall and taking college classes, I enrolled in the food certificate program, a three-month training program in food safety and preparation required to access higher-echelon jobs in the mess hall.

2 See Joe Biden 1993 speech pushing the crime bill. Also "How the 1994 Crime Bill Fed the Mass Incarceration Crisis" by the ACLU.

VERSE

03

Mess Hall Crew

March 1995

I got transferred to D-Block—the assigned housing unit for the food service training program, where, for the first time in my NY state prison experience, there was a Black man assigned to the cell block, which wasn't always a good thing. The few Black COs in The Cat often went out of their way to utilize extreme violence towards Blacks and Latinos, as if to fuel and create dissonance—separation, difference, and positionality in the eyes of the White COs. But thankfully, this Black CO was, for many of us, a big brother who would often stop by our cells to check in and offer support.

Over the next few weeks, I got close to a few people on D-1. Rondoo was from "South Jamaica, Queens"—a poor, destabilized community with high rates of substance use and incarceration that gave birth to infamous crews like the Supreme Team and rap legend 50 Cent. He was big, strong, giving, had untreated mental health problems, wild dreads, and was prone to impulsive acts of violence.

Jus was from a highly criminalized neighborhood in Brooklyn called Bushwick. He was hilarious and a freak athlete who, at 5'7" and about 160 pounds, could dunk a basketball and bench-press 225 pounds for over twenty reps. Jus blew trial for a crime he claimed he didn't commit and often joked, "It's not like I never committed a crime; it's just that I didn't do this one."

My boy Serge was, indeed, in The Cat and housed in B-2, which was the cell block below me when I was locked in B-3. Serge's cell was next to mine, but a tier below. This allowed us to communicate, send messages, food, clothes, and pretty much anything.

Serge introduced me to Bishop, who was from Belize but grew up in another destabilized and impoverished neighborhood in Brooklyn called Flatbush. He was a known stick-up-kid, who embodied Tupac's character in the movie Juice.

Through Bishop, I met Reecy and CI, which was short for cock eye. CI was from Queensbridge Housing—the largest project in the United States. He was about five feet five, cross-eyed, wore huge bifocals, and was always playing spades or gambling for money. He was hilariously funny, but you couldn't play with him too much as he could snap—like the time a new jack to the mess hall jokingly invited him to his private parts during a card game.

Inviting people to your private parts in the communities I come from often leads to a fight; however, in prison, where homophobia is rampant, and *respect* often equates to life or death, the consequences are often far more severe. But even I was caught off guard when CI, with cat reflexes, got to his feet, spat out a razor from his mouth, and cut half the guy's face off.

When somebody gets cut in The Cat, there are only a few choices—one, you hold it down, which is slang for saying you don't go to the CO and tell. And if you do go to the CO, it is only to request medical attention. Either way, the person who got cut will likely get their ass beat by the COs and forced to cooperate by naming the assailant. The other option is to fight back, at which point both participants will go to the box and get their ass beat. In the case of the new jack who got cut, he went to the CO for medical attention, was transferred to protective custody, and was ultimately transferred out of the prison. But he didn't *snitch*.

Reece was a skinny, unassuming dude from Brownsville who sold drugs, extorted people, and ran gambling rings. But Reece was also one of the most giving, kind, thoughtful, and brilliant people I have ever met. We were a motley crew, but working in the mess hall of The Cat, we developed a brotherhood forged out of our shared trauma and collective will to survive.

One night, after a visit with Heather and Keiana, Reece swung by my cell for what we called a post-visit check-in. Sizing me up with his usual perceptive gaze, he asked if I needed the "hang-up box." It was a crude term for a cherished cassette tape collection, a rotating library of soul, jazz, and R&B tracks that we shared when someone needed to dig deep, confront their emotions, or simply get lost in music.

Reece's gesture was small but profound. I told him I had a great visit, but confessed I needed to let some stuff out. A few hours later,

I heard a knock and turned to see him slip the shoebox of tapes through the food slot on my cell door. But as I got up and grabbed the box, I noticed a pack of cigarettes among the tapes. I looked at him, puzzled, but he just smiled and said: "It's a gift."

I took a quick peek inside the cigarette box and counted five sticks of weed wrapped in bible[3] paper. I laughed nervously and quickly slid the cigarette box back to Reece and jokingly offered: "If I start now, I would be your best customer"—which was true, and why I refrained from smoking weed.

I promised my family that I wouldn't do anything *intentionally* to further jeopardize my freedom, which meant that my friendship with Reece and my crew from the mess hall was often an uneasy alliance. But these men treated me, and each other, like brothers—which allowed us to be ourselves, no masks, no pretense, just being—which, to me, at that time, was an immeasurable gift.

April 1995

I was on D-1 till the end of April before a few of us in the food service program strategically transferred to the honor dorm—which was the only non-cell block housing unit for prisoners in The Cat. Serge got there at the beginning of '95 and convinced me to apply. It was a wide-open space, with beds arranged in rows, like at Rikers Island. But everyone there was mostly chill, seeing the dorm as an escape from the violent reality of The Cat.

The perks, such as having pots and pans to cook, and fewer restrictions on movement, were great, but many COs assigned to the dorm had White supremacist tattoos and were known to be openly racist. Some were even alleged to have participated in the killing of prisoners in the Box.

The Cat, and everything in it, was a dystopian reality on steroids. Yet I was happy to be with my crew and Serge. There was also a nostalgic comfort in having a friendship that predated prison—in some ways, it was like a private space, off-limits to the shackles of confinement, where you could reminisce together about the *good old days*.

When we weren't programming, Serge and I would meet up with

3 Small Bibles were usually in every cell and used as a substitute for rolling paper.

Will and other dudes we knew from Queens to work out, play handball, or just spin the center yard and talk.

The "big yard"—the polar opposite of the center yard—had grass, views of the sky and mountains, and what felt like acres of space. It opened in the late spring of '95 and was, I must admit, a strange paradox. For instance, the air quality was so fresh that it made me high—to the point that I often found myself just staring beyond the barbed wire and gun towers at the beautiful, majestic mountains that engulfed Coxsackie in a meditative trance.

As the temperatures rose, I would walk the yard's perimeter until I found a remote area of grass to sit in and just stare at the sky, as if I were in Central Park. In rare moments, I could *almost* forget that I was in prison—until someone got cut, stabbed, or the loudspeaker blared, "Yard closed."

The big yard was my escape—a place where I could daydream and let my mind wander. But when the yard closed, reality came rushing back with a vengeance. Returning to The Cat felt like a slap in the face. By the time the guards barked orders for us to line up and be counted, I was usually agitated and bracing myself for the grim march back into the building and the horrors that awaited.

May 1995

On my 20th birthday, Serge and the crew cooked a feast of fried chicken, mackerel, and seafood rice with shrimp, calamari, and octopus. And for dessert, chunky monkey ice cream and honey buns from the commissary.

I was thrilled for the feast, but a little apathetic about my second birthday incarcerated. Nevertheless, I spent the day celebrating with my comrades, soaking in the moment, and feeling grateful for people who loved, supported, and celebrated me in such a dark place.

The night of my birthday, I took some time for myself to reflect and journal about my arrest, time on Rikers Island, birth of my daughter, conviction, loss of friends, and my time upstate serving a life sentence in a violently inhumane system. When fatigue crept in, I slid *Illmatic* by Nas into the tape deck and got lost in the music. It was a good day. But deep down, I knew that in prison, and places like The Cat, good days never last long!

Coxsackie Correctional Facility 1994-95

1 Keiana and me circa 1994

2 Me, Keiana, and Heather circa 1994

3 Kareem and me circa 1994

4 Me, Keiana, and Heather circa 1994

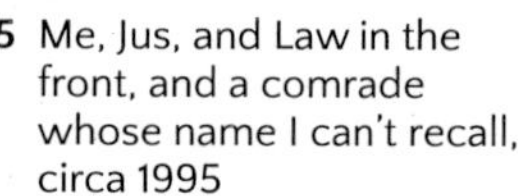

5 Me, Jus, and Law in the front, and a comrade whose name I can't recall, circa 1995

6 Serge and family circa 1995

7 Me, Jus, Messiah (hat), and Reece circa 1995

8 Me, Tata, and Law circa 1994

Full-size photos can be found on https://www.instagram.com/94a6325/

Some individuals have been pixellated for privacy.

VERSE

04

Greene

June 1995

I didn't think much of it when the mess hall CO told me to return to the dorm. The one good thing about a maximum-security prison was that they allowed daily visits—which meant some good and not-so-good surprises. So, in my mind, I was preparing for a *surprise visit*. But when I got back to the dorm, the CO handed me draft bags and said:

"Pack up; you're going to another prison."

I was shocked. He must be joking. It was the middle of June, and I had just seen my counselor, who said I would need to do at least another year in The Cat before I would be eligible for a transfer to a medium-security prison. I initially took the news that I was leaving badly, as The Cat—for good and bad—was now home.

I was leaving a community that accepted, nurtured, and taught me how to survive, many of whom I would never see again. Many of whom, due to their sentences, were destined to die in the bowels of a maximum-security Prison.

My emotions were all over the place. I cried and laughed with Serge as I packed my bags. I also wrote a few messages to people like Pops and comrades I wouldn't see before leaving. I felt anxious, not knowing my next destination, but I slowly embraced the possibilities.

I finished packing and took my bags to the draft room, where I recognized one of the COs from the mess hall and felt comfortable asking him where I was going. Maybe he expected the question, but he answered immediately: "Across the street"—code for Greene Correctional Facility, a medium-security prison next door to The Cat. I wasn't thrilled, but going to a medium meant, at least in theory, that I was one step closer to going home.

The cataloging of my personal items, strip search, and shackling took longer than the short van ride across the street. At first sight, Greene could almost pass as a college campus—dorms, administrative buildings, and walkways set against a picturesque mountain range. But Greene was a violent "adolescent" prison, filled mostly with young Black and Brown teenagers, divided into two sides: the old and the new.

The "old side" is the original prison, with dorms A to G, and the "new side" is the new prison, with dorms H to N. After processing, they sent me to H-I—the reception house. The draft room was on the old side of the prison, which meant I had to use the custom-made wheelbarrow to haul my property unescorted across the jail.

The dorms in Greene were designed for 50 people. But with the passage of the 1994 crime bill and other racialized laws, the prison business was booming. Ten extra bunk beds were added to accommodate the surplus of teenage prisoners with "95" numbers coming into the system, which made the dorms crowded and bristling with adolescent energy.

Upon arrival, I sat on the top bunk with my back against the wall to acclimate myself. There were fewer restrictions in a medium-security prison, allowing for more unescorted movement between housing units and program buildings. In theory, this was a good thing but also dangerous, as it allowed rival factions easier access to one another.

Within hours of my arrival, I witnessed three fights from my top bunk involving "homemade" weapons like the lock in the sock, the can in the sock, and, finally, a metal mop wringer.

The ingenuity behind the weapons was next-level—anything and everything could be turned into a survival tool. I wasn't personally afraid, but my adrenaline was surging, and I barely registered the PA system blaring on and off in the background. When I finally heard the announcement, I had no idea what "red dots"[4] were.

Curious, I made my way down off my bunk to catch the porter sweeping the floors outside the cube and asked him with a straight face, "What's a red dot?" The porter stopped mopping and looked me over to see if I was serious—once his cognitive process was complete, he glanced around, leaned forward as if to tell me a secret, and said:

"Shit is hot son! Summertime is razor tag season."

4 A security code often followed by the location (ex. Red Dot, B-1).

VERSE

05

M-2 Dorm

The porter wasn't lying! Greene was on fire—the walkways, housing units, sick call, mess hall, and any type of recreational activity usually involved at least one fight, cutting, or stabbing. Like The Cat, COs were always central players in the violence. They fanned the flames by providing weapons and drugs and instigating gang wars through Machiavellian tactics. It was basically "divide and conquer"—the antiquated but ever-effective "Babylon" formula. Yet, I felt prepared to navigate the jungle.

A few days after arriving at Greene, I met with the program committee and was assigned to "ASAT," the Alcohol/Substance Abuse Treatment program. I was also assigned to the mess hall because I had a food-service training certificate from The Cat. About two weeks later, I was moved to M-2, one of the program dorms designated for ASAT participants. In M-2, the COs had heightened authority, as every prisoner assigned there needed the program to meet parole eligibility requirements, which meant that completing ASAT meant not only adhering to the program itself but also navigating the dynamics and expectations of all three COs overseeing the dorm.

Prisoners jokingly referred to the M-2 COs as the Holy Trinity: Paul, Mary, and Joseph. Paul worked the overnight shift. We had the least contact with him, but his presence was stifling. He was huge, at least six feet four and two forty; he wore cowboy boots with two-inch heels and spurs, which rattled when he did the midnight count. He chewed tobacco and never looked happy. When he worked, it felt like someone was always getting kicked out or sent to the box. And if he couldn't get anyone, he would penalize the whole dorm for some arbitrary reason usually related to cleanliness. His favorite power play was taking the microwave and TV power cords.

Joseph worked the day shift. He read his daily newspaper and a novel most of the time. He never really messed with us, as long as we didn't fuck up.

Mary was the wild card and often functioned somewhere between Paul and Joseph. She was laid-back and charming but also had a nasty streak. There were people she just didn't like—maybe it was the way they talked, or who they talked to, or where they were from; whatever it was, when Mary didn't like you, something bad usually happened!

Navigating the Holy Trinity was scary, but so was navigating extremely traumatized teenage boys who only knew how to communicate through violence—which, a few weeks after I arrived, became so constant that the prison authorities had to declare a lockdown. We had no movement, no programs, no recreation, and often no talking.

Each housing unit required additional porters to help with food distribution and post-meal cleanup. Normally, I would never volunteer for a porter position because I was uneasy working directly with the COs. However, the opportunity to move around freely during a lockdown came with undeniable advantages.

My boy G was already a porter and a group leader in the house, and he vouched for me with the Holy Trinity. He had the type of clout that everyone respected. G was also from Queens and rumored to have a *thing* with Mary—something I never asked him about, as I didn't want to know. Not that I wasn't curious, but I wanted to maintain plausible deniability to protect my fragile prospect of freedom.

The lockdown had its benefits: it let me slow down enough to process the first six months of '95, learn the lay of the land, and make new connections in Greene. It was also my second summer incarcerated, but my first one upstate. And even though Rikers was fucked up, at least it was technically a part of New York City and easier for friends and family to visit.

July 1995

July 20, 1995, was Keiana's first birthday. Heather sent lots of pictures, and I knew I would see them once the lockdown ended. However, the reality that I missed the first year of my daughter's life was hard to accept and tormented me beyond words. Also, many of the early-release programs our lawyers had promised had not yet materialized and didn't seem likely to do so. So, as I glanced at pictures of my daughter and imagined a future with her, I knew that missing a few more birthdays was a strong possibility.

Music was my lifeline. I spent hours in my cube with my Walkman, smiling and reminiscing about legendary shows in Jamaica like *Reggae Sunsplash* and *Sting*. Or NYC's summer music staples like Brooklyn-Queens Day at Flushing Meadow Park, the Greekfest at Jones Beach, the vibrant vibes at Washington Square Park, and the Coney Island boardwalk. I even found myself missing the electric energy of clubs like *The Palladium* and *The Tunnel*, where I had the chance to see some of my favorite artists light up the stage.

Memories and my deep connection to music fueled my escape from the confines of prison walls. My eclectic tape collection—some gifted and others ordered through prison-approved vendors—spanned genres, from Miles Davis to the Red Hot Chili Peppers. But '90s hip-hop held a special place in my heart, and I was especially obsessed with Raekwon's newly released iconic purple tape, Only Built for Cuban Linx. I played the tape on repeat during the lockdown so much that I worried it might pop. At the time, I didn't fully realize it, but songs like Incarcerated Scarfaces, with their vivid jail and prison references, felt like a raw confirmation of the madness we "*unfortunates*" trapped in the mountains were living, but couldn't find the words to articulate.

Monica's Miss Thang was my jam when I needed a different vibe. It took me back to when being fly, meeting girls, getting numbers, and hanging out was living my best life. However, I had to be careful not to go down the rabbit hole of reminiscing—as once the euphoria subsided, a depressive state often followed. But things started to feel a little brighter once the lockdown ended, and I began to see more familiar faces.

Rondoo, whom I knew from the mess hall in The Cat, got transferred to Greene and ended up in ASAT—right next to me in the adjoining cube. Rondoo introduced me to Bliss, his bunky, and boy from the South Side of Queens.

Bliss was about ten years my senior. An army veteran, he loved guns and was a stick-up kid from the Supreme Team era. Bliss, like many people from historically traumatized and oppressed communities, was complex. He had war stories for days, but also a deep philosophical side.

We'd spend hours debating the teachings of revolutionary leaders—and were particularly fond of Nelson Mandela's *Long Walk To Freedom*—particularly his commitment to the collective, exemplified by his demand and ultimate victory at Robben Island for himself and other prisoners to have pants, which the apartheid regime had denied them to reinforce their alleged inferiority.

I went back to work in the mess hall after the lockdown ended. The hustle was the same as The Cat—but the medium-security classification made movement easier, which allowed more food and swag to be "liberated."[5]

The ease of movement also facilitated a booming underground economy. The COs operated like the mob and offered protection or a blind eye as long as they got cigarettes or food. But I also had "runners" who were unsuspecting and could slip through checkpoints to deliver various swag, including Kool-Aid, which was always in demand and thus never sweet when served in the mess hall.

5 We saw ourselves as oppressed imprisoned people—and did not consider taking food from the mess hall or our captors stealing.

VERSE

06

OJ

October 1995

My boy Jus from The Cat got transferred to Greene and assigned to the mess hall. We worked the lunch and dinner shifts together and did calisthenics between meals. We would argue for hours about sports, hip hop, cars, money, women, name it!? It was all dumb shit, but it helped us pass the time. The "OJ" trial was ending, and we added it to the queue of subjects we pontificated on. But Jus was a loud dude, and our daily chats soon drew in other prisoners looking to weigh in on the matter. For the most part, everyone thought OJ did it. But no one wanted to see him get convicted, as most of us wouldn't wish prison on our worst enemy.

On October 3, we were all anxious for the OJ verdict—expected sometime in the afternoon. Once lunch finished, we quickly cleaned up and rushed back to the dorm, hoping to watch the proceedings, which, by all accounts, had turned into a soap opera. But halfway down the walkway towards the dorm, the prison exploded in a collective cheer. I ran the rest of the way as if the verdict determined my freedom.

As I entered the dorm, I was out of breath and found Bliss amongst the crowd gathered by the dayroom, transfixed by the television. He gave me a fist bump and said, "Don't get too excited; the pigs are watching, and they aren't going to be happy!"

Yet the joy many prisoners felt from OJ's acquittal wasn't racialized, had little to do with his guilt or innocence, and everything to do with our collective contempt towards the system—which we *hated*, but were often powerless to escape. So, at that moment, OJ symbolically became the glitch in the matrix and the instigator of possibilities.

I watched for a little longer before heading to my cube. I tried to avoid "what ifs," but it was hard not to wonder what would have happened if I had gone to trial—and won. I tried hard to imagine the emotions of a "not guilty" verdict. Or the feeling of sleeping at home, eating a meal of my choice, or just simply hanging with my family and daughter after months in a jail cell. The emotions turned into a wave of depression that washed over me for weeks. It became harder to get lost in the monotony of prison life.

I drowned in thoughts of Keiana, family, friends, Moya, and the simplicity of life before jail and prison. I was nearing my second year of incarceration, and the letters and visits had slowed considerably. I was struggling to hold on to hope as 1995 rumbled to a close. I alternated between an unwarranted belief that *something* would happen to liberate me from my confines—and feeling like I was destined to die a violent death in prison.

1996

VERSE

01

Who am I?

January 1996

The upstate winters were long, dark, and cold. They tormented my psyche. Everything felt like a threat—I was hyper-vigilant to the omnipresence of violence. But as 1996 began, I felt a defiant joy brewing—I was no longer a "new jack." I survived two years in prison and was thriving in a space designed to destroy me under the guise of rehabilitation. I even began writing poetry to express my emotions.

I usually wrote at night when everyone was asleep, and the dorm was quiet. My poems were mostly philosophical and focused on love, humanity, and revolution—themes central to my 21 years of existence as a Black man trapped within the confines of White supremacy.

Poetry, journaling, and reading, especially books like *Man's Search for Meaning* by Viktor Frankl, provoked in me a deeper exploration of the human experience, leading me to conclude that even as "civilization" made technological advancements, our progression as humans was stagnant, and tethered to archaic ideological beliefs, often serving as vehicles for the perpetuation of dissonant savagery under the guise of justice and democracy.

I began to probe deeper and reflect on my own life and my desire to be a lawyer—a dream that emanated from an era in Jamaica that dancehall artists like Super Cat spoke about in songs like *Ghetto Red Hot.* A period that saw the tiny island of less than two million people become the murder capital of the world, instigated by the Cold War, guns via the CIA, and Reaganomics.[1]

I was born into a world of political gang warfare: two opposing

1 See "Inside the CIA's Secret War in Jamaica" by Casey Gane-McCalla. The novel *A Brief History of Seven Killings* by Marlon James is also a great source. This is also a pivotal moment for New York City, as the 2025 election of democratic socialist Mayor Zohran Mamdani invites us to revisit and learn from the histories of Jamaica and Grenada—two nations destabilized for daring to imagine a similar political and economic order centered on justice, equity, and self-determination, defying capitalist greed and exploitation.

forces—the People's National Party (PNP) and the Jamaican Labour Party (JLP)—locked in deadly conflict. It was no different from the Bloods and the Crips or the Republicans and the Democrats, each divided, and incarcerated by colors and ideologies—each with people ready to kill and die for them.

In our destabilized community, guns were the ultimate tool of communication—ever-present, loud, and constantly going off. Police raids, tear gas, and lifeless bodies were a regular part of life on trips outside the house. But one day, the violence crept into our home when gunmen from a rival political party opened fire on our apartment complex in Mountain View, Kingston. Mom rushed to hide us in a closet, where we huddled in fear for hours. Eventually, the gunfire stopped, but fear, confusion, and trauma lingered. That night, as Mom tucked me into bed, I asked:

"Why do people kill each other?"

The year was 1981. I was five going on six and had recently moved to Kingston from Montego Bay to live with Mom. I was a curious child, asking many questions, which my family entertained and often encouraged. But that night, Mom just looked at me for a long time—as if unsure herself, or maybe just searching for the right words to satisfy her son's curiosity. Yet after what felt like an eternity of contemplation, Mom hugged me tightly, laughed nervously, and said, "Become a lawyer or someone who can change the world!"

It took a few more questions before I fully understood what a lawyer did. Looking back, I'm unsure whether Mom's answer was meant to satisfy my curiosity or whether she truly believed the law was a tool for democracy and humanity. Either way, her words stuck with me. Aside from a brief period when I dreamed of becoming both an astronaut and an actor, I always believed I'd become a lawyer who would change the world. But now, with a "felony" hanging over me, how could I change the world if I couldn't practice law?

My experience with the so-called "legal" system only further complicated my outlook on life as I was convinced that the law—at least in the United States—was nothing more than a tool designed by and for White men to maintain power. A system much like a theater where everyone had fixed roles, and the outcome was predetermined—by race, class, and access to resources. To me, the legal system was not a tool of justice but a system designed to maintain the status quo.

Frustrated and confused, I spent a lot of time reflecting on the months and years lost with my family, especially my brothers Andre and Kareem, who were babies when I got arrested. And even though they were still very young, I couldn't help but worry knowing the struggles that awaited them as young Black men in the United States—it was a debilitating fear exacerbated by not knowing if and when I would ever get out of prison—this reality added a ton of guilt to an already messy situation. And that guilt was infinitely magnified, knowing that Keiana would soon celebrate her second birthday without me.

VERSE

02

Y.A.P.

May 1996

I was barely 21 years old, having a midlife crisis—exacerbated by an overactive mind, a perceived lack of purpose, and a life sentence in prison. But in the spring of 1996, Bliss told me about the Youth Assistance Program (YAP) he was putting together with a few counselors.

The goal of YAP was to support young people facing criminal cases, also known as "Persons In Need of Supervision" (PINS), in avoiding incarceration. Bliss explained that we would "use our stories to help young people make better life decisions" and believed my story could positively impact the program.

At first, I didn't see the value in my story or understand how it could help anyone else. But Bliss was my big brother and mentor, and I trusted his opinion. I also liked the team he was assembling and felt I could learn from them. So after some thought, I told Bliss I was in.

YAP was scheduled to meet twice a month for about 4 hours with "troubled" teens from the Hudson Valley and Coxsackie region. The agenda was divided into two parts. The first part included introductions, a presentation by Bliss, then lunch. The second half would commence with a prison tour, small breakout groups, and then reconvene to wrap up.

The first YAP meeting occurred a little after my 21st birthday in May. We were all anxious and didn't know what to expect as we waited in the prison's school building for the participants to arrive—yet when they did, I was overcome with sadness, for many appeared no older than elementary school kids. Most were also White, which was shocking, considering how disproportionately Black and Brown my jail and prison experience had been thus far.

We didn't want YAP to become a "scared straight" program, but as the kids entered the school building, many looked terrified, some even crying. This forced the counselors to huddle with us to adjust the day's agenda.

We decided to take a few minutes to ease their fears before diving in. Bliss opened the session by welcoming everyone and setting the tone, explaining what they could expect from the program. It was my first time hearing him speak publicly, and I was immediately struck by the power of his presence and the commanding tone of his voice.

Bliss painted a vivid picture of his life growing up on the South Side of Queens, describing the joy, poverty, violence, and loss that defined his youth. He shared stories of his family, kids, time in the army, and his love for guns, drugs, and fast money—all of which shaped the decisions that eventually led him to prison.

What struck me most was his honesty and vulnerability—qualities I rarely saw in men—especially in prison. Bliss already had the presence of a superhero, with his broad chest and drill-sergeant demeanor. But as he spoke with such raw truth and heartfelt sincerity, he transformed into something even greater—a revolutionary figure of strength, compassion, and hope for humanity.

Bliss followed his speech with a brief Q&A session, but many of the participants were too nervous to ask questions. A few kids, trying to play tough and deflect the message, asked questions like, "What kind of guns does Bliss prefer?"—clearly missing the point.

I was on edge, as I wasn't sure how Bliss would respond. But he didn't skip a beat as he quickly glanced at us and *promised* the tough-talking young men that he would share his gun preference(s) later.

After lunch, we went to a designated housing unit to give an inside look at life in a medium-security prison. But Bliss made sure they knew beforehand about the tough-talking, gun-loving participants. So everyone, from the COs to the prisoners, felt the need to put on a show—the COs even gave the impression they wouldn't prevent assaults and let prisoners get close to the tough-acting participants, whose tones all changed with insight into the realities of prison life.

We returned to the school building and broke into small groups—I had two young Black kids and a White girl. I introduced myself and shared a little of my story—I told them how I felt disconnected from high school, was pushed out, got a GED, went to college, but then got arrested at 18 years old—I told them that the judge didn't see a teenager, or even want to know how I got arrested. I told them the system didn't care about your upbringing, mental health, or other mitigating factors. But it did care about handing out prison time in abundance.

We discussed a range of topics, from prison food, collect calls, visits, loss of friends, and the frequency of razor assaults. We then went clockwise around the small circle so that everyone could introduce themselves and share how they got arrested.

By now, I was familiar with the numerous pathways to jails and prisons, but I wasn't prepared as a 13-year-old girl casually discussed being raped by her mother's abusive, alcoholic boyfriend, turning to crack to escape the pain, and ultimately selling her body to pay for drugs.

None of the boys was older than 16, yet they carried heavy burdens, sharing harrowing stories of abuse in group homes, poverty, drugs, gangs, and relentless violence. Their lives had been shaped by pain and chaos, and more than anything, they just wanted someone to listen and genuinely care. I felt an undeniable connection to them—their stories mirrored my own in so many ways, and I couldn't help but see myself in their struggles.

The conversations were brutally honest and felt heavy in ways I couldn't yet understand or articulate, but I didn't want them to end. We wrapped up and reconvened with the large group for remarks from the counselors and participants before Bliss concluded the day's program.

Bliss stood before the room and asked the participants to lift their hands to their faces, to look closely, and to share what they saw. The room fell silent. A few brave voices muttered, "I see my fingers."

Bliss chuckled, his laughter breaking the tension. "Look again," he said, his voice filled with intention. "What do you see?" This time, he didn't wait for a reply. Instead, his words rang out with power and purpose as he said:

"See hope."

"See possibilities."

"See your dreams."

"It's always in your hands."

"Peace!"

The air in the room shifted. Bliss's words were more than advice—

they were a call to action. Many of the YAP participants cried and hugged us as they left the school building. There was an energy to the day that we all wanted to check into, but our debrief had to wait, as it was almost time for the 3:30 pm count. However, as soon as we left the school building, Bliss asked, “How was it, comrade? Tell me what you think?”

We walked in silence toward M-2 as I searched for the right words. But rather than give Bliss a superficial answer, I told him I was overwhelmed, sad, and couldn’t stop thinking about the kids from my group. Yet I felt grateful for the opportunity and wanted to continue in the program, and we made plans to speak later that night in the yard—which would give us more time to process the day. However, as soon as I got to my cube and sat in the chair, I grabbed a towel from the locker and covered my face to hide the hot tears running down my cheeks.

Future YAP events would carry the same emotional weight,[2] but I was learning to see value and purpose in my story. Yet it would take over a decade for me to overstand just how much *those* moments, and Bliss’s example and words, shaped me for a *purpose* beyond prison.

2 See *vicarious trauma.*

VERSE

03

Killing Me Softly

July 1996

Violence in places like Greene spiked in the heat of the summer as prisoners became more frustrated with being trapped hundreds of miles away from their families, loved ones, and communities. So, in what had already been a violent year, our captors preemptively tried to assuage us with cable television. But don't worry, we didn't get the prime-time stuff like HBO or Showtime. We did get the sports channels, though, which were a huge form of distraction and, at times, tension—especially if multiple games were on.

I wasn't much of a TV person except for sports and wrestling—which I loved unabashedly and didn't care for the haters who debated whether it was real. There was also a rumor that we would get MTV and BET if the first few months went smoothly.

Even though many of us knew that cable TV was a tool of control, there was still a genuine excitement, as we all loved music—which was a huge part of how we stayed connected to the outside world.

We dissected, analyzed, and debated music with the intensity of a contact sport. For many prisoners, arguing was a pastime in itself, and music and sports provided endless topics for debate. But one summer morning, I experienced a rare moment of magic—a song so captivating it silenced all discussion.

It was after breakfast, and we were in the dayroom waiting for the CO to call morning recreation. SportsCenter was on the TV, providing the usual background noise. Then, during a commercial break, Boom—my boy from the Bronx and a hardcore hip-hop head switched the channel to MTV. Technically, we didn't have MTV, but in prison, people were always resourceful and realized that, even though the picture was distorted on music channels we weren't subscribed to, the sound came through loud and clear.

There were about twenty of us huddled in the small dayroom listening to MTV videos when the host introduced "Killing Me Softly with His Song" by the Fugees—and as Lauryn Hill sang, the room became silent, and it was as if time stopped. Even though there was no picture, we stared at the TV, hypnotized by the beauty and power of her voice. The song's energy immediately transported me to memories of distant summers, teenage love, the hot sun, and beautiful melanated skin tones.

Winters and summers spent caged in the forgotten lands inevitably led to a lot of reminiscing. Memories of freedom, family, and better days kept hope alive, even when it felt out of reach. At times, those reflections were bittersweet, a double-edged sword that could either uplift or remind us of all we'd lost. Still, we were realists and learned to make the most of what we had—like "festivals"—special outdoor visits held in a small, isolated area behind the mess hall. The space was outfitted with picnic tables, music, and a play area for children, creating a fleeting sense of normalcy for those lucky enough to have family or friends visit. There was also food—not quite home-cooked, but better than the usual mess hall slop.

Outside, under the warmth of the summer sun, food, music, and family, combined with the laughter of kids running around, made the grimness of incarceration bearable. But festivals also had another reputation: they were rumored to be the best place for an unofficial conjugal visit, depending on which COs were on duty.

Many prisoners and COs knew what went down at festivals, but didn't care unless it was obvious. So as couples navigated the watchful eyes of authority to steal intimate moments, other prisoners, and even their families would often serve as lookouts. It was a reminder that even in places designed to strip humanity away—ingenuity, connection, and love will always find ways to persist.

VERSE

04

1996 Immigration Laws

Greene was crazy in every sense, but I adapted and made strides in all my programs. I even got promoted in the mess hall to a cook position—giving me access to some of the most coveted commodities on the black market outside of drugs—things like Kool-Aid, flour, seasoning, rice, and any type of fish or meat could fetch cartons of cigarettes. But with more money came more problems, and COs looking for bigger payoffs. Most days, I left through the side door of the mess hall with "liberated" swag in every pocket. Or a net bag full of goods if the demand was great. I had a green light through all the checkpoints along the walkway, but I usually brought a tray of food for Mary when she worked the dorm for good measure. She was a fan of the Little Debbie Honey Buns sold in the commissary, so I kept them handy when she worked.

Mary often worked Monday through Friday, so she was the CO who primarily distributed the mail. Outside of a visit, the mail[1] call was the most anticipated moment for prisoners. Whether a letter from your mother, crayon scribble cards from your kids, or a surprise message from a lost flame scented with a hint of perfume, we were all anxious and expected a prompt distribution of the mail.

Many COs understood the importance of outside communication to prisoners and distributed the mail early in their shifts. However, some COs enjoyed the power the mail gave them over us and toyed with our emotions—like Mary, who took pleasure in having us squirm and succumb each day to the monotony of:

"Did you give out the mail yet?"

A little after Keiana's birthday, towards the end of July, I found myself engaged with Mary, asking the *question* upon returning from work. We made small talk before she handed me an envelope. I took

1 Mail is a vital lifeline for prisoners and serves as a connection to the outside world, offering hope, support, and a sense of humanity in the darkness of human cages.

it casually and began to walk away when she mentioned that I also had "legal mail." Call it psychic, but my heart was racing—which often signaled that some drastic event was imminent.

My norm was to read the mail after I showered and changed out of my filthy mess hall whites. But the letter felt heavy as I entered my cube and sat in the chair next to the big locker. I made small talk with some of my people before looking down and seeing that the letter was from Moya, whom I hadn't spoken to since 1994 in The Cat.

Moya's letter was not a complete surprise. I was working through my ego and feelings of abandonment, and wrote to her a few weeks back. I told her that I missed our friendship and could never be mad at her—even though jail and prison had certainly put our *love* to the test!

In my last letter, I thanked Moya for all the visits, letters, phone calls, and packages. I told her I couldn't have survived those initial dark days, which turned to weeks, then months, and now years without her. I didn't want anyone ever to feel sad or burdened by my imprisonment—especially Moya—as I valued our friendship more than the transitional nature often associated with a romantic relationship. I wasn't used to this level of emotional awareness or vulnerability, but Moya was still one of my best friends, and it felt silly not to be honest.

Planted in front of the locker, I reread the four-page letter till I could recite each paragraph verbatim. It made me happy to hear that Moya was going to school, working, and doing well for herself. I also got updates on our mutual friends and their journeys post-high school—and while I was pleased with their success, I couldn't help but think—*what if*—I hadn't gotten arrested? What could my life look like?

I quickly moved from contemplation to laughter as Moya related all the rumors surrounding my arrest while joking that Polo and I were now officially Scarface and Manolo—and according to urban legend, we continued to run our "drug enterprise" from prison.

I took a deep breath, looked up from my locker, and realized it was almost time to pick up legal mail. I quickly took a shower and got dressed, but my head was in the clouds as Bliss, and I strolled in silence along the walkway towards the law library—but as we got closer, Bliss asked if I was "expecting something?" This was a great question, as I didn't get legal mail often. I told Bliss "no," but hoped secretly and irrationally that maybe they reformed the "Rockefeller Drug Laws" and that the letter would signal my immediate or imminent release.

Unlike regular mail, legal mail required a signature before it could be handed over—which meant a long queue of *unfortunates* already waiting when we got to the law library. When it was finally my turn, I glanced at the "Sender" column and saw that the letter was from the Immigration and Naturalization Service—aka the "INS."

The INS interviewed me in September 1994 while I was in Downstate, asking about my family—*why we came to the United States, and what ties I still had in Jamaica.* I didn't think much of the interview, as I had a Green Card.

The INS agent also said I had nothing to worry about, as my crime was not considered an "aggravated felony"[2]—yet my heart ached and my hands shook as I tore open the envelope and glanced at the subject line, which read: "ORDER TO SHOW CAUSE AND WARRANT FOR ARREST OF ALIEN DATED 7/3/96."

Bliss saw the look on my face and asked if I was ok. I wasn't and couldn't speak. But I handed him the letter once we were outside the law library. I couldn't have imagined things getting any worse than a life sentence in prison. But it did. The INS was now trying to deport me!

The letter mentioned a preliminary hearing at Downstate Correctional Facility in mid-October, about two months away.

My dreams of one day picking Keiana up from school, playing basketball in the park with my brothers, or having a Sunday dinner with my family were now being threatened. Confusion soon turned to anger.

I hadn't lived in Jamaica since 1986—and most of my family had migrated[3] to England, the United States, and Canada. Maybe my Dad was still in Jamaica? Either way, we didn't have much of a relationship before prison—and I couldn't see the stigma of deportation helping matters.

---

2 Crimes like murder, robbery and rape trigger mandatory deportation.

3 The migration of Caribbean—and broader diasporic—peoples cannot be understood without examining the historical entanglements of imperialism, capitalism, and colonization. The Caribbean was engineered into a plantation economy built on enslaved African labor that generated immense wealth for European empires while leaving the region structurally underdeveloped. Even after emancipation, global capitalist systems continued extraction through debt dependency, exploitative trade arrangements, and IMF / World Bank structural adjustment policies that weakened infrastructure, slashed social spending, and undermined local autonomy. These forces—combined with political destabilization often tied to foreign intervention—created the economic precarity that has pushed generations of Caribbean people to migrate in search of stability, safety, and opportunity. This long history of extraction also explains why climate disasters like Hurricane Melissa in 2025 are so devastating for Jamaica.

Exhibit C: Immigration Warrant

M.Y

State of New York
Department of Correctional Services
Greene Correctional Facility
P.O. Box 8
Coxsackie, New York 12051
(518)731-2741

Glenn S. Goord
Acting Commissioner

Arthur A. Leonardo
Superintendent

7/29/96

U.S. INS
PO box 415
Fishkill, New York 12524

RE; KIRK, JAMES 94-A-6325

Dear Sir:

The warrant listed below has been received from your office and lodged at our facility against this inmate.

A24 794 790 ORDER TO SHOW CAUSE AND WARRANT FOR ARREST OF ALIEN DATED 7/3/96

The inmates earliest release date will be **4/9/2001**
Your office will be notified prior to his release.

Yours truly,

Diane Warner IRC

cc Dep. Security
parole
central files
guidance
temp. release
file
inmate
Dep. Programs
Supt. Leonardo

September 1996

Against all odds, I knew I was going to fight the deportation order—something, in hindsight, I was angry at myself for not doing in my "criminal" case. Over the next few weeks, I became a regular at the law library, where I learned about the 1996 immigration laws, more aptly titled The Illegal Immigration Reform and Immigrant Responsibility Act (IIRIRA[4])—under which many crimes previously not considered deportable offenses were now made deportable.

Heinous and indicative of the absurdity of US law is the fact that IIRIRA was made retroactive. Thousands of people no longer in jail or prison, with convictions as petty as shoplifting, as far back as the '70s, were now at risk for deportation. Further, IIRIRA created a provision making detention and deportation *mandatory* for immigrants convicted under the *expanded* "aggravated felony" clause.

I was overwhelmed and spent the next few weeks in a mental fog. Then, on Friday, September 13, my boy Boom stopped by my cube and shocked me back to reality with the news that "2Pac died." I initially thought he was joking, but when I saw the tears streaming down Boom's face, I knew it was real.

Boom loved 2Pac even more than I did. Mookie, Panna, Ace, Wayno, Kirk, U-God, Butter, little Malik, Flaco, Isa, and I would spend hours blasting his music while trying to decipher the content. And even though I didn't personally know 2Pac—I knew *him.* And *he* knew and captured better than anyone in my generation what it was like to be a young Black man in America. We understood 2Pac's Gemini polarities and the history of marginalization that fed them.

I was already in The Cat when 2Pac was convicted in New York City and sent to prison towards the end of 1994. Most prisoners there thought he would end up in The Cat before the Department of Corrections sent him to Clinton—another infamous maximum-security prison by the Canadian border.

I played "Dear Mama" repeatedly and decided to write a few of

4 A landmark legislation that significantly toughened US immigration policy. Enacted during the Clinton administration, IIRAIRA expanded the grounds for deportation, introduced mandatory detention for certain immigrants, and retroactively applied harsher penalties for legal permanent residents convicted of crimes, including minor offenses. The law also eliminated judicial discretion in many deportation cases, making it nearly impossible for individuals to present mitigating circumstances.

his verses in my journal late that night. While his words were always powerful, verses like "Who would think in elementary I would see the penitentiary?" felt prophetic.

When the CO turned out the lights after the midnight count, I cried in the dark for 2Pac; I cried for Black mothers with Black sons; I cried for myself; and I cried for every human being trapped in the psychosis of "this White man's world."[5]

I struggled through the second half of 1996. And every time I thought I hit rock bottom, the floor fell out, and there was a drop further into the abyss. The mess hall was usually my solace, but even there, I couldn't shake it. Finally, the civilian head cook recognized I was struggling and gave me a few days off—which I spent oscillating between debilitating depression and anxiety, worrying about the upcoming INS court date. I knew it was only a preliminary hearing and would render no verdict, yet I couldn't sleep and rarely ate.

In an effort to maintain my sanity, I began doing calisthenics in the dorm with Mizzo—a Five Percenter[6] in his 40s who could have easily passed for 20 if it wasn't for his thick bifocals and gray stubble.

Mizzo was one of the funniest people I've ever met. Yet he hated White people and would rant for hours to anyone who was listening about how White men have robbed, raped, and murdered more than anyone else on this planet—yet America and much of the world continue to love, praise, and strive to be like the oppressor while hating and labeling the oppressed as criminals.

Mizzo was fiery like a young Malcolm X and convinced that White women were the key to ending "White supremacy"—which he reasoned White men knew, and thus a huge part of the reason Black men were ideologically demonized, criminalized, and subjected to human cages. He also had many far-fetched beliefs about where White people came from and why they were so driven to destroy the planet—and all its inhabitants.

---

5 See 2Pac's *White Man'z World.*

6 The Five Percent Nation, also known as the Nation of Gods and Earths, emerged in Harlem in 1964 when Clarence 13X—formerly of the Nation of Islam—taught that black people are the original people and, therefore, possess innate divinity. Five Percenters believe that 85% of the population is misled, 10% manipulated through power and deception, and the remaining 5%—the "poor righteous teachers"—are responsible for uplifting humanity through knowledge of self. Their teachings blend Islam, mathematics, Afro-diasporic philosophy, and street wisdom, emphasizing self-mastery, community responsibility, and the transformation of consciousness. The Five Percenters profoundly shaped hip-hop culture, Black urban identity, prison education circles, and contemporary liberation movements, offering an alternative intellectual tradition rooted in empowerment, creativity, and critical resistance.

I didn't agree with everything Mizzo said, but he provoked me to see how deeply anti-Blackness and White worship were programmed into our way of seeing, being, and acting. He pushed me to see the historical savagery rooted in the quest for White supremacy, and maybe most importantly, for the first time in my life, Mizzo forced me to question the *redeemability*[7] of dissonant White men—considering their history in the United States and much of the colonial world over the last 500 years.

October 1996

Fall arrived, and I finally felt a sense of relief as the INS hearing neared—more so for clarity than an expectation that something good would come from it. And even though I was in a marked prison van, shackled, and going to a deportation hearing, I was excited to leave Greene.

I got to see stoplights, cars, people, streets, and restaurants for the first time in almost two years on the two-hour drive to Downstate Correctional Facility. All the *little* things I took for granted now seemed magical. However, the sight of Downstate dissolved the nostalgia and brought back memories of the last time I saw Polo—whom I regularly communicated with through our families, but still felt a lot of guilt and shame towards.

I thought about Judas and wondered if he knew what he did? And if so, how did he truly feel? Did he understand the impact of his actions? And what about the cop masquerading as "Eddie?"—How many more financially insecure Black and Brown people had he set up using promises of easy money?

Downstate triggered many suppressed memories. And once the cell door locked, they began to run free, and it felt like 1994—when I got sprayed, shaved bald, and branded—94A6325—before being auctioned to the plantation.

7 The question of redeemability in the context of White supremacy has long been interrogated across disciplines. Frantz Fanon argued that colonial violence is not an aberration but a structural function of domination (*The Wretched of the Earth*, 1961). Cedric J. Robinson located racial capitalism at the core of global power, rendering reform within such systems profoundly limited (*Black Marxism*, 1983). W.E.B. Du Bois identified the "color line" as the defining problem of modern America, rooted in centuries of racial hierarchy (*The Souls of Black Folk*, 1903), while Saidiya Hartman shows how narratives of White innocence and redemption repeatedly evade accountability for violence against Black life (*Lose Your Mother*, 2007). Taken together, these works and countless others, call into question the premise that White men positioned within violent systems can be redeemed without a direct reckoning with the psychological, structural and historical forces that continue to shape the present.

I was near a meltdown when I thought of Pops, took a deep breath, and teleported back to our conversations in The Cat. I recalled passages from George Jackson and other books we read. I found strength in George's story and my time with Pops—who challenged me not to personalize my prison experience and to always move from a critically informed position—yet I had *no* idea what that looked like at the moment. But I knew I couldn't drown in my emotions if I wanted to survive.

I stood from the bed and looked out the window framed by steel bars. I stared at the highway in the distance before closing my eyes and taking deep breaths of the cold mountain air. I reminded myself of my ancestors and the inherent power within me to overcome insurmountable odds. But when night came, and the darkness ensued, sleep was nowhere to be found.

I tossed and turned for hours, massaging my fears before deciding to read and do calisthenics in the small cell. By morning, I was a nervous wreck, yet somehow functional, when the CO unlocked my cage for the hearing, which was held in a large room in the administrative part of the prison, designed to look like a courtroom.

A White judge and two younger White women sat waiting as we were brought into the room. I was directed to a desk facing the bench. After a few moments of hushed exchanges and the dry rasp of papers being shuffled, one of the women slid a stack of legal documents onto the table in front of me. I scanned them quickly. They were familiar—nearly identical to the papers I had already been served months earlier in the law library.

I sat in silence, observing the banter between the judge and the women before he commenced the proceedings. I nonchalantly went through the formalities, such as my name and place of birth, before finally addressing the "order to show cause." The judge explained that I faced mandatory deportation under the 1996 immigration law and was not eligible for administrative or judicial relief. Yet, he advised me of the right to an attorney at my own expense while repeatedly seeking confirmation that I understood he would render a decision at my next hearing. The judge then asked if I had any questions.

"What's the point of the next hearing?"

I didn't plan on saying it, but I was pissed off and tired of pretending that these laws weren't arbitrary and made up by White men. It all felt maddening, yet I had no choice but to play the game for the possibility of freedom.

After getting back to Greene, I spent the next few weeks obsessed with learning more about the 1996 immigration law. I even found pro bono legal services that my aunt Karen, who was home during the day, would call on a 3-way to discuss my case. Yet no one was optimistic—and most even recommended that I represent myself and save my money for when I get deported!

December 1996

As 1996 came to a close, I spent New Year's Eve in my cube, journaling to capture the year and take stock of my emotional state, which felt incredibly fragile amid all the uncertainty in my life. After a while, the implications of my pending deportation sent a wave of sadness over me, and I began to cry—probably louder than I would have liked, but I felt safe as most of the *unfortunates* were in the dayroom watching TV and waiting for the ball to drop.

I pulled out my Walkman from the small locker and started searching the dials for a college radio station we picked up every once in a while that played hip-hop. I finally found it and was half-listening till they played "If I Ruled the World" by Lauryn Hill and Nas.

I took a deep breath and slowly closed my eyes as they sang about freeing prisoners and sending them back to Africa—and for the first time since I was ten years old, I began to *imagine* a life outside of the United States.

1997

VERSE

01

Deportee

January 1997

I began reading Carl Jung in January 1997. Jung saw dreams as a window into dormant memories and emotions. I stumbled upon the book in the prison library just as my subconscious had begun hijacking my dreams. This strange phenomenon started in the summer of '96, after the INS served me with a warrant, and continued through January 1997. During that time, nearly every dream I had was about Jamaica, traversing different periods of my life there.

One of my most vivid dreams was leaving Jamaica at ten years old to move to the United States in February 1986. I don't remember every detail, but the car ride from our home in Washington Gardens to Norman Manley Airport in Kingston is etched in my memory.

It was the first time I truly remember hearing Bob Marley's *Redemption Song*. To this day, whenever I hear the gentle strum of the acoustic guitar and Marley's voice singing "songs of freedom," I am instantly transported back to February 1986. I can see my ten-year-old self in the car, tears streaming down my face, overwhelmed by the sadness and fear of leaving behind my friends and the only home I had ever known.

Many dreams were in a place called Orange, where I spent my early years, and the place in Montego Bay, where my family traces its roots post-Africa. Orange was where my great-grandmother, Miss Tiny's house, sat on a hill overlooking acres of green pastures once owned by my twice-great-grandfather, Mr T, who allegedly acquired the land from former slaveholders as payment for his job as a sugar-cane plantation overseer.

It was rumored that Mr T was once the wealthiest Black man in Orange. But by 1975—the year of my birth—Mr T was long dead, and my family's claim to the land was gone with him. The only thing we owned in Orange was the small house on the hill—the first place I would ever call home—sometimes living with Mom or just with Miss Tiny and an assortment of cousins and aunts who flowed in and out.

The small house on the hill wasn't luxurious—we often didn't have running water or electricity, and sometimes, we had to go to the river to bathe and wash clothes. But there were always good vibes.

In other dreams, I was with Miss Tiny and her sewing machine—which she placed most mornings on the small patio at the front of the house. As an infant, I remember her balancing me on her lap while threading the needle to operate the machine. Each press of the pedal sent the needle plunging up and down with precision, creating a steady *thuk-thuk-thuk-thuk-thuk* that shook us both.

The patio was where Miss Tiny worked, entertained, and was apprised of the *happenings* as various folks made their way up and down the hill. She knew everyone in the community, and they all knew her.

From birth to about five years old,[1] I lived between Orange and another place in Montego Bay called Granville with my Dad's mom, Mrs Miller, her husband, Mr Miller, and their children Roger, Clifton, and Donna till one day in 1980—when Aunt Karen, my Mom's sister and partner in crime came to Granville to pick me up for the weekend. However, days turned to months, and I ended up staying with Mom in Kingston.

My earliest memories of school were around this time. And even though I was young, specific memories were hardwired, like the first school I attended in Kingston, Arden Primary—I was there for maybe a year, but I kept dreaming about the *day* they took us to Hope Road.

It was May 21, 1981—and while I have a great memory, I only know that date *today* because it represents one of the most memorialized funerals in the history of Jamaica. I was barely six years old, but I remember the strange mixture of sadness and joy vividly as the country gathered to celebrate the late, great Robert Nesta Marley.

The funeral procession passed Arden Primary, which bordered Hope

1 Mom had me at 16 years old and went back to finish high school then college soon after my birth. I didn't go to live with her till 1980, when she finished teachers college in Kingston. Aunt Karen often picked me up and took me back and forth to see Mom in Kingston during this period. However, it was really tough for me—despite being in a loving community—to be away from Mom for weeks and months at a time. Telephones were also not widespread at this time.

Road. I had no idea who Bob Marley was, but I sensed his importance as our teacher discussed the message of his music.

As she played "One Love/People Get Ready," the teacher had us sing the chorus with her. Then, at some point, all the classes went to the front of the school to anxiously await the funeral procession. To this day, I couldn't tell you whether I saw the hearse, but I never forgot how we all stood transfixed along the fence, watching the seemingly endless streams of cars, bikes, and people pay homage to a national hero and global icon.

Other dreams centered around my years at Pembroke Hall, the last school I attended before migrating in '86. At Pembroke Hall, we always fought with the older kids, which seemed to be the norm, as each grade tried to impose its will on the one below it. Eventually, Wayne, Markey, Paul, and a few of us formed a crew and christened ourselves "The Dragons"—an ode to the brown "dragon stout" glass bottles we often used to defend ourselves—or race as boats when it rained, and the gutters and gullies flooded.

In the morning, when we weren't fighting, we pooled money and bought peeled oranges, sweet tamarind balls, or banana chips from the vendors who waited for us outside the school. For lunch, we got patties or a box lunch filled with coconut rice and brown stewed chicken. But the highlight was always crab season. I can't tell you the cost, but it was cheap enough that lines of financially-challenged school kids patiently waited as the vendors performed magic with their self-made, highly portable charcoal cooking stations.

As we approached the front of the line, we would excitedly peer into the ginormous pots filled with fresh crab seasoned with aromatic scotch bonnet peppers, thyme, scallions, and other accoutrements. After we won the prize, we spent what felt like hours methodically eating crab in some nook behind the school, where we shared scary stories and dreams of the future.

Many of us flip-flopped on what we wanted to do when we grew up, but for some of us, the calling was obvious—like my boy Wayne, who with no training could do life-like portraits in minutes, and draw comic book-quality Black superheroes. Markey,[2] we joked, would grow up to

2 He was also my first White friend—though I didn't realize he was "White" until I watched the mini-series *Roots*. I remember going to school the next day, shocked and confused, and confronting him as if something fundamental had shifted. Looking back, that moment reveals just how deeply race is a social construction—something learned, not inherent, something we are taught to see rather than something we naturally recognize.

be a politician. He was friends with people in every grade, knew all the teachers, and was always aware of what was happening at the school.

Many of my dreams also included Paul. At Pembroke Hall, we were required to wear *military-sharp* khaki uniforms—yet Paul's were always tattered, and he rarely had money to contribute to our meals. Paul also lived the furthest from school in a downtown Kingston ghetto called "Jungle."[3]

On nights Mom worked late, Paul usually hung out at home with me—playing Transformers and pretending to be brothers. He was always in awe that I had my room and a color TV—which Grandma gifted me on my first visit to New York in 1983.

Paul was always funny, introspective, and positive. But sometimes I found him weird—especially when he began to talk about "Obeah" and "magical realms beyond Earth." He would also read everybody's palm like some kind of fortune-teller.

I remember one day, Paul grabbed my hands—flipped them over, inspected them, and proclaimed: "You're going to be rich." To validate his hypothesis, Paul used his fingers to trace the intersecting lines converging within my palms that formed the letter "M"—which he reasoned was a sign of money.

As the cold days of January 1997 slowly ticked away, and the INS hearing neared—I was consumed by childhood memories of my prior life in Jamaica. It was more than a decade since I last saw Paul and my crew from Pembroke Hall. And not only was I not rich, but I was in prison with a pending deportation—which felt like a fast-approaching death sentence.

My life felt dark, but the last few months had strengthened my resolve and faith in God—and made the events that transpired over the next few months, years, and decades appear somewhat divine. Yet, on the morning of the INS hearing, I just wanted the suffering to end.

I got on my knees and prayed for a miracle in the small cell before washing my face and getting dressed in my state greens. I went for

3 "Jungle" is the informal name for Arnett Gardens, a neighborhood in Kingston, Jamaica, built in the early 1970s during Michael Manley's democratic socialist government. It was originally designed as low-income housing that would support working-class families and offer an alternative to overcrowded inner-city settlements. But like many urban communities shaped by colonial legacies, global capitalism, and political violence, Jungle became associated with poverty, political tribalism, and neglect. Despite these challenges, Jungle is also a vibrant cultural space known for its music, community bonds, sound system culture, and political consciousness—producing some of Jamaica's most important musicians, organizers, and cultural innovators.

breakfast—but I couldn't eat. I just needed an opportunity to get out of the cell, move nervous energy, and see if I knew any fresh-faced new jacks coming into the system.

An hour after breakfast, a CO stopped by the cell to escort me to the hearing. But my legs felt heavy on the walk over, and I struggled to keep pace. When we finally made it to the courtroom, I saw the same judge from last year and knew there would be no miracle.

As the judge began to speak, my existence became blurred. I don't know how many people he deported. But without emotion, he read what felt like a script—with no consciousness of his role in separating mothers, fathers, brothers, sisters, children—and further destroying marginalized communities.

I laughed internally at the absurdity of it all. But I was shocked and confused when the judge asked if I wanted to "sign out"?[4]—which he explained would look better if I ever wanted to return to the United States.

I asked the judge a few more clarifying questions before deciding that I would NOT voluntarily consent to leave my home, my family, and my daughter. With the formalities out of the way, I got served with a final order of deportation, handcuffed, and led out of the room.

The papers were heavy in my hands as the CO escorted me back to the cell. Once inside, I fell face down onto the bed, curled up in a ball, and cried until I fell asleep.

It was getting dark when I woke up and looked out the window. The cold January air smelled of skunk. Unfazed by the air quality, I took a few deep breaths, sat back down on the bed with my back against the wall, and stared at the INS paperwork in my hands—wondering if it was a blessing or a curse.

The judge mentioned that under the new immigration law, I could be paroled earlier for deportation—which was the last thing I wanted, but the chance of getting out of prison within a few months created exciting possibilities to ponder.

4 This is a very important question and choice for later in the story.

February 1997

When I returned to Greene, I immediately signed up for the law library and did some intel on the legal clerks—a crew of characters with varying degrees of legal aptitude, which they often oversold to fellow prisoners desperate for freedom.

As luck would have it, the 1996 immigration law and the clause allowing for early deportation were so new that no clerk understood them enough to try and hustle me—so I decided to dedicate two nights a week to research.

With each day trapped in Greene, I became more excited at the possibility of early release—even for deportation. The law library was also a way for me to see my boys, Mike from 108th Street, and Jimmy from Rego Park. Both were nearing the completion of short sentences and used the library to get out of the housing unit and the ever-encroaching gang warfare.

A few weeks went by before I understood that the immigration judge was referring to a new "merit time" law that allowed "non-violent" prisoners with deportation orders to qualify for early parole. However, they needed to also meet specific programmatic and disciplinary requirements—which I did.

I did the math and realized I would be parole-eligible by the summer. I reread the memo a few times to ensure I understood it correctly—and even after I felt I did, I kept the findings to myself, but sent a letter to my correctional counselor seeking more information. A week passed, and I was about to send another letter when he showed up at the dorm early one morning.

The counselor had longish, hippie-type hair, wore corduroys with bell-bottoms, and usually walked with his head down, as if in deep thought. He also carried a legal folder between his arms that I assumed held my fate. We sat on opposite sides of a table in the glass-enclosed small dayroom—where private meetings were held in the dorm. Yet even with our proximity, the counselor didn't make eye contact or say anything—instead, he shuffled through the contents of the folder as if struggling to locate his target.

He dug through all the paperwork for a few minutes before letting out a triumphant "Aha!" But before divulging the content of his discovery, the counselor made eye contact and asked, "Are your parents Trekkies?" I played along and smiled as if he hadn't made the same corny joke at least ten times throughout the two years we knew each other. Finally, he dug into his coat pocket, pulled out tiny reading glasses, and placed them on the bridge of his nose. He looked down at the document, cleared his throat, and stated, "We have the final order of deportation from the INS, and according to the new merit time law, you're eligible for parole to deportation in April."

Exhibit D: Deportation Order

04/13/1998 DOP COUNSEL J2

KIRK JAMES
94-A 6325 01-21-97
GREENE
11 CPCS 2ND

U.S. DEPARTMENT OF JUSTICE
Executive Office for Immigration Review
Office of the Immigration Judge

In the Matter of: James, Kirk Anthony DIN: 94-A-6325 RESPONDENT

Case No.: A 24-794-790

Docket: Downstate I.H.P. Downstate Correctional Facility Fishkill, N.Y.

IN DEPORTATION PROCEEDINGS

ORDER OF THE IMMIGRATION JUDGE

This is a summary of the oral decision entered on 1-14-97.
This memorandum is solely for the convenience of the parties. If the proceedings should be appealed, the Oral Decision will become the official decision in this matter.

- [x] The respondent was ordered deported to Jamaica.
- [ ] Respondent's application for voluntary departure was denied and respondent was ordered deported to ______ or in the alternative to ______.
- [ ] Respondent's application for voluntary departure was granted until ______, with an alternate order of deportation to ______ or ______.
- [ ] Respondent's application for asylum was ( )granted ( )denied ( )withdrawn ( )other.
- [ ] Respondent's application for withholding of deportation was ( )granted ( )denied ( )withdrawn ( )other.
- [ ] Respondent's application for suspension of deportation was ( )granted ( )denied ( )withdrawn ( )other.
- [ ] Respondent's application for waiver under Section ______ of the Immigration and Nationality Act was ( )granted ( )denied ( )withdrawn ( )other.
- [ ] Respondent's application for ______ was ( )granted ( )denied ( )withdrawn ( )other.
- [ ] Proceedings were terminated.
- [ ] The application for adjustment of status under Section (216) (216A) (245) (249) was ( )granted ( )denied ( )withdrawn ( )other. If granted, it was ordered that the respondent be issued all appropriate documents necessary to give effect to this order.
- [ ] Respondent's status was rescinded under Section 246.
- [ ] Other ______
- [ ] Respondent was advised of the limitation on discretionary relief for failure to appear as ordered in the Immigration Judge's oral decision.

Mitchell [signature]
Immigration Judge

Appeal Due: 2/13/97

Date: 1/14/97

Appeal: RESERVED/WAIVED (A/I/B)

Form EOIR-37
REV. JUNE 90

VERSE

02

Parole Board #1

March 1997

The reality of a hearing in *April* brought on a paralyzing mixture of euphoria and fear—especially communicating the possibility of parole to deportation with my family. I worried about placing a heavier burden on Heather, who had never been on a plane and was already doing so much on her own to raise our daughter.

I felt overwhelmed by the many emotions and went to Bliss for support. I updated him as we spun the outer perimeter of the yard during night recreation. After processing the news, Bliss joked about joining me in Jamaica when he got out, but reasoned thoughtfully that freedom, even if deported, would undoubtedly be better than a life sentence in prison.

The following day, I began calling and checking in with my friends and family. But I gave only a few details over the phone, knowing the calls were recorded. Instead, I set up a series of visits to fully debrief and plan the next steps. About a week later, the first visit with mom, John, my brothers Andre and Kareem, my sister Alicia, Grandma Yvonne,[5] and my friend "Nat" took place. Yet prison rules stipulated that they could enter the facility only in two groups of no more than four persons. The first group included Grandma Yvonne, whom I had not seen since my arrest, primarily due to my feelings of shame and not wanting her to see me confined.

Grandma Yvonne grabbed my arms as we held each other for the first time in over three years. As I sat down, her eyes probed deep within my soul, trying to discern whether I was in one piece. I tried to hold back my emotions, but couldn't deny tears of joy.

5 Grandma Yvonne was Ms Tiny's daughter who migrated to the United States before my birth to follow her dreams in the fashion industry. Her arrival to the US would create a path for numerous family members from Jamaica to migrate as the political violence in Jamaica escalated.

Grandma was a storyteller, and it didn't take long before she launched into her experiences with the guards and her bra—which they made her remove because it was setting off the metal detector.

Anger bubbled as I imagined Grandma Yvonne's encounter with the guard. Yet her tremendous faith in God and the oneness of humanity allowed her to move through most spaces with joy and grace. I also didn't want my emotional state to rob me of precious time with my family.

Grandma was catching me up on all the happenings when mid-sentence she paused, scanned the room, leaned in, and whispered in a hushed tone: "I didn't know what to expect, but all the men here look so healthy and handsome." We all laughed, especially Nat, whom I met as a freshman at Forest Hills High School in 1990.

Nat and I met when I dated her best friend, Carmen—and while our relationship was short-lived, we remained friends, largely because of our shared Jamaican ancestry and immigrant experience. I was happy to see her, whom, like Grandma, I hadn't seen since my arrest. But the meeting was also strategic, since Nat often traveled to Jamaica, and I wanted her to contact my dad, whom I hadn't spoken to since 1993.

My relationship with Dad was complex, but I knew I would need his help if I got deported. I could have just mailed him a letter, but the prison usually reads them. I wasn't hiding anything, but I was paranoid and preferred to sneak the letter into the visiting room and hand it directly to Nat—who would then attempt to locate his address on her next trip to Jamaica. It felt like a long shot, but with an order of deportation hanging over my head, I was desperate.

I spent the rest of the visit being silly, playing games with Andre, Kareem, and Alicia. It was hard to see how much they were growing up without feeling like I was missing out. Overall, it was a great visit, and I felt a lot better with a plan in motion.

In the spring of 1997, I saw Moya for the first time since The Cat. I was still in love with her, probably more than ever, but we kept it fun and light as it was rumored she was dating a member of the Wu-Tang Clan.

Moya and Jimmy's girlfriend, Grace, often made the two-and-a-half-hour trip from Queens to Greene together. She joked about moving to Jamaica with me and opening a shack on the beach in Negril to sell

Peruvian food. I didn't know how serious she was and didn't want to get my hopes up, but it was impossible not to dream.

Heather and I spoke over the phone, and my family shared details with her after our visit. She was supportive and reassuring, and said, "We will always figure things out." We also planned a visit around Keiana's third birthday in July—after the parole hearing—so we would have greater clarity.

While I felt better after updating my family and friends, I had to be careful with dreams of the future—when my now was filled with cuttings and stabbings. I was also still traumatized from last summer when my boy "Monster"—known for his Mike Tyson-like knockouts—was scheduled to be released, but ended up getting a "dirty urine" for smoking weed. He was weeks away from going home when his release date was revoked, and he was sent to the box.

With all my trepidation, I rarely went to the yard and did little beyond working in the mess hall—I even stopped moving swag, as I didn't want to do *anything* to further jeopardize my freedom. I spent much more time in my cube, reading and contemplating life in Jamaica—especially the deportee narrative, which was, understandably, not very welcoming.

Every moment of my existence became consumed by my upcoming parole hearing until the morning of March 9, 1997, when I woke up and found out that "Biggie Smalls," aka "Christopher Wallace," aka "The Notorious Big," aka "The King of New York" was shot and killed in California—almost six months to the date after Tupac was shot and killed. And just like *that*, my generation lost—also to the bullets of assassins—our Malcolm and our Martin.

Like Tupac, I didn't know Biggie, but I knew *him*. And still, remember how I felt in 1991, the first time I heard "Party and Bullshit" on a Ron-G mixtape. To this day, no other song symbolizes my time on Rikers more than "Juicy," which played on the bus radio every time I went to court. It was a song that kept me grounded in the truth of who I am—and not what the system said I was.

Juicy, if you listen closely, is a song about young, traumatized, misunderstood, poor, and desperate to survive Black men—who, in the 1990s, were being hunted throughout the varied ghetto plantations across the United States. It was a song of hope and resistance—a reminder that, despite their plight, young Black men should define themselves, reach for the stars, and never stop believing that they can overcome the confines of White supremacy.

April 1997

I was dreaming of a better life, but caught in the "everyday struggle," stressing over my parole hearing—I wasn't eating, sleeping, or thinking straight as the date approached. I couldn't even read anymore. My potential freedom and its implications occupied every moment of my existence.

Thankfully, on the eve of the hearing, Bliss dragged me to the yard to work out and kick it. We superset pull-ups, abs, and shoulder presses—which he knew I enjoyed. After we finished working out, I took some time for myself and spun the outer perimeter of the yard, stared at the moon and stars, and communed with God.

I prayed for strength and faith that something better awaited. I continued to spin until the loudspeaker crackled and announced, "Yard closed." Returning to the dorm, I took a long, hot shower, letting the water wash away the weight of the day, then settled in to read until the 10:30 pm count and the call for lights out.

Afterward, in the stillness of the night, I got up from my bed and pulled a fresh pair of state-issued green shirt and pants from my locker. I carefully folded them at the seams, smoothing out each crease with precision, and tucked them between the mattress and steel bed platform to iron out the wrinkles.

I prayed again and, surprisingly, fell asleep quickly. But that night, I had a recurring dream that usually began with some unknown force violently snatching me off the Earth—and towards the outer perimeter of space. In the dream, I had superpowers and wasn't worried—even though I had no control. I intuitively knew there was something for me to see. Yet when I got *there,* I could never remember anything!

The part of the dream that I often remembered was free-falling miles and miles back to Earth in the most peaceful state, only to be jarred awake after realizing I was no longer dreaming, still in prison, and had fallen off my bed.

Highly embarrassed and unable to go back to sleep, I spent the rest of the night mostly tossing and turning. In the morning, I contemplated walking to breakfast but didn't feel like talking to anyone, so I spent a little time journaling and getting lost in a way-too-hot shower, which often triggered my eczema.

I got out of the shower, took my state greens from under the bed, got dressed, and began the trek towards the administration building on the old side of the prison. The parole hearing was scheduled to begin at 10 am. The walk was about a mile from M-2 but took longer than usual. Profusely sweating from the hot sun and a host of nerves, I felt like Spike Lee's Malcolm X character—walking slowly towards an assassin's bullet at the Audubon Ballroom.

When I finally got to the administration building, they directed me to a holding room—where prisoners waiting to see the parole board were seated in a "u" formation. The holding room was also adjacent to the room where parole hearings were held. I nodded to a few guys I knew, but no one spoke.

After a few anxious minutes, they summoned the first *unfortunate* into the hearing room. I tried to hear the proceedings but couldn't make out the tone or the words. The hearings had an assembly line pace—everyone was in and out in less than 5 minutes. I didn't know whether that was good or bad. However, I noticed everyone kept their heads down and avoided eye contact as they left the room.

I was the second-to-last person called in. It wasn't cold, but I was shaking, and my legs were weak as I moved towards the door and into the small room—where I sat at the long table as instructed.

I looked around the room before settling my gaze on the all-White tribunal with the power to decide my fate. Another White woman sat adjacent to the tribunal and took notes. They appeared in a festive mood as they finally addressed me and got the formalities quickly out of the way.

"How did you get involved in a series of drug and gun sales?"

In some ways, I was expecting the question, but I paused and took a deep breath to consider its depth and find a response worthy of the entire truth. But for brevity, anxious, and fearful that they didn't want the *truth,* I said, "The opportunity presented itself..."—which, for me, considering the circumstances that led to my arrest and conviction, felt like an appropriate balance of truth and accountability, to begin a deeper conversation. But they didn't see it that way, and I was quickly cut off before I could explain further.

The commissioners started cursing and telling me I was "bullshitting" and not taking accountability for my actions. Yet every time I tried to answer their questions, they cut me off.

Dissatisfied with my perceived lack of remorse, they scolded me brutally. One member of the tribunal compared the hearing to "pulling teeth." Another member joked that I must have tripped and fallen into committing a crime.

It became apparent that mitigating circumstances and clarity held less weight to the parole board than an admission of guilt, which they thought I was shirking by not playing their game. But after beating me up for a few minutes more, the parole tribunal casually enquired how my pending deportation would impact my family and young daughter?

I was confused by the question, considering they had just verbally stomped me out. I tried to collect myself, catch my breath, gather my thoughts, and answer the question. But my lungs were gasping for air, and only God knows if I said anything coherent.

I quickly and somewhat shamefully tried to wipe away the tears before exiting the hearing room. When I got outside the administration building, I looked up at the sun and was almost blinded by the light—when I suddenly realized I had miscalculated!

I should have given more thought to the possibility of a parole denial—a reality my heart all but confirmed. It was Tuesday, April 15, 1997. The parole board's decision usually took 2 to 3 days, so that I wouldn't hear anything before Thursday at the earliest.

With freedom at stake, every moment felt like an eternity—and to make matters worse, my mind tortured me by replaying the parole events over and over. I wasn't suicidal, but I felt like I let myself and my family down—which felt like death.

However, everyone I told about the hearing said they were only trying to scare me because they were letting me go—which was supposedly a typical game they played. Even Bliss reminded me that it was a "merit hearing," meaning I had completed all the requirements they considered essential for parole. He even reasoned, "You have an order of deportation; it makes no sense to deny you parole!"

The civilian cook I reported to in the mess hall gave me off Wednesday through Friday. However, I decided to go to work, as I knew my anxiety would worsen if I stayed in the dorm.

My heart was heavy for days! And I couldn't stop replaying the parole hearing. I critiqued every word I'd spoken and imagined other ways to articulate myself. But there was no going back, and I felt stuck in perdition, anxiously awaiting the fate of my soul.

Thursday passed with no news, and I went to work in the mess hall Friday morning—knowing a parole decision, good or bad, awaited my return later that night.

I tried my best to get lost in work, but found myself constantly checking my watch. It was to *that* point, the longest day of my life. It felt like I was counting each second and each minute of the day. It was a painful experience that was not easily captured in words.

Once the day was over, eager to learn my fate, with my heart and head pounding, palms sweating—I rushed down the walkway, anxious to return before the 3:30 pm count.

Mary was out on vacation, and we had a CO filling in that I knew from the mess hall. I told him my bed number, and he handed me three letters—two from friends, and the other from parole—which wasn't an envelope, but a series of papers folded in half and stapled together in the middle.

I went straight to my cube and placed the envelopes on top of the large locker, which stood by the entrance—before sitting down on the chair to await the mandatory count. Once complete, I went to the last stall in the bathroom—the only place I could have privacy—and locked the door.

I took a few deep breaths to try to relieve the knot in the middle of my chest, which kept getting tighter. I felt like I was having an asthma attack. I sat on the toilet and took deep breaths until I caught up, and the tightness eased.

Once it appeared that most of the dorm had gone to dinner, and no one else was in the bathroom, I got out of the stall, washed my face, and stared into the stainless steel mirror. The eyes of a scared little boy held my gaze—and yearned for peace, safety, and a world where he didn't have to fight to exist.

Bliss greeted me as I exited the bathroom, and we walked back to the cube together. He said nothing but twitched his nose, code for "What's up?"

I entered the cube and handed him the letter from the bed. I told him to "open it" as I sat down. He held it in his hands for a minute and asked if I was sure. I nodded yes, as I already knew.

Bliss read the decision but said nothing. We just stared at each other for a minute—and communicated understanding and empathy in ways I assume people did before words.

Bliss handed the parole decision back to me, and I read it for the first time. The words boldly stated: "DENIED - HOLD TO ORIGINAL PAROLE ELIGIBILITY DATE OF 04/09/01."

I reread it a few times to make sure I didn't miss anything. Then, with clarity and hope exhausted, I placed the decision on my chest and preemptively closed my eyes to halt the onslaught of tears—and as much as I loved Bliss and considered him a brother, I had never cried openly in prison in front of another man.

I was hurting but felt worse for my family and friends, whom I dreaded having to call with bad news. I was mad at the system and myself for putting them in this situation. I felt dead inside and didn't move from my cube for two days except to use the bathroom. If it weren't for Bliss bringing me food and ensuring I ate, I don't know how I would have made it through the weekend.

I made my first call Sunday afternoon to Auntie Karen—and even though I was feeling better than Friday, as soon as she asked how I was doing, I began to cry—again.

I often faked it for my family, but I wasn't okay and needed to lean on them. I knew they would be supportive, but I couldn't help but feel like I let them down—which I knew wasn't true. But I wasn't in my right mind and felt like maybe they were suspicious of me—like maybe I was lying and not doing all the positive things we discussed over the years.

Many of the questions from my family and friends regarding my parole denial begged for understanding. Questions like:

"How can you be denied for the nature of your offense?"

"Isn't that what you're already sentenced for?"

"Wasn't it the nature of your offense that made you eligible for a merit board?"

"Don't they know you have an order of deportation?"

"What sense does it make to keep you until 2001 if you're being deported?"

" Did they tell you something you must do for the next board?"

They were all excellent questions—yet they were rooted in the belief that the system was grounded in rationality. And thus, with each call, I relived the denial and hurt while reassuring everyone that I would be ok. But I needed some time to regroup. I was emotionally raw and vulnerable in ways I hadn't felt since my time on Rikers Island.

Exhibit E1: Parole Denial

INMATE COPY State of New York - Division of Parole Date: 04/16/97
FORM 9026 Parole Board Release Decision Notice

Name: KIRK,JAMES Facility: GREENE
DIN: 94A6325 Interview Date: 04/15/1997
Nysid: 7648252P Interview Type: DEPORT

Earned Eligibility Certificate : INELIGIBLE
Supervision Fee: ELIGIBLE
Certificate of Relief from Disability: ELIGIBLE

Parole Decision:
DENIED - HOLD TO ORIGINAL PAROLE ELIGIBLITY DATE OF 04/09/01

Conditions of Release/Reasons for Denial:

AFTER REVIEW, PAROLE FOR DEPORTATION IS DENIED. RELEASE AT THIS TIME WOULD BE CONTRARY TO PUBLIC SAFETY. THIS DECISION IS BASED ON THE GRAVITY OF THE INSTANT OFFENSE CPCS 2ND WHERE YOU SOLD QUANTITIES OF COCAINE. YOU PARTICIPATED IN A SERIES OF GUN AND DRUG SALES. WHILE WE NOTE YOUR DISCIPLINARY RECORD AND ADJUSTMENT, IT IS CONCLUDED THAT THE GRAVITY OF THE INSTANT OFFENSE PRECLUDES RELEASE AT THIS TIME.

Comments:

FOLLOWING DELIBERATION, THIS DECISION IS BASED ON REVIEW OF THE CASE RECORD AS WELL AS THE INTERVIEW WITH PAROLE BOARD MEMBERS.

FPO II : THOMAS J. BURKE

* * * * * * * INMATE COPY * * * * * * *

exhibit A

Exhibit E2: Transcript

THE STATE OF NEW YORK
DIVISION OF PAROLE
-------------------------------------x

In the Matter of the SP Consdr :
Parole Board Meeting of
:
JAMES KIRK, NYSID No. 7648252P
: DIN No. 94A6325
Parolee.
:
-------------------------------------x

Held on: April, 1997
At: Greene

B E F O R E :

COMMISSIONER TAURIELLO

COMMISSIONER McSHERRY

A P P E A R A N C E S :

JAMES KIRK

Transcribed By:

Vicki Valente

B

COMMISSIONER McSHERRY: Mr. Kirk, please be seated. Sit down. Sit down.

COMMISSIONER TAURIELLO: Sit down, Kirk. I'm Commissioner Tauriello. This is Commissioner McSherry.

You're serving seven years to life for criminal possession of a controlled substance in the second degree, is that correct, Mr. Kirk?

MR. KIRK: Yes, it is.

COMMISSIONER TAURIELLO: You're here today for special consideration for deportation. Do you understand that?

MR. KIRK: Yes, I do.

COMMISSIONER McSHERRY: Where were you born?

MR. KIRK: Jamaica, West Indies.

COMMISSIONER McSHERRY: When did you come to the United States?

MR. KIRK: In 1986.

COMMISSIONER McSHERRY: For what reason?

MR. KIRK: To reside.

COMMISSIONER McSHERRY: For what reason? Did you come with your family?

MR. KIRK: Yes.

COMMISSIONER McSHERRY: How old were you when you came here?

MR. KIRK: Ten years old.

COMMISSIONER McSHERRY: Ten years old. Why didn't you become a citizen of the United States?

MR. KIRK: A technicality, I guess.

COMMISSIONER McSHERRY: No, you just walk in, sign the paperwork, pay the ten dollars and that's it.

MR. KIRK: We were always in the process of getting it, but it just never happened.

COMMISSIONER McSHERRY: Do you have any family in Jamaica?

MR. KIRK: Yeah, my uncle, my aunt.

COMMISSIONER McSHERRY: Okay. I'm sorry, I have nothing else.

COMMISSIONER TAURIELLO: You came here, you said to reside?

MR. KIRK: Yeah, I came with my mother.

COMMISSIONER TAURIELLO: How did you get involved in a series of gun and drug sales over a period of time? Very serious crimes. You're serving a conviction -- you're serving a conviction for criminal possession of a controlled substance; however, part of the record is you were involved in a series of gun and drug sales, is that correct?

MR. KIRK: Yes.

COMMISSIONER TAURIELLO: Why? You're going to tell me you don't know?

MR. KIRK: The opportunity presented itself.

COMMISSIONER TAURIELLO: Oh, bullshit, opportunity.

MR. KIRK: I fell victim.

COMMISSIONER TAURIELLO: Fell victim to who?

MR. KIRK: Me.

COMMISSIONER TAURIELLO: Don't you have something upstairs?

MR. KIRK: Yes, I do.

COMMISSIONER TAURIELLO: How old are you?

MR. KIRK: Right now?

COMMISSIONER TAURIELLO: Any time.

MR. KIRK: I'm going to be twenty-three.

COMMISSIONER TAURIELLO: You're going to be twenty-three?

MR. KIRK: Twenty-three years old next month.

COMMISSIONER TAURIELLO: Did someone force you to do this? They held a gun at your head and said here --

MR. KIRK: Nobody forced me.

COMMISSIONER TAURIELLO: -- sell all these quantity of drugs, illegal drugs, sell all the weapons illegally?

MR. KIRK: No.

COMMISSIONER TAURIELLO: Then why did you do it? Did you understand you were doing something wrong?

MR. KIRK: At the time, I was --

COMMISSIONER TAURIELLO: Oh, you're going to tell me, at the time I didn't know.

MR. KIRK: It wasn't that. I was getting caught up in a materialistic lifestyle and I was ignorant at the time.

COMMISSIONER TAURIELLO: All right. What have you been doing since you were incarcerated?

MR. KIRK: I went to college, before college, I was going to --

COMMISSIONER TAURIELLO: Wonderful. What else did you do?

MR. KIRK: I've been working in the mess hall.

COMMISSIONER TAURIELLO: You've got family? You've got children?

MR. KIRK: Yeah, I have a daughter.

COMMISSIONER TAURIELLO: How many?

MR. KIRK: One daughter.

COMMISSIONER TAURIELLO: How old?

MR. KIRK: She's going to be three years old.

COMMISSIONER TAURIELLO: She's living with her mother, right; not your wife, right?

MR. KIRK: Yes.

COMMISSIONER TAURIELLO: Why do you bring children into the world and then you don't take care of them properly?

MR. KIRK: That's a mistake I made.

COMMISSIONER TAURIELLO: Did you ever work?

MR. KIRK: Yes, sir.

COMMISSIONER TAURIELLO: What kind of work did you do?

MR. KIRK: I had a job at New York City Department of Lawns and Park. I've had a job with the New York City Public -- New York City Department of Transportation. I had a job -- my most recent job was at --

COMMISSIONER TAURIELLO: Well, your most recent job was selling illegal guns and drugs, right?

MR. KIRK: Before I got involved in this.

COMMISSIONER TAURIELLO: Who is taking care of this child?

MR. KIRK: Her mother.

COMMISSIONER TAURIELLO: Her mother?

MR. KIRK: Yeah.

COMMISSIONER TAURIELLO: How is she handling that? How is she doing it?

MR. KIRK: It's hard.

COMMISSIONER TAURIELLO: It's what?

MR. KIRK: It's hard.

COMMISSIONER TAURIELLO: I didn't ask you if it is hard or easy. How is she doing it?

MR. KIRK: She's working.

COMMISSIONER TAURIELLO: What kind of work does she do? It's like pulling teeth, you know. Can't you give me a complete sentence?

MR. KIRK: She's working at --

COMMISSIONER TAURIELLO: Doing what?

MR. KIRK: She's a sales clerk at Macy's.

COMMISSIONER TAURIELLO: She's supporting the child. She's bringing the child up. She's making sure the child does exactly what she has to do and what's right.

MR. KIRK: Yes, sir.

COMMISSIONER TAURIELLO: And how old is the child again?

MR. KIRK: She's three. She's going to be three in July.

COMMISSIONER TAURIELLO: What do you think your responsibilities are?

MR. KIRK: She's my daughter.

COMMISSIONER TAURIELLO: If you're deported, you know, you can't come back here. You know that, don't you?

MR. KIRK: I'm aware of that.

COMMISSIONER TAURIELLO: You're aware of that. How do you feel about that?

MR. KIRK: Well, that's just something that I'm going to have to live with.

COMMISSIONER TAURIELLO: I said, how do you feel about it?

MR. KIRK: I can say I'm not happy, but I'm going to have to live with it. At least, I'll be with some of my family.

COMMISSIONER TAURIELLO: You say you engaged in this very serious criminal activity because of your greed for money?

MR. KIRK: Yes.

COMMISSIONER TAURIELLO: But you knew all the while what you were doing?

MR. KIRK: I never -- to be honest with you, I never sat down and thought about it. It was so caught up, I never sat down and thought about it. I never thought about the consequences. I didn't think I could get locked up.

COMMISSIONER TAURIELLO: Okay. Anything else you want to say to us?

MR. KIRK: No, thank you.

COMMISSIONER TAURIELLO: We'll give you a written decision. Thank you very much. Again -- again, you were here for -- you understand you were here for consideration for deportation?

MR. KIRK: Yes, thank you.

COMMISSIONER TAURIELLO: Thank you.

(Discussion off the record)

COMMISSIONER TAURIELLO: Kirk James is denied. His next appearance date is 2-9-2001.

After review, parole for deportation is denied. Release at this time would be contrary to public safety.

This decision is based on the gravity of the instant offense, criminal possession of a controlled substance in the second in which you sold quantities of cocaine. You also participated in a series of gun and drug sales.

While we note your disciplinary record and adjustment, it is concluded that the gravity of the instant offense precludes release at this time.

He will be above the guidelines due to patterns of similar offenses.

All Commissioners --

COMMISSIONER McSHERRY: Concur.

COMMISSIONER TAURIELLO: --concur.

The foregoing is a correct and true transcript of the hearing in the within matter.

Vicki Valente

Vicki Valente

VERSE

03

Jailhouse Lawyer

August 1997

Over the next few months, I received fewer visits, calls, and letters as I tried to rebuild the armor I had let chip away at the possibility of freedom. Once I felt emotionally stable, I went back to the law library and taught myself how to appeal the parole board decision through a legal procedure called an "Article 78."

I argued that "the nature of my offense" was decided by the courts in determining my sentence—and was the one thing I had no power to change, no matter how hard I tried.

I argued that the parole board abused its power by focusing on my charges and sentence rather than on what I had done while incarcerated.

I argued that denying me parole while knowing that I had an order of deportation amounted to double jeopardy—meaning I was being punished multiple times for the same crime.

I became a fixture at the law library—determined to fight for my freedom. I spoke with all the clerks, studied legal journals and law books, and developed a range of legal templates for appealing parole and administrative decisions. Becoming a jailhouse lawyer wasn't what I envisioned growing up, but my aptitude for law and justice became complementary tools that would serve me and others well throughout my incarceration.

December 1997

I felt good about my Article 78 appeal. But a few months later, it was denied! I wasn't surprised, but it sent me back into depression! As 1997 ended, my journal held an emotional rollercoaster, fixated on questions like: *With a life sentence, would I ever get out of prison? Was anyone willing to see the totality of my humanity beyond my charge? Did anyone care about incarcerated people?*

1998

VERSE

01

El Hefe

January 1998

My boy Boogie from Queens was about to get released and left me a cassette tape of Mobb Deep's *Hell on Earth*, which felt like the title and soundtrack to my life—trapped in prison, an order of deportation, and a fresh parole denial. And did I mention I was losing faith fast?!

I was nearing four years incarcerated and not scheduled to see the parole board again until 2001—which made the denial in '97 that much harder to swallow. For months, no matter how hard I tried, I couldn't stop replaying the parole hearing—torturing myself with all the things I could have said differently. And to make matters worse, I began wondering what would have happened if I had been paroled for deportation?

It was challenging to recondition my mind to prison. I didn't have much motivation for anything until, ironically, *an opportunity presented itself.*

My boy Will from B-3, who I played handball with in The Cat, and knew since Forest Hills High School—was the mess hall clerk and known in some circles as El Jefe. Will's position afforded him a lot of privilege and power—of which he used to run a profitable gambling operation that took daily sports bets, with football season as the real moneymaker.

Will kept a low profile and distance from much of the daily business. But over the last few months, key members of his organization got caught. Some began to snitch on Will, who ultimately decided things were getting too hot and put in for a transfer to another prison. But before leaving, Will trained me and left me his old job as the clerk—one of the most coveted positions for prisoners, requiring an intentional line of succession to maintain—similar to a monarchy, except along racial lines.

Before Will, most of the clerks were White, rumored to be snitches, and protected by the COs. For example, "Moose," the clerk who preceded Will, was White, over 6 feet tall, and weighed over 300 pounds. He was a loner who lumbered around, head down, and slushed his huge feet like he was playing in the snow. Moose had been in prison for over 20 years and was rumored to be an informant. He also had openly homosexual relationships with other prisoners.

In the summer of 1997, Moose even held a wedding in the yard, with guests and a small reception, where rice was thrown at the couple. The wedding was the talk of the prison for weeks, which probably led to Moose's downfall, as his bed was set on fire a few months later, forcing the powers that be to transfer him out of the prison.

With his expedited exit, Moose didn't get to pick a successor, so Will, who was Latino, and the part-time clerk succeeded by default. Will was also the only one who knew how to use the computer database to order food, as the civilian head of the mess hall, who was also the Mayor of Coxsackie, had abruptly retired.

I didn't want Will to leave, as he was among the few people I considered a friend. But as a clerk, you had access to computers. Even though they didn't have the internet, the authorities were wary of him and demonstrated their paranoia by conducting frequent cube searches that never turned up anything, as Will was always a step ahead. But he knew it was only a matter of time before someone set him up.

March 1998

I held the clerk position for a few weeks before they hired a new civilian head of the mess hall, who seemed cool and was somewhat familiar with the job, having worked there years earlier. But soon after they hired him, rumors circulated that he was fond of trading mess hall swag for sexual favors with prisoners—which I didn't initially pay attention to. But as he got comfortable, I noticed my new boss became a tad touchy with me. We also shared an office in a remote part of the mess hall—at the end of a long hallway that didn't get much traffic.

I didn't work every day, but when I did, I mostly used the office computers to do inventory and place food orders. Initially, I thought I was being paranoid and possibly homophobic, but the lingering hand on my shoulder from my boss as he reviewed my spreadsheets became more frequent.

My new boss was also a close talker, which only made my discomfort worse and pushed me to avoid the office as much as possible—often using dentist appointments as my excuse. I genuinely had to go to the dentist, though, as I had ongoing dental work before my arrest in 1994. Since then, many of the temporary fillings had fallen out, leaving me sensitive to hot and cold food, along with excruciating pain from an incomplete root canal. As bad as things were, I really didn't want to go to the dentist while incarcerated. But as my oral health deteriorated, I reluctantly made an appointment.

VERSE

02

The Dentist

April 1998

On my first visit to the dentist, they took X-rays and outlined an extensive plan of action requiring the removal of numerous wisdom teeth, which they claimed were growing into my jaw and would cause problems later in life. Of course, I was paranoid and suspicious, but it wasn't like I could get a second opinion.

I reluctantly showed up for my second session but had to wait over an hour because the dentist was busy with another prisoner, whose screams suggested he was unhappy with the service. After a while, their bickering got progressively louder, and the dentist shouted, "I bet you were tough on the streets while committing crimes."

I looked at the guy sitting next to me, who nodded sadly to confirm he had heard the dentist's words. I began to wrestle with the consequences of leaving and returning to the dorm, but ultimately decided the pain was too great. I also knew the CO assigned to the dentist would write me a ticket for being out of place if I left. I sat with excruciating pain and tension for another hour before the dental assistant took me to an open room to prepare for the procedure. I looked around as I sat in the chair and saw the needle on the adjacent tray—which made my anxiety spike to unprecedented levels.

The dental assistant recognized my discomfort and promised the shots would help with the pain—which I was desperate to end. So, I took a deep breath and reminded myself I had no choice before closing my eyes as she brought the needle toward my mouth. I gripped the arms of the chair tightly as the needle pierced my gums and jaw—which slowly began to swell and lose sensation. The Dentist came in a few minutes later, glanced at the X-rays, and told me to open my mouth. He had an energy about him that was immediately repulsive, and I decided right there that I would never give him the satisfaction of complaining—no matter the pain. And so, for much of spring '98, I sat in silence as the dentist cut into my jaw, tugged violently at my wisdom teeth, and did much of what I was told was *necessary* dental work.[1]

There were even rumors among prisoners that all the dentists were *veterinarians*—and while I can't verify the truth of that, I knew firsthand that they were indeed brutal and sadistic and utilized our vulnerabilities to feed their egos and reinforce the narratives of who they thought we were. To make matters worse, my jaw hurt for months, felt out of place, and made clicking noises—especially in the mornings for years after the experience.

1 Almost 3 decades later, I am still dealing with PTSD from this experience. But in an effort to heal, be vulnerable and allow more men to discuss dental health, I got a few of my damaged teeth covered with gold crowns.

VERSE

03

Exodus

May 1998

I celebrated my twenty-third birthday as spring transitioned towards summer. I was back in a routine, working out with Bliss in the yard, when he told me he was considering putting in for a transfer. I was shocked. Nobody is happy in prison, but we had a good thing going in M-2 with the community and space we had built together over the years. Yet I understood he was getting close to the parole board and didn't want to have a hearing in Greene—widely considered a bad place to have a parole hearing.

Bliss's rationale for wanting to leave made a lot of sense, but I was sad at the thought of being without my brother and comrade, who had helped me find my voice and value through YAP, supported me through my order of deportation, my parole denial, the dentist, and everything in between. There was always Bliss! Yet, as I gave him my blessings, I began to consider if my days in Greene were also coming to a close.

I couldn't believe it was now three years ago that I left The Cat and came to Greene. As violent as it was, it had become a refuge for me. I knew how to move, I knew the players, and I had access to things worthy of a prison scene in Goodfellas. But it was all bullshit when juxtaposed with freedom—and sharing love with family and friends.

July 1998

It was a sad day when Bliss got transferred. I didn't know where he went as his move coincided with a huge shakeup of the prison—which the powers that be did every once in a while to keep us off balance. And so, in a matter of weeks, I lost Will, Bliss, Randy, Lord, and a few other people I considered comrades. However, the losses motivated me to think more strategically about my future.

Part of me felt that a change might be good, but I was also worried about how a transfer would affect my ability to see Keiana—who was now four years old and able to visit regularly with Heather, since Greene was less than three hours away from the city. A transfer would likely make those visits harder, and the thought of losing that connection with her weighed heavily on me.

Another factor influencing my decision was the *new* "merit time law" for nonviolent offenders, which allowed for early parole by reducing a minimum sentence by one-sixth, provided you met specific programmatic and disciplinary requirements. While the merit time provision was promising, it triggered traumatic memories of my parole hearing in 1997. Still, the law meant I'd be eligible for the parole board in December 1999, rather than February 2001, and that was huge. I also knew that if freedom was the goal, returning to the parole board while at Greene might not be the smartest move.

August 1998

As fall approached, I knew there would be some tough conversations with my family and friends. After a few visits and phone calls, they eventually agreed that a change might be a good idea. I then arranged to speak with my counselor, who confirmed I was eligible for a transfer—but he couldn't say which prison. It felt like playing Russian roulette, but I rolled the dice, requested the transfer, and immediately regretted it.

Every other prisoner I told about the transfer thought I was crazy for leaving a "good situation" for the unknown. Even though I lost Bliss and Will, I still had close friends in the mess hall—like Bush, Jus, Marley, Pops, Born, Ugod, and Chad, whom I was grooming to take over the clerk position when I left.

Jus and I had been tight since '94 in The Cat, sharing countless unforgettable moments—like the time in 1997, when my job in the mess hall entailed making food trays and delivering them with Jus to prisoners in the Box. On this particular day, there were rumors of a gang fight between the Neita's and the Crips, and the prison might be shut down.

Jus and I were usually prepared for what we saw in the box when dropping off food, but this felt more like a horror film. Human beings—some stabbed, others slashed with razors, others beaten by COs—sat cuffed and bleeding in holding cells, waiting for medical attention, which was nowhere in sight.

Violence was routine at Greene, so Jus and I didn't even look at each other as we dropped off the trays. Survival in the jungle often demanded a level of dissonance. But as we stepped out of the Box and headed back toward the mess hall, Jus stopped. He turned, locked eyes with me, and said quietly, almost like a prayer, *"We can't let this shit kill our souls."* I stared at him for a moment, took a deep breath, and we kept walking in silence. I probably didn't understand it fully then,[2] but I knew he was right!

December 1998

As 1998 came to a close, I honored my boys by making them a huge Christmas meal of fried mackerel, seafood rice, barbeque chicken, and candied yams—it was the type of meal rarely seen in prison and a reminder of the privilege my positionality in the mess hall afforded me. I was creating a new norm and had almost forgotten about my transfer request—until I got a surprise visit on the morning of December 26.

It wasn't even 8 am when the CO woke me up. He wasn't a regular, and I initially thought he was joking when he told me to "pack up." But he wasn't!

I was shocked, excited, and sad all at once. I was in a daze, packing my bags, making phone calls to my family, and sending messages to my boys, all while mentally preparing for the journey into the unknown.

I left Greene Correctional Facility on the last Monday of 1998. It was an extremely violent prison, and I was happy to leave that level of hypervigilance behind. However, being surrounded by so many young men who could think critically, draw, sing, write, dance, box, play basketball,

2 I think of this moment and how it mirrors the desensitized world we inhabit today—a place where violence, both spectacular and subtle, has become the background noise of our existence. From the endless stream of geopolitical conflicts to the daily acts of brutality in our own neighborhoods, we are bombarded by images of human suffering. Each headline, each video, each loss slowly dulls our collective sensitivity—numbing us to pain that should shake us to our core and provoke us to action!

power lift, and play chess like grandmasters pushed me to grow and evolve different parts of myself—which I was eternally grateful for, and would never forget!

Greene Correctional Facility 1995-98

1 Me, Keiana, and Heather circa 1995

2 Keiana and me circa 1995

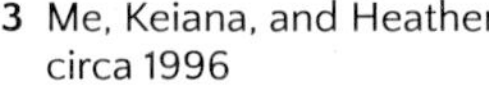

3 Me, Keiana, and Heather circa 1996

4 Keiana and me circa 1996

5 Me, Flacco, and Bliss circa 1996

6 Keiana and me circa 1997

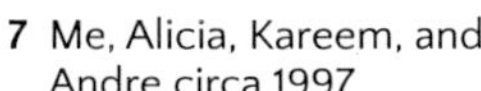

7 Me, Alicia, Kareem, and Andre circa 1997

8 Me, Mom, Andre, and Kareem circa 1997

Continues on next page

Full-size photos can be found on https://www.instagram.com/94a6325/

Some individuals have been pixellated for privacy.

Greene Correctional Facility 1995-98

9 Me and Moya circa 1997

10 Will, aka "El Hefe," and his son circa 1997

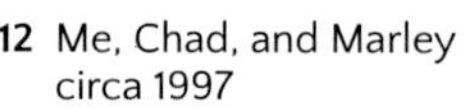

11 Moya and me circa 1997

12 Me, Chad, and Marley circa 1997

13 Jus and I circa 1998

14 Me, Kareem, Nat, and Andre circa 1997

15 Me, Mom, Andre, grandma Yvonne, and Kareem circa 1998

16 Me, John, mom, Alicia, Kareem, and Andre circa 1998

Full-size photos can be found on https://www.instagram.com/94a6325/

Some individuals have been pixellated for privacy.

VERSE

04

Auburn

May 1998

I was happy to be outside a prison for the first time since my deportation hearing in early 1997. I didn't know where I was going, but I heard rumors that it was "further upstate and way up in the mountains!"

I got a window seat on the bus, which stopped at various plantations within the hub to pick up and drop off other prisoners. We didn't stay at each stop for more than 20 to 30 minutes before departing early in the afternoon for Auburn Correctional Facility, which was located right in the middle of the town by the same name and was, ironically, home to abolitionist Harriet Tubman.

Auburn[3] was one of the first prisons ever built in the United States, and is reminiscent of the prisons you see in classic movies like *The Shawshank Redemption*. It was a medieval-looking structure surrounded by high concrete walls decorated with barbed wire, and had a dark cloud fixed permanently above. It was a scary-looking place, made worse by the news from the CO that we had to spend the night, or maybe longer, as the news outlets reported that a major snowstorm was imminent.

I pondered the news and felt more regret, but I knew there was no going back. The only way out was forward, which at the moment meant bracing myself as the slow retracting fence opened and allowed us entrance onto a narrow winding road—running alongside the prison and into its bowels.

Once inside the old prison, they unshackled us before a CO escorted us to the lowest tier of cells called "the flats." Parallel to the tier were huge windows that appeared permanently open—allowing birds and the

3 Auburn Prison (New York) and Eastern State Penitentiary (Philadelphia), framed as humanitarian innovations, served as foundational models for the modern US carceral system. The *Auburn System* emphasized enforced silence, congregate labor, and corporal discipline, while the *Pennsylvania System* relied on solitary confinement as a tool for moral reform and penitence.

cold winter air to roam as they pleased. The cells were small, dirty, and double-bunked. Some are occupied by what we call "cell gangsters"—a term given to prisoners, who, while locked in the safety of their cells, would hurl various profanity, or in extreme cases, "shit-you-down" as you were escorted past.

There were also tiers of similar cell blocks stacked—one on top of each other like Lego blocks—all filled to capacity with general-population prisoners. My bunky was standing at the front of the cell when I arrived—he appeared Central American and was probably gang-affiliated by the visible facial tattoos. We nodded to each other as I moved by him to enter. Double-bunking in a cell was new, and my adrenaline was high. But after a few minutes, we began to make small talk and outlined a working agreement that allowed us to navigate the space respectfully.

My Bunky's name was Alex, and he was indeed Central American, hailing from Guatemala. He had been in Auburn for two days, awaiting a transfer, and wasn't sure where he was going. But had just completed two years in the box and was just happy to be out.

It was only about 4 pm, but it was already getting dark—and with the darkness came colder temperatures and a bone-chilling wind that hissed like a snake as it slithered through the tier. I began to worry as the only clothes they allowed us to wear in transit were a hat, state greens, a jacket, boots, and socks—all made of the cheapest polyester and utterly ineffective.

I was shivering when I jumped down from the top bunk and checked in with Alex, who confirmed that it was getting colder and that he had been sleeping in all his clothes, including his boots. He then pointed to the flimsy, infectious blankets they gave us and suggested I could get some extras from the porter after the count cleared, which was a good idea, but it meant I had to do calisthenics in the small cell to stay warm in the interim.

A few hours later, the count cleared, and the porter began to make rounds—handing out tiny bars of soap, sponge toothbrushes, and toothpaste. I stood by the cell door, listening to the various conversations as the porter made rounds. As he approached my cell, I heard his voice and was sure I knew him.

The porter went by "Beezo," and we were in The Cat together.

We weren't exactly friends, but we knew many of the same people. However, our relationship was a little dicey because he was a suspect when a few items from my boy Serge went missing while we were all in the honor dorm. But when Beezo saw me, he greeted me fondly—which made me nervous, as I knew he had the upper hand. But I gave him a fist bump through the cell bars and played along. He told me he had been in Auburn for a few months and that a few dudes from The Cat were here, too.

Beezo and I spent some time catching up before I asked him to find out where I was going and when I would leave. He told me he would look into it, but spoke of the incoming snowstorm and the possibility that I could be stuck in Auburn until after the New Year. But he promised to look out for me and said that after three days, the COs would let me take a shower and make a phone call.

However, surviving three days in transit on the flats in Auburn wouldn't be easy, even with extra blankets and me sleeping in every item of clothing I had. The extreme conditions and the lack of communication made me feel like I was in solitary confinement. But worse, we didn't have personal property, weren't allowed recreation, and weren't allowed to leave the cell to eat, attend programs, or use the shower.

When I wasn't stressed, talking to Alex or doing calisthenics to stay warm, I stood anxiously by the front of the cell, waiting for the CO to make rounds—which he did intermittently throughout the day to inform the lucky ones who were leaving.

I made peace with ending 1998 in Auburn Maximum Security Prison, which was not on my list of possibilities after leaving Greene. Thankfully, Beezo was true to his word and brought me a few books and old magazines to help with the anxiety and pass the time.

I began reading an abridged version of *The Count of Monte Cristo* that immediately transported me to a reality far from Auburn. But a reality that, though fictitious, depicted a narrative that closely mirrored my own and implored me to wonder whether I would get out of prison in 1999—or the coming decade? And if I did, what would my return home look like? I didn't know the future, but the story of Edmond Dantes dared me to dream big!

1999

VERSE

01

Attica

January 1999

It was finally New Year's Day 1999, and we were on the precipice of the year 2000 and the great unknown—but instead of partying with Prince, I was in Auburn Maximum Security prison lying on the top bunk reading as the countdown reached one.

It was my first New Year in a "max" since The Cat in '95. The years since then felt fast and slow and showed me why Pops always emphasized the "importance of doing time, and not having time do you."

I was now a veteran of doing time and more than halfway through my seven-year minimum sentence. Being trapped in the bowels of Auburn made me sad but eternally grateful for Pops and other "lifers" who spent decades in human cages—many, who knew they would never go home, but had not given up hope, or their humanity.

Deep in the bowels of darkness exists the revolutionary "Lion Vanguard," who chose to share their love, wisdom, knowledge, and understanding with chosen disciples, who, in theory, had a possibility of parole. It wasn't purely altruism; it was a strategic plan going back to Chattel Slavery, rooted in the uncompromising belief that, in time, our collective knowledge, strength, and embodiment of freedom would finally break the bondages of White supremacy!!!

On January 1, 1999, stuck in Auburn, reading *The Count of Monte Cristo* fueled thoughts of redemption and probably made me somewhat delusional—yet I was genuinely giddy at how parallel the story was to mine. Pops was to me what Abbé Faria was to Edmond Dantes. Yet I didn't have a fortune awaiting me on release. But I was optimistic that 1999 would be the year I finally got free—in every sense!

However, the first few days of 1999 were spent just trying to stay warm in the small cell. I'd been in Auburn for about a week when Beezo found out I was being transferred to Wyoming—a medium-security prison across from Attica, closer to Canada than to New York City.

The bus ride to Wyoming felt endless, giving me plenty of time to regret my transfer request. But I refused to let myself start the year with negative energy. I kept telling myself that things would work out—which in my dystopian reality meant spending a year in Wyoming before my second merit parole hearing in December—and, ultimately, being deported to Jamaica shortly after.

The physical, mental, and emotional gymnastics of surviving and navigating prison, especially over the last few months, were taking a toll on me—especially my sleep, which never felt like enough. So I figured I would grab a quick nap on the bus ride. But I was jarred awake as someone in front of me yelled to no one in particular: "We at Attica!"

I looked up just as the electric fence was retracting to allow us entrance into another medieval-looking structure—which triggered a strong sense of déjà vu, a feeling probably connected to the fact that the last documentary Moya and I watched in '94 was about the "Attica Riots." And now, the irony was that five years later, here I was, rolling through the gates of Attica, imprisoned with fourteen other men, divided into seven shackled pairs. Half of us were going to Wyoming, while the other half would stay in Attica for the foreseeable future.

As we disembarked the bus onto hallowed ground, I looked up at the massive concrete walls and imagined the stories trapped within them. I thought again of Pops and the stories he told me about the riots in 1971. I imagined the courage of the Attica Brotherhood,[1] who demanded to be treated like men, only to be tear-gassed and slaughtered by state troopers.

It was easy to see that Attica was a dark place—and this was with clear skies on a sunny day. I could feel the tension in the air as the CO led us into the building. I stared at the other prisoners we passed in the long hallways and wondered how they maintained sanity and hope in a place so desolate.

1 The Attica Brotherhood was a group of prisoners who came together and demanded to be treated like human beings—which was not heard, and led to the 1971 Attica Prison Uprising, a pivotal moment in the history of US prisons. See *Blood in the Water: The Attica Prison Uprising of 1971 and Its Legacy* by Heather Ann Thompson.

VERSE

02

Wyoming

We made it to the receiving room in Attica, where prisoners were exchanged. We then boarded a smaller bus for Wyoming and arrived less than five minutes after leaving Attica. Wyoming looked much like Greene, with a vast campus divided into two sides. But where Greene was primarily flat, Wyoming appeared to be perched on two sides of a U-shaped hill, with the housing unit and program buildings located on parallel sides, connected by the base of the "U," which served as the walkway.

Once we got to the receiving room in Wyoming, we were unshackled and individually interviewed by a high-ranking CO. It was a standard procedure: the CO asked questions to determine whether you had any known enemies in the prison. Once that was complete, he ensured you knew where you were, their rules, and what would happen if you didn't comply.

After the intake interview, the CO informed us that our property wouldn't arrive for a few days, which was frustrating, as I had been wearing the same clothes and had only been allowed one shower in over a week since I left Greene. But I knew complaining would do more harm than good, so I kept my mouth shut.

I got assigned to the reception dorm in the back of the prison. The sun was down, and the January air was frigid as we began our journey to the far side—which was at least two miles away and got progressively colder as we climbed out of the valley and trekked up the hill.

I was frozen and sure I was sick when I reached the reception dorm. My body ached for a hot shower—which would be the last thing I did upon entering a new housing unit. But I felt a little reckless after a week in Auburn and five years in adolescent gladiator schools. However, out of habit, I casually scanned the dorm as I moved towards my assigned bed—a bottom bunk along the perimeter wall with good views of the dorm and the CO station.

I took out the dingy bedding they gave me in the receiving room and began to make the bed when I heard a familiar voice. I glanced over my shoulder and couldn't believe my eyes, but I casually continued to make the bed while watching him in the distance. As he got closer, I sat out of sight in the chair adjacent to the large locker and kept a low profile as he mopped closer and closer to my bunk. And just as he was mere feet away from me, and paused to ring out the mop, I moved on him.

VERSE

03

Bliss & Kye

Mere feet away from him, in an almost whisper, I said, "You can never get away from me, old man!" Bliss stared at me in disbelief. We hadn't seen each other in over six months, and in many ways, his decision to leave triggered a butterfly effect. Even though neither of us had manifested coming to Attica, New York, the uncertainty of the journey ahead felt much less daunting knowing my comrade was by my side again.

Bliss and I went to the yard the following day to work out and catch up. He loaned me a hoodie and warned me about the cold. Yet, I still wasn't prepared. 20 minutes into our workout, I realized I wasn't warming up. As the temperature fell, giant congealed snowballs began to fall from the sky and pounded the roof of the weight shack.

Maybe five other people were in the yard, including the COs. My face, feet, and hands were numb and prickly. We couldn't escape the elements, but kept working out harder in hopes of staying warm. Bliss also used the opportunity to give me a rundown of Wyoming—which he succinctly summed by declaring, "They're still mad about Attica!"

Bliss also warned of specific COs who targeted prisoners from New York City. He said I had to "be extra careful if the Jets or Giants beat the Bills," which made me stop working out and look at Bliss to see if he was joking. But with a straight face, he looked at me and declared: "These motherfuckers are crazy here, Rah!"

I took it all in and processed as much as possible while watching the snowfall accumulate—in a way so foreign to me that I felt compelled to step out of the weight shack to investigate. But this was a poor decision, as I was immediately knee-deep in snow and my feet, already cold, were now threatening to freeze. Thankfully, a few minutes later, the PA system announced that the yard was closed. The short walk back to the dorm was treacherous, as the sloped walkway was covered in at least three feet of snow. When we returned to the dorm, it looked and felt like we had just survived an avalanche on Mount Everest.

I stood on a mat in the vestibule, dislodging the snow from the crevices of my clothing. I took off my boots and shook them out while glancing at the nearby wall strewn with rules, a mess hall menu, and a program call-out list for the day, when I saw a familiar name. *He* was on the list for "sick call," and his name was "Kye."

The guy I knew, named Kye, was from 57th Ave in Lefrak City and infamous. He had "unforgiven" tattooed across his back and was known as "Killer Kye." He was about 5 feet 5 inches, known to rock trench coats with sawed-off shotguns, and had a reputation for destroying crews single-handed with a Bruce Lee-inspired martial arts game.

When I arrived yesterday, I thought I spotted someone who looked like Kye, but I couldn't be sure. I even asked Bliss about him, but he didn't have much to offer, only that the guy kept to himself. If it was Kye, he'd picked up a few more facial scars since I last saw him—on Rikers Island in 1994. Back then, my boy Spider would always talk about a guy he played ball with from Lefrak City, they called "Unforgiven." I was curious, so I eventually went to the yard, and sure enough, "Unforgiven" was Kye. He'd just gotten out of prison, but a few months later, he caught a gun charge on 108th Street in Forest Hills, not far from where Polo lived.

I hadn't seen Kye in half a decade, but I thought about him a lot listening to *The War Report* by Capone-N-Noreaga, especially the prison epics "Live on Live Long." "Parole Violators" and "Capone Phone Home." Noreaga (aka N.O.R.E.) was also from Lefrak City and the uncle to Kye's child.

I decided to approach Kye when the moment felt right. Yet I had to be strategic, as I had just arrived, which meant that he would have noticed me—and if I appeared *similarly* familiar, he was probably trying to decide if I was friend or foe. Also, the guy I presumed was Kye was a porter and had a corner cube, indicating he had been in the house for a while and had seniority. Finally, one day I noticed he didn't go to lunch, and I seized the moment. He was in the small dayroom watching TV when I approached him, but before I could say anything, he casually looked up from his chair and said: "What's good, Rah?"

I couldn't help but laugh as we embraced. Kye knew it was me when I arrived, but played it cool. We spent the next few days catching up and playing Scrabble, which I was good at, but Kye destroyed me. He was brilliant, well-read, and competitive about everything—yet had spent most of his teens and adult life in various juvenile and adult prisons.

Kye painted a bleak picture of Wyoming but mentioned many people from Queens were here—even the rapper Capone from CNN, who caught a charge before *The War Report* album was released.

Having Bliss and Kye to ease my transition was good, but Wyoming felt far away from family and friends. It was also cold and snowed every day for two weeks. The only promising thing was a private college program—which was an extremely rare commodity since the 1994 crime bill and the loss of aid to incarcerated people. But luck was not on my side, and I arrived too late for registration, so I would have to wait until the summer session to take classes.

VERSE

04

The Mountains

February 1999

I was surprised when my former boss from Greene—the close talker with the lingering hand—reached out to his counterpart in Wyoming and secured me a clerk position in the mess hall. So after a few weeks in reception, they moved me from the back of the prison to A-1—the mess hall house dorm, where I began working in early February.

In the mess hall, I knew a few people from Rikers, The Cat, and Greene. I knew a few people through varied Queens and Brooklyn associates, but didn't mingle much and mostly stayed to myself. It was also rumored that some people opposed me getting a prime position and wanted me out. I also got bad vibes from one of the civilian cooks—who went out of his way to make small talk—as if to feel me out and prove his intellectual superiority.

The snow started again and continued into April. I learned new terms like "lake effect snow" and gained a clear understanding of "seasonal affective disorder." I felt depression and hopelessness on another level in "The Mountains"—which was how prison veterans from New York City refer to places like Wyoming and plantations bordering Canada.

I did my best to adjust and develop new routines. But being far away from home in a very racially charged environment, and now in the front part of the prison, away from Bliss and Kye, the two people I knew had my back—was tough, especially in such a morbid place.

Outside of work, I spent most of my free time in my cube sleeping, reading, listening to music, and thinking more critically about the role of religion in my life. I was having an existential crisis when I needed *faith* the most.

I wrote more letters over the first few months of 1999 than in previous years. Many were to Heather, who could not visit as much due to the distance. But we had grown a lot closer as Keiana approached her fifth birthday. We used letters to co-parent, offer emotional support, and update each other on our life. Writing letters also helped offset the cost of collect calls, which would run as much as twenty-five dollars for a 30-minute call.[2]

My proximity to the Canadian border allowed me to see Oronde—a few months younger, and my favorite cousin, who lived in Toronto, where we had a lot of family, including my great-grandmother. Oronde and I spent many of our early teenage summers together at Tryall Beach in Montego Bay, where my great-uncle and Oronde's father, Zero, owned and ran a dive shop right on the beach. It was a magical place where we would hang out all day, canoeing, listening to reggae music, snorkeling, and eating fresh seafood that Zero and his boys would catch and grill on the beach.

May 1999

Spending time with Oronde made me nostalgic about Jamaica—and a little less worried about my pending deportation. But seeing him as an adult made me hyper-conscious that I was no longer a teenager. I was a grown man on the precipice of my 24th birthday—which felt surreal and somewhat depressing, considering I had spent what would have been my college years imprisoned.

On the night of my birthday, I called Mom, who answered excitedly, saying she had a surprise for me. Laughing, I took the bait and asked, "What?" But I was genuinely shocked when, in her customary Jamaican patois, she announced that she was pregnant, quickly adding, "It was an accident." Stunned, I couldn't help but crack up as she explained.

Teasing Mom, I joked about Keiana having an uncle younger than her, and we laughed even harder. I was happy for Mom—she was due in December, around the same time as my next parole board hearing. Yet beneath my happiness, a pang of sadness lingered, knowing my family was growing and changing without me.

2 Charging outrageous rates for calls, which are often the only way for people separated by miles, walls and prison sentences to stay in touch with their families—exemplifies the inhumanity and racial capitalism which undergirds the carceral complex.

July 1999

Everyone in the prison, and I surmise the planet, was talking about "Y2K" and the uncertainty surrounding the year 2000. So, with speculations running rampant and doomsday pundits predicting the end of the world, I felt a *little* extra pressure to make the parole board in December. The Y2K talk also made me hyper-conscious of time. Yet winter persisted stubbornly into spring—who was determined to keep summer away with minimal sunshine, freezing temperatures, and an occasional snowstorm.

The bleak weather pushed me further into solitude, giving me more time to read and reflect. During one of my study sessions with the dictionary, I came across the word *anthropomorphic*—a term that reignited my struggles with religion. I found myself tumbling down a rabbit hole, contemplating the long history of humans attributing their behaviors and characteristics to God.

Questions swirled in my mind: Had we shaped God in our image rather than the other way around? Was our perception of the divine merely a reflection of ourselves? Terms such as "my god is a jealous god" or "my god is a vengeful god" provoked me to think deeper on the ways religion and God were often utilized to justify the division and oppression of the "other."

I struggled with the realization that religion was often a tool of oppression and control. Incarcerating more people than jails and prisons could ever hold. But I continued to go to Jummah services on Fridays—where, late in July, I noticed a new member of the ummah (Muslim community) who looked familiar. It took a few minutes to rolodex his face and connect "Wali"—who had just been transferred from Attica after serving time in the box.

Wali was a member of the Muslim community in Greene—specifically the mujahideen, the *unofficial* Muslim security team. Wali was also good friends with "Little Malik"—who lived with me and Bliss in M-2 and was the heartbeat of our community and spiritual practice, and someone I trusted dearly—all things which made seeing Wali a welcome sight.

With Bliss and Kye in the back of the prison, I was excited to see an old face I shared mutual friends with. Wali's presence interrupted my deep depression and daily monotony, which revolved around work in the mess hall, hoping for mail, reading, journaling, listening to music, sleeping, and stressing. With Wali, I had a new comrade to navigate Wyoming and everything that came with being trapped in the mountains.

VERSE

05

The Consortium

September 1999

My college semester began in the fall with courses in Economics and English. I was extremely excited to attend college—located in the school building at the front of the prison—and it was unlike anything else I had experienced in an educational setting.

There was a strong sense of community and pride for everyone associated with the college. And even though no one used the word "healing," trauma-informed approaches were naturally interwoven within everything we did—like check-ins before class and designated rooms for yoga, meditation, and mindfulness. The classes were highly competitive, due in part to the history and legacy of the 1994 crime bill, which reduced access to higher education in prison and labeled those with education as "smarter criminals."

While it was never stated or expected, we knew our educational performance was the only way to discredit the false narrative and advocate for widespread access to higher education across all jails and prisons.

Our economics professor was Nigerian and reminiscent of the tough Jamaican teachers of my youth. Yet, we all made time—in the yard, the library, or the dayroom—to study and support each other. In the English class, we read and analyzed stories by writers worldwide and across genres with great curiosity—while sharing critical, honest, and vulnerable feedback—which blew my mind and expanded my love of literature and writing.

Many of my papers came back covered in red ink, courtesy of Roman—the English professor who challenged me to become a better writer and storyteller. While the feedback was often ego-bruising, I kept showing up, practicing, and began to experience curiosity, joy, liberation, and a degree of catharsis as a writer.

VERSE

06

Parole Board #2

October 1999

The college semester allowed my mind not to dwell on parole—but I was ready to go. I didn't even care where anymore; I just wanted to see my family and friends outside a prison, which had begun to feel like the only reality I'd ever known. It was as if "freedom" and "the good old days" were but a distant dream—to be desired but never attained.

In October, I had my customary check-in with my counselor, who reviewed my folder, said everything looked good with the parole board, and insisted that my college classes would help my case. But I didn't trust him or the system. However, trying to temper the *possibility* of freedom—after nearly five years incarcerated—was an impossible task.

December 1999

Fear and anxiety grew as December commenced and my parole hearing neared—which coincided with Mom's due date—making me desperate for some positive news. But my *gut* didn't feel good.

On the morning of the hearing, I was nauseous, shivering, and just wanted to lie in bed with the blanket over my head and cry. But I pulled myself together, trudged through the snow to the administration building, and took my place amongst a group of somber, anxiety-riddled prisoners.

Similar to my parole hearing in Greene, no one made eye contact. We sat in silence, heads bowed, almost prayerful. I stole glances at the faces around me and wondered—quietly, and with a tad of jealousy—who among us might make it home. And to make matters worse, the parole board in Wyoming was as ruthless as Greene, if not worse.

Imagine a room dominated by dissonant, self-righteous White officials—empowered to decide the fate of Black and Brown men whose lives had already been shaped by centuries of violence they refused to acknowledge. The parole board played with our futures, and that of our family and children, mistaking punishment and the perpetuation of a racialized system of control and labor exploitation for justice and public safety.

I fought to be optimistic, but I was in the belly of the beast, and my gut was sounding the air-raid sirens—and sure enough, when it was my turn, the accusations came in rapid succession like laser-guided rockets.

I tried to dodge, tried to defend myself, but the parole board either refused to or was unable to see me beyond my charges!

It didn't matter to the parole board that I was a human being, incarcerated since I was 18 years old, with a daughter—now five—who didn't know her father outside a jail or prison.

It didn't matter to the parole board that my mother—with more *at-risk* Black sons at home—couldn't sleep at night knowing her firstborn was trapped in a cage.

It didn't matter to the parole board that I faced deportation, had completed all my programs, had an excellent disciplinary record, and had received letters of recommendation from all the civilian employees I had worked with over the years.

In the eyes of the parole board, I was a mere stereotype—a dangerous, disposable Black man whose fate, like all the rest, could be reasoned and sealed by White people in a heartbeat.

I was mad and left the parole hearing, not wanting to be around anybody. But Wali sent a kite for me to come to the yard that night. I didn't want to go, but I knew that if I didn't talk it out with someone, I would end up down the rabbit hole of "what ifs," which I knew wouldn't be good for my mental health.

It took me a few hours to pull myself together, but I felt better the moment I got to the yard and saw Wali, who was adamant I was going home. He reasoned it made no sense to deny me parole *again* if I was getting deported! But I wasn't optimistic, and I spent the next few days in limbo, avoiding the phone.

Things were getting dicey in the mess hall with the civilian cook. And two days after the parole hearing, another prisoner in the mess hall named "Horse" pulled me aside and told me to be careful, as he knew the cook was "grimy" and was trying to get rid of me—which meant a lot of things, and none of them good.

I was worried about the drama in the mess hall and planned to quit regardless of the parole decision.

I didn't feel confident that I was going home, but the anxiety of not knowing began to feel like its own sentence. With the decision imminent, I took Friday off and stayed in my cube listening to Mary J Blige, Dru Hill, Usher, R. Kelly, and every other depressing tape I owned. And when I wasn't listening to music, my mind played tricks on me and induced extreme paranoia—like *every* time the phone in the dorm rang, I just knew the CO was talking about me. Even when he hung up and said nothing to me, it felt like he was hiding something. And I repeated the same pattern with every call—I was torturing myself but couldn't stop.

I probably checked my watch every 10 minutes from when I woke up straight through the 3 pm shift change. And by the time the CO put up the mail list, I was sweating, jittery, lightheaded, and pretty sure my heart would run out of gas. But I played it cool and waited a few minutes before checking.

Parole board decisions never came in an envelope—and were usually a few papers folded over and stapled together. A thick packet was often bad news, as it meant appeal papers (which you don't get if you made the board) were attached to the decision. So, as I held up the letter and glanced at the appeal papers—without reading the decision, I knew I wasn't going home in 1999.

My cube was only a few feet away from the CO station, but the walk back felt like an eternity. My paranoia was still high, and I felt all eyes on me. I lay on the bed so no one could see me open the envelope. My heart was racing, and my chest was tight. I took a few deep breaths to calm myself before reading the rationale for denial—which read almost verbatim from my first hearing:

"The nature of your crime precludes release at this time."

I slowly placed the papers into my small locker and sat on the chair. There was a relief in knowing. Yet, I was still hurt and mad that the parole board had such disregard for everything I'd done to prove my humanity and right to freedom.

After my second denial, I began seriously considering whether I would leave prison alive. It was a fucked-up thought, but none of the denials made sense, and the parole board never gave any instructions on how I could improve in *their* eyes.

I, more than anyone else, wished I could go back and tell Judas and Eddie, "Hell NO!" But I couldn't undo the sequence of choices and consequences leading to my arrest—leaving me stuck and unsure of how to proceed.

After the count cleared and most people went to dinner, I went to the last stall in the bathroom and cried, then got in the shower and cried some more. I was starting to go down the rabbit hole, so I sent Wali a message to meet me in the yard later that night.

It was frigid and windy even for Wyoming, but I felt the walls closing in and needed to be outside. We met by the pull-up bar and walked silently towards the perimeter fence. I didn't have to say anything to Wali—he knew my body language and hugged me after we got far enough away from everybody. We talked and lapped the yard a few times. Eventually, the tears subsided, but faith and hope, both cornerstones of my survival, were depleted. But thankfully, Wali, like Bliss, held me like a brother and created space for me to re-anchor.

Exhibit F: 1999 Parole Denial

INMATE COPY State of New York - Division of Parole Date: 12/08/99
FORM 9026 Parole Board Release Decision Notice

Name: KIRK,JAMES Facility: WYOMING
DIN: 94A6325 Interview Date: 12/08/1999
Nysid: 7648252P Interview Type: MERIT TIME

Earned Eligibility Certificate : INELIGIBLE
Supervision Fee: ELIGIBLE
Certificate of Relief from Disability:

Parole Decision:
NOT GRANTED

Conditions of Release/Reasons for Denial:

AFTER A CAREFUL REVIEW OF YOUR RECORD AND THIS INTERVIEW PAROLE IS DENIED FOR THE FOLLOWING REASONS. YOU ARE CURRENTLY SERVING A SENTENCE FOR CPCS 2ND. YOU DESCRIBE BEING INVOLVED IN A SERIES OF TRANSACTIONS WHERE YOU SOLD SIGNIFICANT AMOUNTS OF DRUGS AND WEAPONS TO AN UNDERCOVER POLICE OFFICER.
DURING THE INTERVIEW YOU SHOWED LIMITED UNDERSTANDING AS TO THE RISK YOU PLACED ON COMMUNITY SAFETY.
DUE TO THE SERIOUS NATURE OF THE INSTANT OFFENSE, AND LACK OF INSIGHT AS TO YOUR ACTIONS AND THE EFFECT ON THE COMMUNITY, YOUR RELEASE AT THIS TIME REPRESENTS A SERIOUS RISK TO THE PUBLIC SAFETY.

Comments:

FOLLOWING DELIBERATION, THIS DECISION IS BASED ON REVIEW OF THE CASE RECORD AS WELL AS THE INTERVIEW WITH PAROLE BOARD MEMBERS.

FPO II : JOHN SIKORA

* * * * * * * I N M A T E C O P Y * * * * * * *

VERSE

07

The Box

I was feeling better and talking with Wali when the PA system announced that the yard was closed. While walking out of the yard, Wali and I continued to speak until the CO barked at me:

"Boy, stop talking!"

The CO was notoriously racist and known to bait prisoners as they went in and out of the yard—which I knew and often moved accordingly, but I was not in a rational mind. Things escalated quickly. A crowd gathered, and I stopped walking and turned to face him as if we were going to have a shootout.

The CO and I locked eyes in a stare-down, my heart racing and fist clenched. I asked, "Who you calling a boy?" My adrenaline was on a hundred, and I felt prepared for *whatever.* But thankfully, the CO just looked me over, turned his back, and returned to his post.

"Rah, you ok?" I don't know how long Wali tried to get my attention, but I was still motionless as he pulled my wrist and urged me to keep moving. I wasn't okay, but I trusted him enough to heed his words. Yet, everything in my already fragile existence was crumbling.

To add insult to injury, I returned to the dorm that night after being denied parole and surviving a potential life-altering encounter with the CO in the yard to discover that my cube got selected for a "random" search—which felt extremely invasive and magnified just how powerless I was to the whims of the carceral system.

As mad as I was, I could only stare in disbelief at my belongings sprawled about the floor and cube. To top it all off, a tier 3 ticket—the highest prison infraction—was planted on my locker. I gingerly stepped over my belongings and read the charges, alleging that I was in the "possession of contraband."

It was a setup!

I knew instantly that there would be no justice, and I was going down! So, I got draft bags from the CO, packed my belongings, and spent the weekend communicating the parole denial—and preparing my family and friends for the strong possibility that I would end up in solitary confinement before the year ended.

After receiving the ticket, I was placed on "keep lock," which meant I couldn't leave my cube unless going to the bathroom or the mess hall for meals. So, over the next few days, I mostly slept, read, and hoped to wake up in a faraway dimension. Yet there was no escaping my reality—and even the good news, like a letter from Mom telling me Polo was home on "work release,"[3] sent my mind spiraling into the abyss with fears that I was destined to spend my adult life in prison.

I was happy for Polo! He deserved to be home with his family and children for the holidays. But his release proved just how unreasonable it was to deny me parole under the guise I was a threat to public safety—not once, but twice—even though I was scheduled to be deported.

Regardless of what the parole board said, I wasn't a threat, except to my own physical and mental health, both of which were drastically declining by the time of the ticket hearing—which took place two days before Christmas.

I was a defeated fighter, resigned to my fate, when the CO came and got me. On the way to the hearing, he asked what I was being charged with, and I explained it was for "possessing contraband," which, in truth, was a sample legal document with someone else's name that I had gotten from the law library to use as a template. It was such a bogus charge that he looked at me and laughed—yet to the kangaroo court and the White man with the authority to determine my fate, it was no laughing matter.

I was determined not to play along or beg for mercy. So, I sat expressionless as the highly agitated CO in charge of the shenanigans scolded me for my transgression. He was so self-righteous and angry that I wanted to interrupt to make sure we were discussing the same thing. Ironically, I had survived almost five years in Coxsackie and Greene with no tickets—and these were prisons coined "ticketron" by prisoners due to how often you received them. But again, I knew it was a farce,

3 Primarily for non-violent offenders who met eligibility criteria, like completing most of your minimum sentence, maintaining good conduct, having stable housing plans upon release, and securing a job opportunity. Prisoners who qualified were transferred to prisons close to home where they were able to leave—during work hours to gain employment or work, after which they returned to the facility. I was not eligible due to my immigration warrant.

and he was putting on a show. The ticket was only an excuse to get me out of the mess hall and, possibly, out of the prison.

As expected, the CO found me guilty and gave me 14 days of solitary confinement in the segregated housing unit (aka the box). The sentence commenced immediately as I was filmed, handcuffed, and escorted to the dungeon—a box within a box within a box—a place where time and space ceased to exist. A place where artificial light did little to mask the darkness within men who conceive, operate, and rationalize barbaric practices intended to separate mind from spirit and body from soul. And if you think I'm exaggerating, there's a good reason why the first thing they take from you when you get to the box is your shoelaces and belt.

They took off my handcuffs and locked me in a tiny cell with nothing but a Bible, which I immediately picked up and tried to read, but couldn't.

I put the book down and slowly began pacing the small cell, counting steps and reading messages scribbled on the wall by past inhabitants. While some were funny, many were grim, like the one deeply carved into the concrete above the bed that read: "Kill yourself now before it's too late!!!"

I stared at the words and ran my finger over the engraving, wondering how many prisoners read those words—and how it made them feel?! For me, in that moment, it felt like a direct order—and sadly, one I contemplated.

For maybe the first time, I began considering a strategy to kill myself. But I couldn't even access enough imagination to make a plan.

I was broken into a million pieces and wanted my life to end. But *faith* and *hope* wouldn't let go. In the darkness of the cell, and the depths of my soul, I recalled the story of "Mike P"—a guy from junior high school who got locked up in the early 90's and allegedly hung himself in his cell. I remembered the *ambiguous loss* and pain we all felt—it was a feeling I knew I could never intentionally inflict on my family and friends.

I made it through the first 24 hours and eventually got access to the prison library after three long days of pacing my cell, doing calisthenics, and re-reading the writing on the walls.

The solitary confinement library didn't contain many options, but I chose a book on religion—which was surprising, as I was mad at God, and my relationship with Islam and religion was nearing its end!

The box gave me time to wonder and question why a just and benevolent being could allow people he created to toil and suffer for centuries under the brutality of White supremacy, delusions of scarcity, hate, and all the *isms*?

My feelings for God aside, I loved and devoured the book, which examined the principles and main points of all the "major religions." I re-read it nonstop, day and night.

Eventually, I got my hands on some paper and a pen. I began to journal—wrestling with questions that seemed to summon me.

Questions like, *Who am I? Who created us? Who created the creator? And what is the purpose of human beings on this planet, within this fragile consciousness we call life?*

In the depths of darkness with nothing to do but think, I evolved—my mind traversed distant galaxies and dimensions where I found sadness, pain, joy, possibilities, and freedom beyond prisons and ideological walls.

On the morning of December 31, 1999, a strange feeling took hold of me—I woke up in solitary confinement, but I knew in every pore of my being that a change was coming!

2000

VERSE 01 Phoenix

January 2000

1999 was a fire—and every illusion I held on to in life burned to ashes. But on the last day of the year, I experienced a rebirth and a light that guided me into the new century!

Please forgive my archaic, religious, and metaphysical hyperbole, but saying I experienced a "miracle" is the most succinct way to describe what happened on New Year's Eve 1999, when I woke up in solitary confinement—*happy*—a feeling that felt like the return of a lost lover. But this struck me as weird, considering my circumstances and the uncertainty of Y2K.

Perhaps it was the endless isolation and time spent in darkness, but I emerged feeling fearless—ready to embrace a life filled with infinite possibilities. And this transformation wasn't just in my head; the universe itself seemed to be conspiring in my favor. On Friday, New Year's Eve, for example, I received a stack of loving, supportive letters from family and friends, which was my first time receiving mail while in solitary confinement.

My favorite message was from Grandma Yvonne, whose words felt like a shot of adrenaline for my mental, physical, and spiritual health. Grandma concluded her letter with: "Don't worry about a thing, cause every little thing is going to be alright!"—which were verses from Bob Marley's song "Three Little Birds" and lyrics we often sang together during my youth.

Something in my life shifted on New Year's Eve 1999. Even though I decided to move away from formalized religion, I knew more than ever that "God," the "universe," "spirit," or whoever *you* referred to as the creator was with me—and that I would always be protected on the path of *love*—even in the belly of the beast!

And to affirm the power of *infinite possibilities*, on that same day, New Year's Eve, just after 8 pm, a CO stopped by my cell and told me to pack up.[1] With no hesitation, I quickly gathered my few belongings. I was hoping to be transferred to a new prison, but was told that I would remain in Wyoming.

I got assigned to K-dorm in the back of the prison—which I damn near ran to, unpacked, and got lost in the shower trying to scrub away the energy of the box and any remnant of 1999. However, I was still on "keep lock," meaning I couldn't leave my cube except to use the bathroom or go to meals. Mercifully, the CO didn't care and allowed me to watch the New Year's Eve celebration.

As 2000 began, and Ja Rule reigned supreme, I deeply massaged how quickly life ebbs and flows upstream—wondering what highs and lows awaited me over the next 365 days. But I wasn't anxious—it was more a boyish curiosity inspired by sci-fi fantasies that linked the year 2000 to flying cars and technology seen in *The Jetsons*.

I knew a few people in K-dorm through acquaintances who looked out for me with food and toiletries. But I mostly stayed to myself and began plotting goals for the year while assuring my friends and family, who were all concerned for my safety, that I would be okay. I saw my counselor in late January, who confirmed that there would be no transfer—meaning I would likely have my third parole hearing scheduled for 2001 in Wyoming.

February 2000

I got off keep lock by mid-January, but didn't have new programs to occupy my time. Not being active was weird, but I was happy not to be in the box. I spent most days in my cube reading, writing, and listening to music.

On February 7, I was in my cube with my Walkman, tuned to a Buffalo hip-hop station, half-listening when they announced that "Big Pun" died. I initially thought this was one of those stupid radio pranks until they began playing his music repeatedly.

Pun was only 28 and left behind a wife and three kids. I wasn't

1 A few weeks later, I learned that a gang fight in the prison, requiring beds in the box, was a factor in my release

obsessed with Pun like I was with Biggie and Pac, but I knew that hip-hop was losing a generational talent and a dope MC. A few dudes in Wyoming from the Bronx were down with Pun's crew, the Terror Squad. And there were occasional sightings of Fat Joe,[2] Pun's mentor, in the visiting room.

Pun was Puerto Rican, and racial lines were strong in jails and prisons. But on the night of his death, hip-hop heads all across the spectrum got together in the small dayroom with mixtapes and albums to celebrate his life and legacy—which was one of the dopest nights of my life—and showed how powerful music can be as a unifying force.

Bliss and Kye were both still in the back of the prison when I finally got off keep-lock. I was grateful to process the events of 1999 with two of my closest comrades, who agreed that returning to work in the mess hall was no longer an option.

Thankfully, I continued with the college program for the 2000 spring semester, which was a blessing, as I could have lost my spot while I was in the box. But I only had classes twice a week in the evening, leaving me an entire day to fill.

2 I remember driving around in the early 90's rocking Fat Joe's first single "Flow Joe" on repeat in our hatchback hooptie with a booming system. So to see him visiting friends in prison, and holding them down was so so dope!

VERSE

02

Human Relations Therapeutic Program

January 2000

I was figuring out what to do with my extra time when I received a message from the Muslim chaplain (Imam) requesting a meeting. This caught me off guard, as the Muslim community did not always view people who left the community (aka apostates) favorably.

The Imam was a tall Black man with a dark chocolate-brown complexion who spoke in melodic tones and was a Jazz musician. He seemed nice, but we didn't interact much during my time in Wyoming. I wasn't sure what to expect from our meeting, but he was welcoming and mentioned that he had heard about my experiences over the last few weeks.

The Imam asked whether he could be of support and appeared genuinely concerned. To my surprise, we spoke for almost two hours, discussing a wide range of topics, including my decision to leave the Muslim community—something he was more supportive of than I expected.

After hearing about my experiences in the mess hall, the Imam offered me a job within the Human Relations Therapeutic Program (HRTP) he had developed. The program consisted of group work with imprisoned men on various topics, such as anger management, healing, budgeting, communication, and building healthy family relations in and out of prison.

HRTP sounded amazing, but I was apprehensive about accepting the offer as I had little experience with the topics or running groups. However, the Imam felt I would be a good fit because of my "curiosity" and "temperament." I asked for some time to consider the offer, but ultimately accepted it and began working in early March.

I was thrust immediately into conversations discussing childhood traumas, parenting, substance use, and surviving all the mitigating factors that come with being incarcerated. Many discussions also touched on parole denials, pending deportations, and healing while imprisoned. The conversations and themes we covered in HRTP prompted deeper reflection on how we were all shaped and conditioned by "culture" and by varied, politically motivated educational agendas.[3] They also showed me how we, as Black men, accept and normalize violence and trauma.

Thankfully, HRTP was one of the few spaces in the prison that allowed men—including myself—to express vulnerability and participate in opportunities for healing. I remember one conversation about our childhood where a group of 7 men all shared stories of horrific personal and systemic abuses that left us all in tears. Another time, towards the end of a session, a participant left me speechless when he asked:

"The system is always talking about accountability, accountability, but who is going to be accountable to us?"

3 bell hooks and Paulo Freire understood education as a practice of freedom—where students learn to question power and imagine more just worlds. Today, the dismantling of the Department of Education, the rollback of DEI, and political attacks on academic institutions represent an effort to shut down that critical consciousness. hooks warned that systems of domination fear classrooms where race, gender, and power are examined honestly. Freire noted that authoritarian forces always try to replace liberatory education with models that demand obedience. The current assault on public education isn't about learning—it's about controlling what people are allowed to know and who they are allowed to become.

VERSE

03

Jedi School

March 2000

Around late March, I moved to C-dorm, which was in front of the prison, and my sixth housing unit in a little more than a year in Wyoming. While the housing instability was rough, I was back to reading, journaling, and working out in the yard—all of which fed my mental and physical health.

C-dorm was where I first encountered "Ninja"—a fascinating human being who would become one of my greatest teachers. Ninja was slim, about six feet three inches tall, and had a hairline that receded into dreadlocks that he kept in a ponytail. He wore thick bifocals, which he squinted through as he spoke.

Ninja slept on the top bunk next to mine in the dorm. At first, I didn't pay him much attention, as he slept most of the day. But I began to notice him reading and writing when I made my nightly 3 am pilgrimage to the bathroom. To this day, I am not sure when or how Ninja and I first spoke, but I grew to love and cherish our conversations.

Ninja didn't look very smart and went out of his way to play the fool. He often appeared spaced out in conversations but was always listening, usually ten steps ahead. Ninja was well-versed in most subjects but rarely expressed his position on issues. And even when he disagreed with you, he would never directly challenge you but instead ask, "Why?"

Ninja's communication style was initially maddening to me. But as time passed, I realized he was planting a seed to induce greater intellectual labor, hoping to move me beyond axiomatic beliefs.

As we got to know each other better, Ninja shared that he had earned a Ph.D. before prison—but lost everything after a battle with depression and mental health led to drugs.

Ninja was well-traveled and shared amazing adventures through

Asia and Africa. He also had Jamaican ancestry—and could trace his roots to West Africa and the Maroons. I nicknamed him "The Teacher" and called our sessions "Jedi School." We read books on the Egyptian Dynasty, Nubia, Kemet, and Kush. We also studied the transatlantic slave routes and the histories of resistance throughout the diaspora. Ninja was particularly fond of the Haitian revolution, often citing the significance of Haiti and Toussaint Louverture for defeating Napoleon and ending France's colonial rule as a catalyst for Black liberation.

June 2000

I was cautious in navigating prison, but observing Ninja utilize his limited interactions in the dorm with the precision of a grandmaster taught me the true meaning of *intentionality*. Ninja often saw things before they happened—like when they moved "Tata" to the dorm, and he immediately warned me not to mess with him—which I didn't initially heed, as I knew Tata from Queens. He grew up in Elmhurst and ran with cats from Lefrak. And while we weren't close, we knew many of the same people, which sometimes, in prison, *made* you close, whether you wanted to or not.

Tata had just gotten out of the box in Attica and transferred to Wyoming with little to no property. Feeling obligated, I set him up with cosmetics, sweats, and some food to get him through to the commissary. However, I didn't know that Tata was a member of the Bloods and had allegedly stabbed a few members of the Latin Kings in Attica. But pretty soon, Wali, now head of the Muslim security team, got news that the Latin Kings had a bounty on Tata's head.

I couldn't get mixed up with anyone else's beef—especially anything gang-related. It was hard to turn my back on Tata, but he was placed in protective custody before I could get his side of the story, leaving me with more questions than answers.

A similar situation occurred a few weeks later when Ninja again pulled me aside and warned me about a dude we called "Akhi"—an Arabic word for brother. We became cool through Wali—who knew him from their time together in Attica. He was affable, well-read, and spoke numerous languages. Akhi was only in his mid-twenties but had been incarcerated for more than a decade under a juvenile conviction. Wali, Akhi, and I began working out together—a big deal in prison—where your associations often defined you.

Ninja again cautioned me as rumors began to circulate of Akhi having homosexual relations with someone in his dorm. The rumors turned out to be true, but took on another level when Akhi's accuser outed him to the Muslim community, alleging sexual assault.

We were shocked!

Wali and I met for night recreation to debrief and try to make sense of things, but neither of us had words. My experiences were not like the movies, where dropping the soap becomes a prelude to a sexual assault—in my six years incarcerated, this was the first time I was forced to consider *why* someone we worked out with and shared meals, hopes, and dreams, would allegedly have committed such horrific actions.

But sadly, like Tata before him, Akhi signed into protective custody, leaving us all to wonder…

August 2000

The abrupt departure of Tata and Akhi from Wyoming reminded me of the *intentionality* I needed to navigate prison if I wanted to be free. But sadly, in 2000, the only thing I had physically free was my hair, which I decided to grow out after leaving Greene. I had now transitioned from an Afro to short locks, which I spent much time trying to maintain as summer approached.

People saw my transformation and began to wonder whether I had become "Rasta," which I had considered, as the motto "one love" was always dear to my heart.

Reggae music and Rastafarian ideology were staples of my youth in Jamaica. But Rastafarianism lost me with the inconsistency between its proclamation of "one love" and its *hate* of homosexuality—themes Ninja and I spent hours intellectually massaging to try to reconcile the dissonance.

VERSE

04

Family

September 2000

Visits with my family often brought me equal parts joy and sadness, especially when they left without me. However, due to the distance from New York City, it had been almost two years since we last saw each other—and I missed them dearly. Luckily, they visited family in Canada and drove down during the summer to see me.

I was super excited to meet my youngest brother, Aaron Jordan Alexis, a big, light-skinned baby with huge eyes who took in everything. He was only a couple of months old, but his energy was strong, and it felt as if he had always been part of the family. I bounced him on my legs and simultaneously marveled at how big Andre, Kareem, and Alicia had grown during my imprisonment.

I missed my siblings a lot and was happy to see them. But I also felt sadness and anger at the years lost—a feeling that washed over me at various points during the visit.

We laughed and joked when Andre found an opening in the conversation and asked, "When are you getting out?" I got this question a lot, but it felt tougher coming from my 11-year-old brother, who could no longer recall a time when I was free.

Over the past six years—a huge amount of time in a child's life—Andre and the rest of my siblings had only known me through phone calls, pictures, stories, and prison visits—a sad realization that made me struggle even more to find the appropriate words to answer my brother's question.

I took the easy way out and told Andre, "Hopefully, next year." I told him that my next parole hearing was in February 2001—and if parole was granted, the government wanted to deport me.

Andre couldn't understand the logic of it all—and kept asking more questions—till Mom jokingly told him to stop. However, my siblings were babies when I got arrested, and we never spoke directly about my case. I never considered what they knew about my case—overheard or made up. Did Mom talk to them?

My siblings probably had many questions. I began to wonder, but did not ask, if my siblings told their friends about their brother in prison? And if so, what did they tell them? Was I a bad guy?

I quickly fell down a rabbit hole!

I got to see Keiana a lot more over the summer. But it was a lot of labor for Heather—who had to take the train from Coney Island into the city, catch a bus at midnight, then ride upstate with poor, marginalized Black and Brown families and children for at least 8 hours each way to see their loved ones—trapped in human cages.

Heather was also having some health complications from her ongoing battle with sickle-cell anemia, which impacted her work, finances, emotional health, and ability to take care of our daughter—all of which made me more desperate to get out of prison. And so, with the fall approaching, I began to obsess over my upcoming parole hearing—my third, marking the completion of 7 years in prison—more than 2,222 days trapped in varied human cages throughout New York State.

VERSE

05

Pre-Honor Dorm

October 2000

I applied for the pre-honor dorm in the back of the prison with its yard, weights, and a cooking station with pots and pans. It was a different world from much of Wyoming, and when *unfortunates* got there, they often didn't leave unless it was to a new prison or to go home—which meant the waiting list was long. However, around Halloween, I got moved to the dorm, which sat adjacent to the honor dorm and served as a holdover space. To get to the honor dorm, you had to be ticket-free for a year, but to get to the pre-honor dorm, it was only six months.

Living in the pre-honor dorm was the first time I felt a *degree* of safety in Wyoming. This allowed me to focus more on and prepare for my college classes, which were academically rigorous and further challenged my concepts of self, truth, and norms. Books like *The Teachings of Don Juan, Stranger in a Strange Land,* and *The Crack in the Cosmic Egg* were among our assigned readings.

The books implored me towards greater inner dimensions of freedom—so much so that I began questioning everything. I was deeply unsatisfied with the present version of reality. I was determined to be free of ideological boxes—and anything which negated critical inquiry into the human experience—with self, each other, the planet, and all sentient beings.

"Believe, but don't believe"—a Buddhist axiom became my motto.

However, the *insanity* of the *world* made me question sanity[4]—and who gets to define it in such a dissonant, dystopian world?

4 We often speak of "sanity" as if it were an objective condition, yet the behaviors we label rational or healthy are deeply shaped by the society we inhabit. In a dystopian reality where violence, exploitation, and environmental destruction are normalized—where capitalism and imperialism demand that we suppress empathy to keep systems of harm running—those who cannot adapt are often pathologized and punished. However, the real insanity may lie in our unwillingness to question a world that celebrates domination and extraction.

I didn't know all the answers, but "grokked" that a commitment to love,[5] abundance, humanity, and oneness was the path.

5 Love is often dismissed as sentimental, yet the greatest freedom movements have treated it as a radically transformative force. bell hooks taught that love is a political act—a deliberate commitment to nurturing our collective growth and resisting systems that thrive on domination and disconnection. Bob Marley reminded us that love is the courage to remain human in an inhumane world. Even the story of Jesus frames love as a revolutionary ethic powerful enough to confront the empire itself. Across history, activists have understood that love is not merely emotion but praxis—a daily act of reflection, reforming theory, and action that disrupts violence and creates the conditions for liberation. In a society organized around fear and exploitation, choosing love becomes one of the most radical (aka gangsta) acts we can make.

2001

VERSE

01

Parole Board #3

February 2001

"The nature of the crime precludes release at this time."

It was February 2001, and I had been incarcerated for seven years. This was my third parole hearing—and third denial—all for the same reason. I had one major ticket in seven years, completed all my recommended programs, and was close to earning an associate degree. I also had a pending deportation order. But none of this mattered to the parole board.

The parole denial was for two years. Again, they told me nothing about what I needed to make myself a better candidate—only that I'd see them again in 2003. The lack of clarity and humanity fed my ever-growing fear that I was destined to die in prison like George Jackson.

I was devastated by the denial and spent a lot of emotional labor with family and friends speculating why I couldn't get paroled. I was putting on a good show for my family, but I was hurting. I never imagined, even after being sentenced in 1994, that I would serve seven years in prison.

I always thought God, the system, or some semblance of *justice* would come forward and save me—sure, it felt irrational at times, but when my faith wavered, I came back stronger. But how much more could I take? How much more positive hyperbole could I swallow to justify the violence I was experiencing? I was drowning in anger at the system and pissed at myself for subjecting my family to its cruelty.

Exhibit G: 2001 Parole Denial

INMATE COPY
FORM 9026

State of New York - Division of Parole
Parole Board Release Decision Notice

Date: 02/15/01

Name: KIRK,JAMES
DIN: 94A6325
Nysid: 07648252P

Facility: WYOMING
Interview Date: 02/14/2001
Interview Type: INITIAL

Earned Eligibility Certificate : INELIGIBLE
Supervision Fee: ELIGIBLE
Certificate of Relief from Disability:

Parole Decision:
DENIED - HOLD FOR 24 MONTHS, NEXT APPEARANCE DATE: 02/2003

Conditions of Release/Reasons for Denial:

PAROLE IS DENIED FOR THE FOLLOWING REASONS THE SERIOUS NATURE OF YOUR INSTANT OFFENSE OF CPCS 2ND. YOU WERE INVOLVED IN AN IN CONCERT POSSESSION OF A LARGE AMOUNT OF COCAINE. YOU WERE ACTUALLY INVOLVED IN THE SALE OF ILLEGAL DRUGS AND ILLEGAL FIREARMS. THIS CONDUCT REFLECTS A TOTAL DISREGARD FOR THE HEALTH AND SAFETY OF THE COMMUNITY. THESE FACTORS LEAD THE PANEL TO CONCLUDE YOUR RELEASE TO THE COMMUNITY WOULD NOT BE IN THE BEST INTEREST OF SOCIETY.

Comments:

FOLLOWING DELIBERATION, THIS DECISION IS BASED ON REVIEW OF THE CASE RECORD AS WELL AS THE INTERVIEW WITH PAROLE BOARD MEMBERS.

FPD II : JOHN SIKORA

* * * * * * * INMATE COPY * * * * * * *

VERSE

02

Honor Dorm Crew

March 2001

The long, cold, dark upstate winter transitioned to spring, and I slowly began to refocus and prepare myself for at least two more years in prison. In late March, I moved to the honor dorm, where I began to create some much-needed stability while building relationships that would play a pivotal role in determining my fate post-prison.

Many people in the honor dorm would normally have beef in the general population—but in the honor dorm, an unwritten and sometimes fragile peace treaty governed our engagements. There was also a large segment of prisoners from Jamaica and other islands, which, surprisingly, brought up a lot of unresolved childhood and immigrant tensions surrounding my "Jamaicanness."

"X" was the head of the Caribbean crew, and we knew each other from Greene. He was Jamaican, short, and the leader of our workout team: "the Silverbacks." X was light-skinned and unassuming. But he was a warrior and fiercely protective of his community—even if that meant occasionally bringing knives to the yard.

There was Haitian Rich, who was from Queens, who looked Spanish but repped Haiti harder than anyone I ever met. Scully was a tall Jamaican loner with long dreads, unpredictable, spoke to himself sometimes, and would get mad at us over petty shit for weeks. Yet no one took umbrage and always treated him like a brother.

"John Wayne" was Jamaican and a "shotta," which earned him his moniker in the streets. But Wayne was a natural comedian, always willing to broker truces when someone got mad. There was also "Baz" from Elmira, New York. He and Bliss were among the few non-Caribbean people down with the crew.

We cooked together on Sundays—which was my favorite day.

However, Sunday dinners in the Caribbean often began days earlier with the seasoning and marinating of various dishes. I went to bed on Saturday nights, excited to know that by 6 am, X would be up, prepping food we got from the commissary or packages.

It was pure alchemy as X transformed box chicken from the commissary into coconut brown stew rundown, garnished with scotch bonnet and thyme. X even made rice and peas with coconut cream and fried dumplings to complement the meal, which took hours to prepare and made the entire dorm smell like a Jamaican restaurant.

VERSE

03

INS v. St. Cyr

April 2001

The crew and the community we created sustained me amidst my parole denials and extreme distance from my family. But sadly, like myself, most of the crew were born outside of the US and had orders of deportation—even though many of them were US war veterans, had partners or children who were citizens, and had *legally* lived in the US most of their lives.

My ever-looming deportation always felt like an *extra* life sentence and created tensions I struggled to understand and put into words. But with the honor dorm crew, I found a family that overstood—and their collective knowledge of immigration law would guide me to "INS v. St. Cyr"—a case about a Haitian brother who got locked up in 1996 for drug possession before the passage of IIRIRA. He argued successfully in Federal court that the law shouldn't apply retroactively. However, the government appealed, and the case was scheduled for a hearing before the Supreme Court on April 21.

If the Supreme Court upheld the prior court's ruling on retroactivity, I would be able to appeal my INS decision and request a waiver hearing. If my hearing request is granted and I win, my deportation order would be voided. However, the ruling wouldn't impact people with what the government deemed "violent crimes" or aggravated felonies—which was pretty much everything except a few drug exemptions.

June 2001

April 21 came and went, and I forgot about the case until Haitian Rich, whose cube was adjacent to mine, placed a copy of the Supreme Court decision on my locker amid our daily chess game. It was June 30, and I remember the date as I wrote it down in my journal. Yet the decision, which favored *me*, felt surreal.

I re-read the June 25 decision with the precision of a legal editor in search of misleading jargon. It was hard to sleep that night. The next day, I went to the law library to read newspapers and journals to deepen my understanding. I also engaged with the law clerks and anyone who looked remotely astute. I was desperate for affirmation, but it took a few days to confirm that the Supreme Court did indeed rule against the retroactive application of the 1996 immigration laws.

The decision felt like my first victory in a long time. I quickly put together a legal motion to reopen my INS case. I had a lot of help from my crew and a few Dominican brothers, including "Poppy," an alleged drug kingpin from Washington Heights who attended college with me and lived in the honor dorm.

Poppy also had INS troubles, but went on visits often and had unlimited access to collect phone calls and lawyers on standby. Poppy was always in the know and thankfully shared his resources with me and everyone else in need.

Cabeza was an unlikely ally: the head of the Dominican gang and a Red Sox fan, yet incredibly knowledgeable about immigration law. He was the first Dominican I knew who openly acknowledged the African diaspora in the Dominican Republic—he also knew and spoke openly about the intentional utilization of racism to facilitate anti-Blackness, segregation, and oppression amongst Dominicans and Haitians.[1]

September 2001

With the help of my crew, Ralphy and Cabeza, I filed a motion to reopen my INS case. I was beyond excited, but decided not to share the news with my family until I received a decision. I did my best to temper my expectations and spent most of the summer working out and practicing with our flag football team to pass the time. But it was more than a distraction. I loved football, as did most of the honor dorm. We had a history of winning the Wyoming flag football championship—and we were determined to carry on the legacy.

1 See Franco, F. J. (1969). *Los negros, los mulatos y la nación dominicana.* Santo Domingo, Dominican Republic: Editora Nacional. Mayes, A. J. (2014). *The mulatto republic: Class, race, and Dominican national identity.* Gainesville, FL: University Press of Florida. Ricourt, M. (2016). *The Dominican racial imaginary: Surveying the landscape of race and nation in Hispaniola.* New Brunswick, NJ: Rutgers University Press.

VERSE 04

9-11-01

When I wasn't training for football, I was facilitating HRTP programs. Although I was not yet an expert, I was getting better and enjoyed leading challenging conversations. I ultimately got to teach more classes and was navigating a discussion on de-escalating violence when the PA system announced that all programs were closed.

Instructions were given for all prisoners to return to their housing units—which I found strange, as it was only 10:15 am on the morning of September 11. I was frustrated and upset with the announcement—as it was a commissary day and I planned on going after HRTP.

I sought clarity on why we had to return to our dorms, but everyone had a different story. There were even rumors that a small plane had flown into the side of the World Trade Center. Other stories had the US under attack by terrorists. Whatever it was, everyone was talking!

I arrived at the dorm around 10:45 am to find some *unfortunates* and the CO glued to the TV. I quickly found Bliss in the crowd of people in the small dayroom and made my way towards him. He saw the questioning look on my face and immediately shared, "Two planes flew into the World Trade Center!"

I looked at Bliss in disbelief before turning my attention to the TV—the footage was straight out of a horror movie and challenged my perception of reality. I watched in disbelief for a few more minutes before, suddenly, remembering that Heather worked in the financial district. I ran to the payphone and tried her house number, but the call went unanswered. I tried a few other numbers with no luck. Other people reported being unable to reach their loved ones before we realized the phones were down.

The uncertainty was sickening, even before we watched the World Trade Center Tower collapse. I could only stare in disbelief as a staple of the Manhattan skyline, one I had viewed countless times from our

17th-floor terrace in Lefrak City, disappeared. The twin towers were within ten blocks of my first two jobs, and I spent a good portion of every summer from 1990 to 1993 having lunch and listening to music with friends—many of whom still worked in the area.

The next few hours were paralyzing as we watched news station after news station feed us trauma porn—and prepare us for war. Opinions amongst prisoners varied drastically. Many politically conscious people felt that the US should pay for its foreign policy practices, which they argued were genocidal and destructive for much of the world. Others felt patriotic and angry, wanting retribution. I was somewhere in the middle, as I knew all about the impact of US imperialism. Still, I couldn't condone killing innocent people and was adamantly opposed to the developing narrative of Muslims and immigrants as "terrorists."

VERSE

05

212c

Thankfully, the phones began to work two days after "9/11," and I got to speak with Heather, who recounted the terror she felt evacuating lower Manhattan under a cloud of smoke and burning buildings. She described having to cross the Brooklyn Bridge with frantic people covered in soot and blood. She described walking for hours, unsure of what was happening—not knowing if Keiana and her family were okay as she did mile after mile from "Ground Zero" to Coney Island on foot.

The world was on the brink of war, and my family was in danger—and I felt powerless to help! However, a few hours after I spoke to Heather, on the night of Thursday, September 13, divine timing aligned and intervened on my behalf.

I had no expectations when the CO informed me that I had legal mail. I was preparing for the worst, as the anti-immigrant and Muslim sentiment post 9/11 was growing stronger by the day—which we all reasoned would undoubtedly impact our immigration processes. But I was finally wrong.

I opened the legal letter and read that my motion to reopen my INS case had been granted! I had a "212c"[2] hearing in less than five months.

2 A 212(c) hearing is an INS administrative review conducted by immigration officials where the applicant is allowed to demonstrate why they should be granted relief from deportation.

2002

VERSE

01

A Change is Gonna Come

January 2001

I was on a mini-win streak!

With the arrival of the New Year, I began most mornings playing Sam Cooke's "A Change is Gonna Come," which captured my pain and frustration with the present while gripping tightly to a profound belief in the possibility of a future free of cages or deportation. However, I knew I would need help to bring about the change I desired. So, when the INS reopened my case in September 2001, I excitedly called a man I had never met but had spoken to numerous times.

Manny Vargas was an attorney who ran a weekly hotline providing immigration advice. I got his information from a bulletin in the law library in Greene sometime in 1997 after my order of deportation. The hotline Manny ran was free but could not accept calls, so I had Aunt Karen call him on 3-way, which was against the rules, but it was a chance I was willing to take to fight my immigration case.

Manny was incredibly generous with his time and knowledge of immigration law, and he often provided valuable legal updates more quickly than I would have received in prison. He was also the first attorney to see me as a human being and to have my back. So I won the lottery when Manny decided to represent me pro bono (aka free!) at my 212 (c) waiver hearing.

Manny believed I had a solid argument to remain in the US and assigned his legal intern, Kevin Lapp, to gather information and build my case for the hearing. Kevin and I hit it off instantly and spent the last few months of 2001 on numerous calls so he could better understand who I was, how I got to prison, and how deportation would impact me, my family, and especially Keiana. Kevin also spent considerable time interviewing and requesting letters from family members and friends to provide a holistic picture for the 212(c) hearing scheduled for February at Downstate Correctional Facility.

February 2002

I knew my family's presence and testimony would be critical to the hearing's outcome. So, we decided Mom, Grandma, John, Heather, and my good friend Ed would testify on my behalf.

I had the *dream team* and trusted our chances of winning—or at least of putting up a valiant effort against *Goliath*! However, the speed at which things were happening felt kind of trippy—leading me to pause at various points in my day and question whether I was dreaming or possibly delusional? And it certainly wasn't lost on me that the hearing—and the possibility to *now* remain in the United States—happened *only* because they denied me parole three times!!!

And as much as I talk about *faith*, I was still a Black man in Amerikkka with a life sentence, an order of deportation, and trapped in prison since age 18—so it literally took everything for me not to internalize an oppressive reality—in which the outcome was often trauma, drama, disappointment, and hopelessness.

With so many people supporting me, I embraced the audacity of hope—and the yet unseen promise of victory—that beckoned from beyond the great wall of fear. I was super optimistic, and my crew sent me off from Wyoming with a ton of positive vibes.

I needed all the energy for the journey to Downstate—which was at least a three-day trip each way with an overnight in Auburn—and while I was still traumatized from being stuck there in '98, I unconsciously knew that an opportunity to experience life in maximum security prison, where the likelihood of going home was slim, should be honored, captured, and utilized in my quest to one day destroy the narrative and ideologies that legitimize their existence.

Music was a huge part of survival in max prisons, and the range was eclectic; however, *You Got It Bad* by Usher was the current song of choice when I arrived at Auburn. A prisoner on a tier above the flats, probably going through it, played the song over and over until it permeated my subconscious, and I began to sing along silently.

Max prisons are often as dark as the minds that create them. But if you look closely enough, you can find a beautiful, creative, resilient, and loving ethos that prisoners have made to occupy space and time while trapped in human cages.

There is always energy flowing up and down the tiers—recapping favorite movies, sporting events, and neighborhood drama; soliciting parenting or relationship advice; theatrical re-readings of old Dear John letters and the drama that ensued; making acoustic music with cell doors, steel beds, and concrete walls; and playing chess together over different tiers using a combination of letters and numbers to guide pawns and kings in magical combinations.

There was an ever-evolving stream of voices and consciousness emanating from the human cages—and you could never tell who was who or what was real. But it was fascinating and probably somewhat voyeuristic to sit and listen—especially knowing that I wasn't staying.

Thankfully, there were no snowstorms or delays on the way out of Auburn, and I arrived at Downstate a day before the hearing. Kevin drove up that same day and arranged a legal visit to catch up and go over last-minute details.

Kevin and I spent hours talking over the phone, and he knew more about my family, my charges, and my immigration case than anyone else. But there was an initial awkwardness as it was our first in-person meeting. My experience with attorneys over the years jaded me towards the profession. But I enjoyed the honesty and humility with which Kevin and Manny operated. As I sat down with Kevin to review my defense folder, filled with personal letters from family and friends, it confirmed how hard they had worked and honored the totality of my humanity.

I was excited to leave the meeting with Kevin, but felt prepared in every way except emotionally. So I prayed, did calisthenics, meditated, and read most of the night. I didn't sleep much, but I was up and energized as the sun's light permeated the cell's darkness. I felt like a child on Christmas morning, *unsure if I was getting a Nintendo or a bag of unwanted clothes from Alexander's Department Store.*

I was ready and anxiously pacing the cell when the CO came for me at 9:30 am—thirty minutes before the start of the hearing, as Manny and Kevin arranged for me to have some time with Mom, Grandma Yvonne,

John, and Heather—who were waiting and excitedly greeted me as the CO led me into the room.

I smiled and hugged everyone, especially Manny—as it was our first in-person meeting. I was overjoyed until I realized Ed was missing and wasn't allowed into the facility to testify. Still, I couldn't help noticing my family's strength and optimism. I didn't know what they would say on my behalf, but I knew Manny and Kevin worked with everyone on their testimonies—with the hope their narratives would allow the court to see me beyond my charges.

The hearing began promptly at 10 am, when another CO arrived, escorted us from the holding room, and led us to the courtroom. I immediately noticed that the judge was younger and more affable than the one who ordered me deported. Two women assisted him and captured the proceedings for the record. And, somewhat ironically, there was a Black woman representing the INS.

We all sat in different sections of the makeshift courtroom facing the judge. He called my name and docket number, stated the purpose of the hearing, and then allowed the INS attorney to present their case.

There were no surprises; it was a retelling of my arrest charges and conviction. My family was then allowed to testify on why, irrespective of my charges, I shouldn't be deported.

I cried as Mom shared the story of us migrating from Jamaica in February 1986. It was a story I knew well. However, I never heard it from her side, or thought about what it must have felt like for her as a 27-year-old Black woman—to leave her home, profession, friends, family, and partner behind for a dream of a better life in New York City with her 10-year-old son.

I continued to cry as Grandma, who also left Jamaica in the '60s to follow her dream of becoming a fashion designer, weaved stories of my early years in New York. I was immediately thrust back to the excitement I felt as a kid, waiting on the terrace in Rego Park, watching and waiting to spot her in the distance coming home after work—often with freshly baked, still hot ham and cheese croissants.

Grandma shared tales of our weekend trips into Manhattan to shop at Lord & Taylor, peruse antique shops, and hang out in the West Village at her favorite Parisian restaurants—where we sat for hours as she told stories, discussed all the new fashion trends, and people-watched.

John spoke about my relationship with Andree, Kareem, Aaron, Alicia, and the impact of my arrest. He pleaded with the judge to consider how my deportation would further harm our family. In his trademark jovial, Caribbean, reflective, and soft spoken voice, John discussed our love for music—which often led us on Saturday morning excursions from Lefrak City in his 1988 gold Toyota Cressida—to VP Records on Jamaica Avenue in Queens—where we dug through the crates for new and old vinyl reggae classics before grabbing beef patties for the family up the block from the Queen's Coliseum on 165th St.

I was deeply emotional witnessing my family cry and share personal memories and reflections with the court—which, in some ways, felt invasive, but necessary—in a system refusing to see my humanity.

Heather discussed how we met in '93 at the Mid-Manhattan Library and the process of co-raising Keiana throughout my incarceration. Listening to her speak about Keiana—and the struggles she endured to maintain our relationship across jails and prisons for almost a decade—deepened my love and appreciation for her and my family.

If I had superpowers, I would pause the hearing, lovingly embrace my family, and transport them to a world where Black people didn't have to constantly prove to systems rooted in White supremacy that we deserve to be treated like humans.

I was in a heavy emotional state and was the last one to testify. My recollection of what I said is spotty, but I am pretty sure I told the court who I was before prison, the circumstances that led to my incarceration, and what I did with my time over the last eight years. Including the Associate's Degree, which I was on track to complete in May. The judge listened with what seemed like empathy, making the legal proceeding feel more like a conversation.

The Black INS attorney, however, was not interested in any pleasantries. She dismissed the testimonies, arguing that my criminal charges alone were sufficient grounds to uphold my deportation order. In a moment of irony, I swore I could detect a slight Caribbean accent in her voice.

I was nervous when the judge recused himself. Manny huddled us and thanked everyone for their testimony, and Grandma Yvonne led us in prayer, asking that we put our faith and trust in God's hands. Manny also mentioned that the court could postpone rendering an immediate decision to gather more information. Hence, no one knew what to expect when the judge returned to the courtroom an hour later.

The judge reconvened the court and began summarizing the INS charges. I was holding my breath when he began discussing the merits of the application and the stories my family shared that morning—and others via letters from friends like Gav, Eric, Jav, Ed, Rodney, and Nat.

The judge spoke of Keiana and acknowledged the impact of my incarceration—and how that would be exacerbated if I were deported. He even thanked Heather for all she did to raise our daughter throughout my incarceration. The anticipation in the small makeshift courtroom peaked as the judge wrapped up his review and signaled that he was ready to decide the case. He then asked that I stand and face the court.

My legs were wobbly, and my heart was erratic, but I stood proudly, knowing that my family was watching—and had my back no matter the outcome.

The judge read some legal jargon I couldn't decipher before declaring:

"Your application for a 212 (c) waiver is granted…"

Time stopped!

There was no further recollection of what the judge said. All I remember is tearfully turning toward Manny and Kevin, standing by my side, smiling and beaming joyfully. I quickly embraced them before turning to my family—who began to cry, which made me cry harder, and pretty soon, all the emotions came flowing out.

Exhibit H: 212c Document

U.S. DEPARTMENT OF JUSTICE
EXECUTIVE OFFICE FOR IMMIGRATION REVIEW
IMMIGRATION COURT
121 RED SCHOOLHOUSE ROAD
FISHKILL, NY 12524

In the Matter of: Case No.: A24-794-790
*S-JAMES, KIRK ANTHONY
94-A-6325
RESPONDENT IN DEPORTATION PROCEEDINGS

ORDER OF THE IMMIGRATION JUDGE

This is a summary of the oral decision entered on Feb 19, 2002. This memorandum is solely for the convenience of the parties. If the proceedings should be appealed, the Oral Decision will become the official decision in this matter.

( ) The respondent was ordered deported to the alternative to

( ) Respondent's application for voluntary departure was denied and respondent was ordered deported to or in the alternative to

( ) Respondent's application for voluntary departure was granted until , with an alternate order of deportation to or

( ) Respondent's application for asylum was ( )granted ( )denied ( )withdrawn ( )other.

( ) Respondent's application for withholding of deportation was ( )granted ( )denied ( )withdrawn ( )other.

( ) Respondent's application for suspension of deportation was ( ) granted under section 244(a)(1) or (2) ( ) granted under section 244(a)(3) ( ) denied ( ) withdrawn ( ) other.

( ) Respondent's application for waiver under Section ______ of the Immigration and Nationality Act was ( )granted ( )denied ( )withdrawn ( )other.

(X) Respondent's application for 212c was (X)granted ( )denied ( )withdrawn ( )other.

( ) Proceedings were terminated.

( ) The application for adjustment of status under Section (216)(216A) (245)(249) was ( )granted ( )denied ( )withdrawn ( )other. If granted, it was ordered that the respondent be issued all appropriate documents necessary to give effect to this order.

( ) Respondent's status was rescinded under Section 246.

( ) Other ______

( ) Respondent was advised of the limitation on discretionary relief for failure to appear as ordered in the Immigration Judge's oral decision.

Date: Feb 19, 2002

ADAM OPACIUCH
Immigration Judge

Appeal: RESERVED (Alien/INS/Both)
Appeal Due by: Mar 21, 2002

CLD

VERSE

02

Victory!?

The 212 (c) hearing was my Heavyweight championship, my Super Bowl, World Series, Olympics, and World Cup all in one—and I just won!

I couldn't even wrap my head around all the implications. I just knew that with the help of Manny, Kevin, my family, and friends—I persevered and fought for six years against an order of deportation from the INS, and on February 19, 2002, I finally won the right to remain in the United States!

The Court and CO graciously allowed us a little more time together, but my hearing was over, and other prisoners were awaiting their turn. As we left the courtroom, the judge gave me well-wishes and a copy of the decision. I hugged everyone quickly and shared words of gratitude once we got outside.

I watched Manny, Kevin, and my family walk through the open gates towards the administration building and out of prison without me. Yet, for the first time, I didn't feel sadness. It was replaced by an inner knowing that the doors were wide open, even if I couldn't see it yet.

I was floating and giddy as the CO escorted me back to the cell. Everything felt a little surreal—except that I had a physical copy of the decision in my hand—which I reread over and over and over again once I got into the cell and sat on the bed.

The isolation and privacy of the cell allowed me to indulge in an emotional catharsis. For hours, I cried, laughed, danced, smiled, and finally allowed myself to dream of a life outside prison. I was happiest for my family and for the opportunity to be a father, doing simple things like picking Keiana up from school or hanging out with my siblings.

My heart raced at the thought of New York City—Queens, Manhattan, Brooklyn, Coney Island, hip-hop, summertime, food, the Knicks, Yankee games, and everything else I had missed over the years. I spent most of the night joyfully hysterical and was unusually talkative in the morning as I boarded the large prison bus back to Wyoming.

I was shackled to a teenager with a "2002" number—which meant he was recently processed into the system. We began with small talk, but as the bus set out upstate through the mountains, I learned he was gang-involved from Long Island and was heading to The Cat.

It was hard not to see myself in the young man. I shared my story, my sentence, my parole denials, and my journey through Rikers Island, The Cat, Greene, and Wyoming. I shared some of the advice Pops gave me during those early years in the mess hall—especially the part about *not letting time do you*—all of which he appeared to understand and appreciate. But he got quiet and seemed lost in thought. So, I gave it a few minutes before asking him about his prison sentence—which wasn't something I usually did, but I shared enough about myself, at least in my mind, to warrant the question.

The young man paused to consider my question before sharing that his sentence was "35 years to life." I felt sick to my stomach as he explained the details of his case—which were gruesome, yet so was sentencing a child to 35 years to life!

Racism and anti-Blackness were so pervasive that few people ever stopped to ask why gangs, guns, drugs, robberies, mental health crises, and cycles of harm take root and persist in marginalized communities. Instead of examining the structural violence that produces these conditions, society dehumanizes and incarcerates the people forced to survive within them.

I was mad, and I knew no words could help the young man face the darkness that awaited him. But, for my own comfort, I discussed the appeal process and the importance of not giving up hope!

My prospect of freedom was becoming clearer, but it was hard to truly feel joy in the moment, knowing that so many more men, women, and children were trapped in this heinous system.

I got back to Wyoming and couldn't get "35 years to life" out of my head—which made me a little more reserved about discussing my INS hearing. But my crew was excited and celebrated my victory like it was their own—which was the ultimate sign of love, as many of them, deprived of the opportunities I had as a "drug offender," would be deported.[1]

1 Many people also gave up their rights to an appeal by "signing out"—which I refused to do in 1997.

VERSE

03

The Graduate

May 2002

Three months after my INS victory, I celebrated my 27th birthday—and became a college graduate: I earned my Associate Degree with honors. I was so happy and thankful for Bob, who ran the college[2] and worked tirelessly to raise money to maintain the program despite the 1994 crime bill.

Jails and prisons often shackle the body and the mind. However, the college experience engendered an infinite outlook on life—which became exponentially brighter with my INS victory.

My part-time job in the prison library exposed me to Black fiction authors like Erick Jermone Dickey and stories of young Black professionals navigating life and love in ways that were foreign to me—having spent most of my adult life in prison.

I was *now* a student of life, so I read everything I could get my hands on. I especially devoured urban magazines praising crime lords while selling capitalistic and genocidal epithets like "money, cash, hoes" under the illusion of culture and art. I was trying to catch up with my generation, but I began to fear that we were growing apart.

I dared to dream of freedom but was unsure of the path and eager for guidance. But what I did know, and wrote down in my journal, was that upon release, I would honor and support my family, continue to heal, and be the best father to Keiana. I also knew that I would work tirelessly to expose and destroy systems of oppression.

I began writing to various social work programs in NYC on the advice of Aunt Karen, who was completing her degree at York College

2 Much gratitude to college administrators like Debby and Roman. And guys in the program like AZ, Glenn Martin, Scar, Baz, Little Rich, Elder, X, and comrade "Hotep," who always kept the bar high. I'm incredibly grateful to my favorite professor, Dr. Gregory Peck (RIP), a brilliant, kind human being who abdicated his power in the classroom to ensure that the voices of historically marginalized men of color were heard.

in Jamaica, Queens, and often shared with me the profession's human-rights values.

I felt deeply committed to giving any future position and power to collective liberation, knowing that no one could be free until we all had the right to self-actualize. I knew deep down that social justice, freedom, humanity, and all the things I desired began with me. I had to evolve to become the best version of myself—a commitment tested before the ink even dried on my immigration victory.

VERSE

04

Evolve

October 2002

I didn't have many possessions or things of value throughout my incarceration—just some books, journals, pictures, a typewriter, and my army jacket, which I had since The Cat. It wouldn't even be a stretch to say that on numerous occasions, the jacket saved my life—and had the scars to show where its fabric bettered an attacker's blade and spared me bodily harm.

I loved my army jacket—so it felt like I lost my best friend when it disappeared one day while working in the library. But soon, sadness turned to anger when I heard about a possible suspect. I quickly set up a reconnaissance team and began to plan a mission before deciding it didn't matter—neither the jacket nor my ego was worth the risk of catching another charge and more prison time.

Self-restraint in a predatory environment is neither easy nor the norm. To survive, it is often necessary to violate those who violate you. However, the Jacket wasn't the only test.

In late October, right as I was about to leave for college classes, the CO handed me a letter from my boy Gav, who, in his introduction, warned me to sit down before proceeding further. He begged me not to do anything after I read the letter, which was confusing, as he knew I wasn't reactive.

Considering my circumstances, I couldn't imagine anything Gav could say to make me lose it. However, I debated delaying reading the letter as it was almost time for my chemistry class. But curiosity got the better of me, and I methodically scanned Gav's letter until I got to the part where he said:

"Your boy Will, and your ex-girl Moya, are together, and having a baby."

What!

My boy Will!!!

The one I called on the day I got locked up—and begged to call Moya??

Will, the one that I got into my mad fights because of his mouth and propensity for fucking his boy's girlfriends???!!!

I looked up from the letter and suddenly realized I was standing in my cube—which was in the far right corner of the square dorm with two windows looking out into the dark, snowy mountain range.

I took a deep breath as I stared out the window. After some time, I sat in the chair adjacent to the large locker. I looked at the letter in my hand and re-read Gav's words—allowing them to paint images and possibilities within my consciousness.

Will and Moya *together* triggered an atomic blast of painful emotions I thought were dead!!!

Fuck!

Carlito was right!

Life didn't stop with me in prison—a truly heinous place—that destroyed so many bonds I assumed were sacred.

I was messed up, but I knew I couldn't afford to lose it now. I shook it off and quickly got myself together for class. But the soul of the body, in the seat, was a space cadet far away, suffering in silence.

I returned to the dorm later that night and crumbled into bed. I attempted to block out the world with a fleece blanket over my head. Amid my emotional meltdown, I repeatedly played "Song Cry" by Jay-Z, which, surprisingly, spoke to my soul and my struggle to honor the depth of my pain.

The song also set my mind racing and compelled me to reconsider my relationship with Jay-Z as an artist—a tension I once attributed to others comparing him to Biggie, who, along with Nas and Tupac, formed my own holy trinity. Yet as I listened to Jay-Z's music more deeply for the first time, I discovered my feelings were far more nuanced, and soon the sources of that juxtaposition and tension became clear.[3]

3 Jay-Z, the biggest star in hip hop—made millions under his Roc-A-Fella label, celebrating capitalism, the drug game, and the art of not getting caught. Meanwhile, I was sitting in a prison cell, broke, with a life sentence under the very Rockefeller Drug Laws that criminalized generations of Black and Brown youth for the same hustles that fueled the culture's mythology. One of us became a symbol of entrepreneurial brilliance; the other became a statistic of "mass incarceration."

Hip-hop, like Moya, had grown up and changed!

This new *hip-hop* became commodified and synonymous with glorifying a *life* that cost me and countless sellers, users, and "civilians" their lives and loved ones. The *culture* normalized capitalism and even revered—selling drugs within our communities to oppressed people seeking to escape the perpetual traumas of oppression. Yet I was not without sin. Like many others, I knew that my decisions were often rooted in scarcity and individualism—and thus not in the best interest of my family and community.

Hip-hop, like religion, provided multiple lifelines throughout my life and incarceration. But like religion, I began to have questions: primarily, *why were we being fed the same violent, divisive, overly sexualized, capitalistic, homophobic, drug-abuse-norming, and misogynistic music over and over as art, or worse, culture*? A tension we explored in my psychology course with my favorite professor, Dr. Peck.

In class, we were encouraged to create topics and lead discussions. So I suggested we research with the help of Dr. Peck, "The 1995 Telecommunication Act"[4]—which commodified hip-hop and destroyed the *mainstream* diversity of the genre. Commodified music, aided by the ubiquitous movies of my generation (in the ethos of Scarface, King of New York, Goodfellas, and The Godfather), sold historically marginalized people a myopic and genocidal view of what it means to *survive* oppression.

It was sad and overwhelming to think about hip-hop being weaponized as a tool of racial capitalism. However, I began to overstand that our collective *evolution* demanded not only a transformation of oppressive systems, but also the decolonization of self and the emancipation of minds that George, Malcolm, Baldwin, hooks, Lorde, Fanon, and Marley have illuminated for us.

4 As large conglomerates with artist interest controlled the radio airwaves, programming became more standardized—hip-hop, which emerged as a powerful voice for marginalized communities, historically thrived on independent and community-based radio stations that were more open to socially conscious messages and diversity within the genre. With consolidation, these independent outlets dwindled, limiting the opportunities for many artists to reach a broader audience.

VERSE

05

Christmas Gift

December 2002

Gav's letter reminded me that the world I left in 1994 was no longer the same. I didn't know if my family and friends would embrace this evolved version of me. Or if I would embrace them? Lingering questions that only time could answer. But I was in good spirits as December rolled around.

With an order of deportation not hanging over my head, I was more joyful, appreciative, and present with my crew—especially X, who spent hours cooking our Christmas meal. I even made cheesecake for dessert using commissary products.

Christmas 2002 was the best one I had while incarcerated, which coincided with me dreaming that night of past holidays at Aunt Yola's house in Mo-Bay—perched atop Bogue Heights looking into the ocean. It was a place of family and community, no matter who was there. It was where love, vulnerability, faith, hope, food, laughter, joy, and pain existed as life lessons, and tools—that I now knew worked even in dark places.

The morning after Christmas felt chaotic, as many prisoners were transferred out of Wyoming—as the authorities had been shaking up the prison over the last month. I even lost Bliss a few weeks ago to Ulster—a prison in the middle of New York State. There were rumors that he may have made it home for Christmas.

My fourth parole hearing was coming up in February—and the Department of Corrections didn't often move people that close to their hearing. I also had a "transfer hold" while attending college and was resigned to another parole hearing in Wyoming. However, as I was about to get out of bed, the CO stopped by my cube and told me to pack up.

I didn't know where I was going, but I gave most of my possessions to the crew. My typewriter—a gift from Heather and, next to my army jacket, my most prized possession went to X—who knew I was sad to leave but reminded me that I was one step closer to home. And even though I believed him, it never felt right to leave behind the people who had held and cared for me during dark days.

I left Wyoming in transit for a night in Auburn, then Downstate. And on December 30, 2002, I crossed the Triborough Bridge into New York City for the first time in over eight years!

Tears ran down my face as I looked out the window, but when the radio picked up Hot 97, and "Welcome to New York City" by Cam'ron and Jay-Z blared out the speakers, I lost my fucking mind!!!

I was hype!

I wanted to scream, laugh, and cry with joy.

I spent countless seconds, minutes, hours, days, months, and years dreaming of *my return*—minus, of course, the part where I was on a prison bus, shackled and bound for Arthur Kill Correctional Facility in Staten Island. To be honest, though, none of that mattered.

The energetic vibration and distinct smell of New York City embraced me, and held me tight—and I knew then, in my heart, in my soul, that I was finally home!

Wyoming Correctional Facility

1 Me circa 1999

2 Kye circa 1999

3 Me, Wali, and a comrade whose name I can't recall, circa 2000

4 Me, Oronde, and friend circa 2000

5 Me, mom, Andre, Kareem, and baby Aaron circa 2000

6 Me, Heather and Keiana circa 2001

Continues on next page

Full-size photos can be found on https://www.instagram.com/94a6325/

Some individuals have been pixellated for privacy.

1999-2002

7 Me, Jav, and Ed
circa 2001

8 Me, Heather, and Keiana
circa 2002

9 Me, Wali (kufi), and
comrades circa 2001

10 Haitian Rich, X, and Bliss
circa 2002

11 Me, Heather and Keiana
circa 2002

12 Keiana and me
circa 2002

2003

VERSE

01

Arthur Kill

January 2003

January 1, 2003, marked my 3,185th day incarcerated!

I felt immense gratitude for the long, hard lessons learned and the friendships gained along the journey.

I watched the New Year's celebration in Times Square and could no longer imagine myself *there*. My memories of past New Year's were now in The Cat, Greene, and Wyoming. Prisons, where I found teachers, friends, comrades, and values to guide my life.

I was optimistic about the future, but the weight of almost a decade in prison was heavy. I also had a gruesome infection that caused my scalp to flake, itch, and hurt when I lay on certain parts of my head. I suspected that the questionable prison beds and the infectious-looking blankets over the years played a role. But theorizing on the genesis of my scalp infection did little to stop the pain, which ultimately forced me to seek medical attention—which in prison was always a last resort.

I watched the ball drop, nauseated by antibiotics yet hopeful of 2003. When the spectacle became overbearing, I slipped into the bathroom. Standing at the sink with my tools, I studied my reflection. My locs fell past my shoulders, heavy with memory, growth, and the quiet victories no one else could see.

Thirty minutes went by before I found the courage to take the trimmers to the roots. It was a prolonged and methodical process. I examined each severed loc before placing it in a plastic bag set over the sink.

Sixty minutes later, I looked in the mirror and saw a familiar face—*maybe older? Younger? Wiser? I couldn't tell!*

I was traumatized—and ready for the war to end. And there were *curious* events in the weeks leading up to the parole hearing that I couldn't stop ruminating on…

Let us begin with my last-minute transfer from Wyoming—where, because of my college status, I was, in theory, ineligible to be transferred. I was also two months from my parole board, which, like my college hold, often blocked transfers.

The proverbial icing on the cake was when, upon my arrival at Arthur Kill, the CO asked:

"Do you know why you got transferred?

The intake CO obviously knew more than I did, making his question seem silly and rhetorical. But I nonetheless played along, looked confused, shrugged my shoulders, and said, "I don't know?"

Convinced, the CO gave his attention to what I presumed was my file on his desk. He quickly reviewed it while making small talk, then concluded the interview. But just as I stood to leave, he looked at me with a straight face and said:

"You're at Arthur Kill because you're going home. Don't fuck up!"

I had many questions, but my interview was over—and I was left to carry the weight of his revelation.

Being at Arthur Kill—the only State Prison with a general population in New York City—gave me a lot to think about. For many prisoners who called the five boroughs home—Arthur Kill was often impossible to get to by transfer, which added to the urban legend. In fact, my boy Kye was the only person I knew who got transferred there—and that was only because he performed the Heimlich maneuver and saved a CO's life in Wyoming.

Most of the prisoners in Arthur Kill were heavily medicated and zombie-like in appearance. The prison had little to no programming—and felt like a warehouse—made worse by the fact that, no matter the weather, we were all forced to leave the dorm.

We had two options for recreation. First, there was the yard—which sat on the Bay, was freezing, and frequented by flocks of birds dropping shit-bombs from overhead.

The second, and most popular, recreational option was a colossal gym—with multiple TVs—where prisoners seeking to numb their consciousness *fought* to watch their favorite soap operas and daytime talk shows.

Don't get me wrong, I was thrilled to be in New York City, but the weeks leading up to the parole hearing lacked routine and were torturous.

It was rumored that the parole board in Arthur Kill was better than other prisons, which made the wait a little more manageable. I even heard stories that parole decisions came the day after the hearing, rather than two or three days later.

Waiting days to know whether you will be granted freedom from prison was unimaginably painful and beyond words. So, for someone with three parole denials, the prospect of learning my fate in as little as a day after seeing the board was great news.

VERSE

02

Parole Board #4

February 2003

My parole hearing was on February 11, 2003—a Tuesday morning, and a mere three days before Valentine's Day. I was optimistic, even joking with Mom that I might be home to celebrate with her. And as much as I didn't want to get her hopes up falsely, jails and prisons had taught me to trust my heart, which, at the moment, wasn't feeding me clairvoyant whispers signaling danger ahead.

I was still taking antibiotics on the morning of my fourth parole hearing, and my stomach was a mess. But my spirits were good, and my head was high as I entered the waiting room, where I acknowledged a few other prisoners I knew—including an "old-timer" from Queens named "KG" who transferred into Arthur Kill with me.

KG was incarcerated for over *thirty years* and was well-known in and out of prison. We met on the bus ride down from Wyoming and knew many people in common. I wanted to check in to see how he felt before the hearing, but I kept the conversation light to honor the enormity of the moment.

I sat peacefully as I recalled the journey to my fourth parole hearing. I smiled as my mind recalled Imam Malik Shabazz from Greene Correctional Facility. He was the Muslim Chaplain and a godsend to me and so many young men.

Everyone looked forward to the Imam's Jummah Friday talks. He fed us hope and courage and fueled our will to survive. Among the things he taught us was the 5 Ps: *Proper Preparation Prevents Poor Performance.*

Rooted in spirit, I refused to let others define me. In 1994, I knew who I was—I understood my actions were wrong, but I also recognized the circumstances and the deeper truth behind my arrest. I knew that in a true system of justice for and by the people—mitigating factors matter!

I knew the man molded by fire. In 2003, I was clear about my values and how they drove me to strive for my best self. Most importantly, I recognized that my actions during nine years of incarceration spoke volumes, revealing more about me than words ever could.

I was prepared and ready to go home—but when it was finally my turn to see the parole board, my anxiety spiked, and things got a little hazy.

To this day, I can't tell you how many people were in the hearing room. What I do remember is this White woman who looked at me and spoke in a loving voice—as if she knew me—and wanted to make sure that I was okay.

Before the interview began, the woman sat close to me and mentioned looking over my file—and being "outraged" that this was my fourth parole board hearing.

I stared at the woman in disbelief as she spoke. While I can't speak for her intention, her words and actions felt like an apology—for the parole board's refusal to see *me*—a human being—and all the factors which led to my incarceration.

A wave of emotions washed over me and threw my equilibrium off. But for once, I didn't need to be on guard. The parole hearing commenced—and no one shouted or screamed at me; no one told me I wasn't showing enough remorse or taking enough accountability.

I discussed with the board how I ended up in prison, the lessons learned, and what I did while incarcerated. We discussed my family, my daughter, and my presumptive plans post-release. And I can't tell you how long it lasted, but I felt seen when I walked out.

VERSE

03

The Dragon

Hip-hop, like religion, was getting complex, but I still loved her. I spent most of the night after the hearing alone in my cube.

I sat on the bottom bunk with my feet on the bed and listened as New York City Radio stations played a steady rotation of 50 Cent, a formerly incarcerated hip-hop artist whom I admired for his drive, determination, and ability to reinvent himself.

I scanned through *Source* and *Vibe* magazines and imagined myself touching down in a Sean John velour tracksuit, fresh construction Timbs, and a Yankee fitted cap—rocking out to instant classics like "In Da Club" and "Lose Yourself."

The possibility of freedom after nearly 9 years of incarceration was intoxicating. I was high—literally for hours before I got tired.

My eyes were hurting when I put down the magazines and took out from my locker the box of tapes I borrowed from Mohamed—A Muslim Brother—who had been incarcerated for over 33 years, with whom I played chess and Scrabble.

I had no preference, but the artwork of a cassette case caught my attention. I slowly put the Earth, Wind, and Fire tape into my Walkman. Eyes closed, I bopped my head as the intro of *Fantasy* summoned me towards a past-present-and future rooted in one love, one heart, and one humanity.

I thought of Miss Tiny—and laughed as her wisdom echoed in my mind.

To no one in particular, I said, "God willing"—And proceeded to let my imagination run free.

I envisioned:

Reuniting with my daughter.

My family.

Friends.

The beach.

The warmth of the sun.

Ocean breeze.

Live music

Savoring the foods I missed.

Reconnecting with my community and exploring the world beyond prison walls!

I was deliriously drunk with the prospect of freedom—a euphoria so consuming it defied sleep, and carried me into the early hours of the morning. But as the morning neared, something in me began to shift.

The energetic expansion felt uncontainable. I was vibrating with a power I could only describe as the very essence of life itself.

As I floated in a dreamlike, ethereal space—with no beginning and no ending—I was blinded by a sudden flash that saturated my physical being and expanded outward into an all-encompassing field of light.

Particle by particle, I felt myself being transformed.

Unshackled—I slowly reclaimed my essence—wise, strong, young, ancient, infinite, untethered by time—an eternal member of the "Lion Vanguard" of Freedom!

For the first time *awake,* I remembered and overstood the *dream.*

I held in my hand the ancestral baton of hope—and with it, the duty to carry it further along the journey toward a world where all people can self-actualize—regardless of race, class, or creed.

Hot tears of joy ran down my cheek. The consciousness and responsibility felt overwhelming. But I felt the ancestors—holding, and urging, *forward ever*—on the eternal exodus—to the *promised land*!

TO BE CONTINUED

Exhibit I: Release paper

Kirk, James
94A6325

STATE OF NEW YORK
EXECUTIVE DEPARTMENT - DIVISION OF PAROLE
CERTIFICATE OF RELEASE TO PAROLE SUPERVISION

SENTENCE: INDETERMINATE [XX] DEFINITE [ ] NYSID NO. 7648252-P

KIRK, James 94A-6325, now confined in Queensboro C.F. who was convicted of CPCS 2nd and sentenced in the county of QUEENS at a term of the SUPREME Court, Judge CHETTA presiding on the 24th day of AUGUST 1994, for the term of 7-0-0/LIFE the maximum term of which sentence expires on the LIFE day of ________, 20____, has agreed to abide by the conditions to which (he) (she) has signed (his) (her) name below, and is hereby granted ☐ Conditional Release/ ☒ Parole by the Board of Parole, by virtue of the authority conferred by New York State Law.

It is therefore directed that (he) (she) be released and placed under legal jurisdiction of the Division of Parole until the LIFE day of ________, 20____.

Signed this 11th day of FEBRUARY, 20 03, at ARTHUR KILL C.F.

Date of Release: March 25, 2003 Board of Parole: [signatures]

I, KIRK, James (94-A-6325), voluntarily accept Parole supervision. I fully understand that my person, residence and property are subject to search and inspection. I understand that Parole supervision is defined by these Conditions of Release and all other conditions that may be imposed upon me by the Board or its representatives. I understand that my violation of these conditions may result in the revocation of my release.

CONDITIONS OF RELEASE

1. I will proceed directly to the area to which I have been released and, within twenty-four hours of my release, make my arrival report to that Office of the Division of Parole unless other instructions are designated on my release agreement. REPORT TO: Central Long I Office 81 Executive Blvd., Farmingdale, NY, 11735; PH# (631) 420-5110
2. I will make office and/or written reports as directed. SPO Washington, PO L. Lauture
3. I will not leave the State of New York or any other State to which I am released or transferred, or any area defined in writing by my Parole Officer without permission.
4. I will permit my Parole Officer to visit me at my residence and/or place of employment and I will permit the search and inspection of my person, residence and property. I will discuss any proposed changes in my residence, employment or program status with my Parole Officer. I understand that I have an immediate and continuing duty to notify my Parole Officer of any changes in my residence, employment or program status when circumstances beyond my control make prior discussion impossible.
5. I will reply promptly, fully and truthfully to any inquiry of or communication by my Parole Officer or other representative of the Division of Parole.
6. I will notify my Parole Officer immediately any time I am in contact with or arrested by any law enforcement agency. I understand that I have a continuing duty to notify my Parole Officer of such contact or arrest.
7. I will not be in the company of or fraternize with any person I know to have a criminal record or whom I know to have been adjudicated a Youthful Offender except for accidental encounters in public places, work, school or in any other instance with the permission of my Parole Officer.
8. I will not behave in such manner as to violate the provisions of any law to which I am subject which provide for a penalty of imprisonment, nor will my behavior threaten the safety or well-being of myself or others.
9. I will not own, possess, or purchase any shotgun, rifle or firearm of any type without the written permission of my Parole Officer. I will not own, possess or purchase any deadly weapon as defined in the Penal Law or any dangerous knife, dirk, razor, stiletto, or imitation pistol. In addition, I will not own, possess or purchase any instrument readily capable of causing physical injury without a satisfactory explanation for ownership, possession or purchase.
10. In the event that I leave the jurisdiction of the State of New York, I hereby waive my right to resist extradition to the State of New York from any state in the Union and from any territory or country outside the United States. This waiver shall be in full force and effect until I am discharged from Parole or Conditional Release. I fully understand that I have the right under the Constitution of the United States and under law to contest an effort to extradite me from another state and return me to New York, and I freely and knowingly waive this right as a condition of my Parole or Conditional Release.
11. I will not use or possess any drug paraphernalia or use or possess any controlled substance without proper medical authorization.
12. Special Conditions:

SEEK, OBTAIN, MAINTAIN EMPLOYMENT AND /OR ACADEMIC/VOCATIONAL PROGRAM.
SUBMIT TO SUBSTANCE ABUSE TESTING AS DIRECTED BY P.O.
PARTICIPATE IN SUBSTANCE ABUSE TREATMENT PROGRAM AS DIRECTED BY P.O.
I WILL NOT CONSUME ALCOHOLIC BEVERAGES

Epilogue

Do you think making the parole board, after almost a decade in various New York State prisons, would finally make me free?

I didn't—at least not yet!

In 2003, after leaving Arthur Kill and going to Queensboro Correctional Facility, I heard the term "re-entry" used to describe people returning home from prison. As a sci-fi geek and avid comic book reader, I was puzzled. To me, "re-entry" meant a spaceship returning to Earth's atmosphere—a complex process requiring precision to avoid burning up.

Prisoner re-entry, on the other hand, is a deeply flawed process that rarely accounts for the stigma, discrimination, and lack of resources that incarcerated people face when they return home. Not to mention the trauma of spending years in human cages, hundreds of miles away from family and friends, in the forgotten lands.

Prisoner re-entry is a perilous journey. National statistics reveal that approximately 600,000 people are released from state and federal prisons each year, and within three years, nearly two-thirds (68 per cent) are rearrested. I was determined to avoid this fate, which led me to pursue my education at various academic institutions. My goal was not just to improve my life, but to sharpen my tools to help dismantle a carceral system that continues to impact millions of Black and Brown people in disproportionate measures.

In 2013, a decade after my release, I earned my doctorate from the University of Pennsylvania's School of Social Policy and Practice. I went on to develop reentry programs for the city of Philadelphia and create educational curricula on mass incarceration for academic institutions across the country.

I have been blessed to speak and share my story on the world stage—achievements beyond anything I once imagined—made possible through intention, faith, relentless work, and the unwavering support of family, friends, and comrades, many of whom are no longer in the physical essence, while others remain trapped in human cages or have been deported to countries they no longer know.

Please don't be fooled by my accomplishments. My return to New York City on March 25, 2003, as a Black immigrant and formerly incarcerated man, was far from easy. The challenges were numerous, and the shadow of incarceration loomed over me, often blocking out my light and casting doubt on my efforts to rebuild relationships, find employment, and navigate a world that seemed intent on reminding me of my past conviction and prison number at every turn.

Despite the systemic hurdles post-incarceration, nothing has been more difficult than learning to be a human being, father, brother, and son to a mother who endured nine years of sleepless nights while her firstborn was trapped in a human cage. This is the context for my next journey. I invite you to join me in the sequel to this story:

Return of The Dragon – Abolition is Freedom

About the Author

Dr. Kirk "Jae" James is an activist, scholar, writer, and speaker whose work sits at the intersection of love, critical consciousness, and collective liberation. Grounded in lived experience and academic research, Jae challenges systems of oppression through abolitionist scholarship, public storytelling, and transformative pedagogy. His work invites communities to confront the legacies of colonialism, imperialism, mass incarceration, structural violence, and racial capitalism—while radically imagining futures rooted in healing, justice, and shared humanity. Whether in classrooms, on stages, or through the written word, Jae embodies a deep commitment to truth-telling, love, and liberation for all.

EU Safety Information

Publisher: Daraja Press, PO BOX 99900 BM 735 664 Wakefield, QC J0X 0C2, Canada

info@darajapress.com | https://darajapress.com

EU Authorized GPSR Representative: Easy Access System Europe - Mustamäe tee 50, 10621 Tallinn, Estonia, gpsr.requests@easproject.com

For EU product safety concerns, please contact us at info@darajapress.com